NATURAL LAW AND INALIENABLE HUMAN RIGHTS

A Pathway to Freedom and Liberty

Third Edition

By Jack Forbes

JAFO PUBLISHING
2010 West Avenue K, PMB 520
Lancaster, CA 93536

NATURAL LAW AND INALIENABLE HUMAN RIGHTS
A Pathway to Freedom and Liberty
Third Edition

TABLE OF CONTENTS

Preface

In 2022, I participated as a guest speaker/civil rights lawyer in a symposium about civil liberties and specifically concerning governmental entities and employers mandating inoculations with Emergency Use Authorization "vaccinations" against Covid-19. In the question and answer portion of the event, I was asked about the origin of human rights.

The question was whether a government, or employer, could make a legally enforceable rule that violates a citizen's natural law right of privacy and liberty. It was a good question and was thought-provoking. My answer was that there were written and unwritten boundaries beyond which governments and employers could not pass, regardless of any rules or laws they may wish to construct. In America, we refer to constitutional rights such as due process, the right of privacy, the right to be free from unreasonable searches and seizures, the right to be free of cruel and unusual punishment, and the right to life, liberty and the pursuit of happiness as being "fundamental" rights. Similarly, there are statutory laws, rules and regulations which protect us in employment and housing, for example.

However, exactly what those essential legal boundaries are, and whether they depend on written law or unwritten tradition, vary to an extent from culture to culture, nation to nation. Nevertheless, certain *boundaries* are universally considered to be absolute. I commented that scholars of natural law and human rights differ not only on the *specifics* of those boundaries, but also upon the *origin* of that natural law.

What are the inalienable (or, "unalienable") rights to life, liberty and the pursuit of happiness, and what is the ultimate origin of such "natural law" for humans? Can we know the legitimate boundaries of governmental (or employer) action in *absolute* terms, or do we require reference to *historical events* to give *shape* to the concept of human rights? Are human rights the same as ethical *duties* to others? What role have *world religions* played in the origin and shaping of natural law? What *use* is there for natural law without there also being an effective means of *enforcement* of the resulting human rights? Can nations legitimately subvert human rights under the auspices of *national security interests*, and if so, to what extent? Answers to these important questions are the focus and subject matter of this book.

Jack Forbes
Author

INTRODUCTION

IN AMERICA, we have, what is widely considered to be, a rich history of freedom, individual rights and justice. But the tradition of human rights surely did not start in America. What is the journey of human rights as it has *evolved over time*? Clearly, these rights and their meanings do not owe their existence to any one person or document. Instead, the unalienable rights have arisen in some manner from relationships with our fellow man, our societal framework, notions of right and wrong, of religion and accountability, and, to an extent, from the balance between one person's welfare and the welfare of a community, nation or world.

One of my songs, *"There Come a Time,"*[1] speaks of a time when liberty has sustained severe challenges, in a way that would call upon all freedom-fighters to stand up to and against oppression. The song cries out:

> "Banding together, as proud as we're strong, that's how our enemies fell. We stand up and fight on, forever as one, ringing that Liberty *Bell!*"

---

1 WARNING, Dangerous Moves, "There Come a Time" (Jafo Publishing 2010), Jack Forbes.

A people, challenged in their freedoms, charged with a responsibility—indeed, a *necessity*—to *fight back*, through coordinated, unified resistance to tyranny. For what purpose? To secure liberty, freedom from oppression. To secure—**human rights**. For what are "human rights" without the ability to enforce them? Merely words on an ephemeral piece of parchment. One may well have *duties* to afford others rights, but it is the *rights themselves*, and more specifically, the *enforceability* of those rights, which is the gravamen of liberty. For example, without the right to bear arms, a community (such as the Australian people in present times) *are virtually helpless* against a government Hell-bent on oppression under the pretext of universal Covid-19 vaccination. The *difficulty* with natural law has been described:

> "...[I]f the natural law has any weakness, and it has, that weakness is that everything about it cannot be said all at once. It is a philosophy of life, of law, of conduct and of living, not a phrase, nor a simple theory, nor a theorem that can be pulled out and applied to a problem for an automatic solution."[2]

One would think that perhaps the essential basis for natural law and human rights could be exposed by abstract thought as to a philosophy of freedom and justice. *Or, can it?*

---

2   David C. Bayne, The Supreme Court and the Natural Law, 1 DePaul L. Rev. 216 (1952) Available at: https://via.library.depaul.edu/law-review/vol1/iss2/3.

CHAPTER ONE

Philosophy and Natural Law

HUMAN RIGHTS arguably encompass both natural law and what has been described elsewhere as "positive" law, referring to governmental written law and edicts. Positive law has developed and evolved over the millennia and differs from region to region within the world. Natural law, theoretically, is a constant; it is thought to be "inherent" or "endemic" to life generally or human beings in particular. The natural law component of "human rights," then, are rules, moral precepts and social conventions which purportedly have their origin in the human condition itself.

This natural law concept has been a topic of *philosophical discourse* for thousands of years as men and women attempt to find *an inexorable value of existence* and *a baseline for freedom and liberty*. A rule against imprisonment[3], for example, could be a "positive" law of society, but it also could have its origins in "natural law" as an indispensable aspect of human dignity, freedom and liberty. Presumably, most everyone would agree that false imprisonment

---

3 Whether the imprisonment is "false" or "acceptable" obviously depends on one's point of view, and this fact should give a hint of the problem with describing bright-line rules as to what is considered to be "natural law."

and kidnapping[4] by a person or group is intolerable. Upon close examination, however, the rule against imprisonment is not so clear.

A simple example of controversy, in a natural law discussion, could be the following:

> One should **never** wrongfully imprison another against their will by force.[5]

> However, if someone *does* wrongfully imprison *another* against their will by force, then it is **permissible** for *society* to imprison that perpetrator against their will by force.

On the one hand, we can understand that false imprisonment and kidnapping are evil in themselves, inherently. Each deprives the victim of liberty and safety and it typically leads to more heinous crimes against that person or against their loved ones (*e.g.*, in ransom situations, robbery, rape, murder, and pain and suffering of others dealing with harm to their loved one).

On the other hand, however, virtually every society, nation state or governmental entity throughout the world has positive laws proscribing **crimes** of false imprisonment and kidnapping. Punishment for such crimes includes forced confinement in a jail,

---

4 Kidnapping typically denotes movement of a person, falsely imprisoned, from one place to another. It is generally considered to be a more serious crime than mere false imprisonment.

5 In the parent-child relationship, this conundrum becomes even more complicated, since at some point in a child's life, they are entitled to make their own decisions. This is not an age issue, since as we know, different nation-states and cultures designate different ages as designating adulthood. Also, it could be argued that forced education of minors is a form of "wrongful imprisonment," for a child (or their parents) who wishes to self-educate/home school. This raises the question of what a "false" imprisonment is, and with that, we find ourselves drifting back to pure philosophy.

prison, hoosegow, slammer, joint, cooler, gulag and so on. So, a *society* may impose imprisonment, but an *individual* may not impose imprisonment. If safety and security from imprisonment is an inherent human right arising from natural law, it should be *absolute*, but it is not. There must be a deeper through-line to "natural law" that accounts for this discrepancy and similar discrepancies in applying inherent rights to real-life scenarios.

American versus Islamic Law

In American criminal law, there is a bright-line judicial distinction[6] between laws which are *"malum prohibitum"* and *"malum in se."* *Malum in se* means that which is intrinsically and morally wrong or evil in itself. *Malum prohibitum* means that which is wrong *because* it is prohibited.[7] The distinction is believed to have first arisen in the late 1400s in England, where,

> "...it separated crimes [for] which the king could grant leave to commit [*i.e.*, pardonable prior to commission], from those for which he had no such power. [fn omitted] Therefore, at least theoretically, malum in se crimes derive from a source higher than the king [i.e., than malum prohibitum]. Since the king was God's representative on Earth, [fn omitted] the logical source of malum in se crimes would be God Himself. [fn omitted]"[8]

---

6 Positive law never contains express reference to whether a particular statute or rule is malum in se or malum prohibitum. Such an interpretation, or categorization, falls to the judicial branch through case-law decisions.

7 *See*, BLACK'S LAW DICTIONARY, 959-960 (6th ed. 1990).

8 Washington University Law Review, Vol. 73, Issue 3, January 1995, *Eliminating the (Absurd) Distinction Between Malum In Se and Malum Prohibitum Crimes*

Forced sexual intercourse against the will of the victim should universally be considered *malum in se*, since it is wrong in itself. Jaywalking in a commercial district across four lanes of traffic would be dangerous, and prohibited, but it would not be morally wrong in itself. Thus, even judicial interpretation of positive law recognizes a distinction between things that are *inherently* wrong and things that are wrong because, as a society, we *say* they are wrong.

In American jurisprudence,

> "...the phrase 'moral turpitude' appears to serve the same function and have the same meaning as malum in se. [fn omitted]"[9]

The Merriam-Webster online dictionary defines moral turpitude as,

> "1: an act or behavior that gravely violates the sentiment or accepted standard of the community
>
> 2: a quality of dishonesty or other immorality that is determined by a court to be present in the commission of a criminal offense"[10]

Placing flexible copper pipe beneath a residential concrete slab may no longer be compliant with a state's plumbing code, and that is clearly *malum prohibitum*. But deliberately constructing a high-rise building with substandard (weaker) concrete in order to save

---

("*Absurd Distinction*"), at 1374, Richard L. Gray.

9 Id, at 1377.

10 Merriam-Webster, www.merriam-webster.com, "moral turpitude" noun.

construction-funds money at the risk of lives to be lost when the building collapses is undoubtedly *malum in se*. In the latter example, there is an unmistakable element of reckless disregard for the health and safety of others. Intentional harm or reckless disregard constitutes the "moral turpitude," or evil intent, component of *malum in se*. Perhaps intended harm or reckless disregard is a key in understanding the origins, or more appropriately, the *parameters* of natural law.

The distinction between a crime of moral turpitude and a crime *not* of moral turpitude can be important in proving "scienter" (criminal intent) or can be decisive in an immigration law context.[11] The Board of Immigration Appeals, through a legion of case decisions, vaguely defines "moral turpitude" to constitute an act that was done recklessly or with evil intent, and which shocks the public conscience as inherently base, vile, or depraved, or contrary to the rules of morality and the duties owed between people or to society in general. Despite this detailed and colorful description, however, a Ninth Circuit Court of Appeals astutely observed:

> "Morality is not a concept that courts can define by judicial decrees, and even less can it be defined by fiats issued by the Board of Immigration Appeals, to whose decisions the courts must give great deference."[12]

Concepts of "morality" and intrinsic good or evil *seem to change with the times*, and as observed by the Court in *Nunez v. Holder*,

---

11 Any alien shall be removed (i.e., deported) if the alien is within the class of deportable aliens of a person who has committed a crime of moral turpitude. 8 United States Code Sect. 1227(a)(2)(A)(i).

12 *Nunez v. Holder* (9th Cir. 2010) 594 F.3d 1124, 1127.

"...[W]e are limited by precedent as a court of law. Furthermore, any answer based on other considerations would in all probability be unacceptable to one or another segment of society and could well divide residents of red states from residents of blue, the old from the young, neighbor from neighbor, and even males from females. There is simply no overall agreement on many issues of morality in contemporary society."[13]

Searching for answers, as to the origin and parameters of natural law, in the legal concepts of *malum in se, malum prohibitum* and moral turpitude proves to be a hopeless, circuitous and bootstrap task, bombarding semantics with subjective cultural preferences. To a significant extent, "morality," like beauty, appears to be in the eye of the beholder.

Worse yet, the shifting sands of "morality" may become *a powerful tool for tyrants* should they be allowed free rein to interpret and enforce vague standards of right and wrong. If natural law has an actual, intrinsic basis in the human condition, why not simply appoint learned jurists and instruct them to "seek justice" and rule accordingly?

"The first issue that Aquinas takes up about human law in his set-piece discussion of law, *Summa Theologiae*, I-II, q. 95 a. 1, is whether human law [positive law] is beneficial—might we not do better with exhortations and warnings, or with judges appointed simply to 'do justice', or with wise leaders ruling as they see fit? ... Classic and leading contemporary texts of natural law theory treat law as morally problematic, understanding it as a normally indispensable instrument of great good

---

13 Ibid.

but one that readily becomes an instrument of great evil unless its authors steadily and vigilantly make it good by recognizing and fulfilling their moral duties to do so, both in settling the content of its rules and principles and in the procedures and institutions by which they make and administer it. Natural law theories all understand **law as a remedy against the great evils of, on the one side anarchy (lawlessness), and on the other side tyranny.** And one of tyranny's characteristic forms is the co-optation of law to deploy it as a mask for fundamentally lawless decisions cloaked in the forms of law and legality."[14] (bold added for emphasis)

Shari'a law, the Islamic code of law and moral conduct, is a contemporary example of an *exceptionally vague set of laws* implemented by Muslim clergy, purportedly with justice as its objective, but often resulting in the kind of arbitrary, capricious and indeed, *prejudiced* whim according to the particular religious or personal beliefs of the jurist. Shari'a law decisions are subject to virtually no review, and may subject one side or another to exceptionally harsh and *undeserved* consequences.

In the United States, allowing a jurist *absolute and unfettered discretion* without regard to good faith would constitute a denial of procedural due process of law,[15] and a statute which is so ambiguous as to allow virtually unlimited discretion in enforcement

---

14 Stanford Encyclopedia of Philosophy, *Natural Law Theories*, John Finnis, February 5, 2007, revised June 3, 2020.

15 Procedural due process of law centers on the question of whether a person, who is threatened with a loss of life, liberty or property, receives fair treatment. A formal, adversarial proceeding, however, is not necessarily required. *Wilkinson v. Austin* (2005) 545 U.S. 209, 224-230.

is considered to be *unenforceable* as, "void for vagueness."[16] Positive law within the United States must be adequately specific to give *fair notice* to people to allow them to conform their conduct to the law, and must *limit enforcement* narrowly to that which is clearly proscribed so as to fairly eliminate selective prosecution of the law by authorities. State and federal constitutions provide the broad outlines of limits on government and of fundamental rights of the people. Statutes and implementing rules create the detail in positive law requiring conformity by members of society.

Certain countries adhering to Shari'a law, on the other hand, are loath to tie their religious hands and restrict their virtually unlimited authority in seeking and implementing justice.

> "...[Th]e Islamic heritage bequeaths to modern constitution writers a relatively weak idea of natural law, on the one hand, and a robust notion of divine law, on the other. The higher law of the man-made constitution thus has the potential to clash with the higher law of God, the *shari'a*. And insofar as the *shari'a* is understood to contain specific and immutable legal rulings, as it is according to many influential theorists, this clash seriously limits the ability of Muslim reformers to revise the *shari'a* according to their understanding of what good government and human rights require.

---

16 A statute is void for vagueness and unenforceable if it is too vague for the average citizen to determine who is regulated, what conduct is prohibited or what punishment applies, or if it could facilitate arbitrary or biased prosecutions. *See, e.g., Champlin Ref. Co. v. Corporation Comm'n* (1936) 269 U.S. 210, 243 and *Connally v. General Constr. Co* (1926) 269 U.S. 385, 391. *And see, United States v. L. Cohen Grocery Co.* (1921) 255 U.S. 81 (holding that section 4 of the Lever Act was void for vagueness insofar as it proscribed the making of "any unjust or unreasonable rate or charge in handling … any necessaries").

This clash has ancient roots in the Islamic intellectual tradition. Perhaps from the time of the prophet Muhammad himself, the Qur'an was viewed in part as an expression of divine law. The Qur'anic text may not explicate a constitution for the Islamic state, but it does contain verses on a variety of subjects, ranging from marriage and inheritance to war and peace, that have legal import. Some injunctions are preceded by the words *kutiba 'alaykum* ("it is written for you"), suggesting that God is directly legislating for humanity."[17]

To Islamic purists, constitutionalism was *inherently contrary* to Islamic Law as contained within and defined by the Qur'an:

"Beginning in the nineteenth century, the ideology of constitutionalism began to creep into Islamic political thought as more and more Muslims visited and studied in Europe. The need to reopen the *shari'a* to reinterpretation and reform was one of the driving forces underlying the advocacy of constitutionalism among reformers. For these men, constitutionalism was the supreme manifestation of neo-*ijtihad*, a legitimate vehicle for the reconceptualization of Islamic polity and the creation of new and more effective political institutions that reflect the true purposes of an Islamic ethical system. But from the beginning, the reformers faced concerted opposition from many ulema and other conservatives, who viewed constitutionalism **as the latest assault on the sacred law**. According to this view of Islamic polity,

---

17   LAW & LIBERTY, *Islam and Constitutionalism* ("*Islam*"), February 1, 2013, Sohail Hashmi, https://lawliberty.org.

the Qur'an and Prophetic *sunna* provide the immutable Islamic 'constitution,' and human engagement with these sources is limited to 'law finding' rather than lawmaking. In his treatise *Islamic Law and Constitution*, Abu al-A'la Mawdudi declared:

'It is beyond the purview of any legislature of an Islamic state to legislate in contravention of the directives of God and His Prophet, and all such pieces of legislation, even though approved by the legislature would *ipso facto* be considered *ultra vires* of the Constitution.'[fn. omitted]

And Ayatollah Khomeini continued his statement quoted earlier as follows:

'The fundamental difference between Islamic government and constitutional monarchies and republics is this: whereas the representatives of the people or the monarch in such regimes engage in legislation, in Islam the legislative power and competence to establish legislation belongs exclusively to God Almighty…No one has the right to legislate and no law may be executed except the law of the Divine Legislator.'[fn. omitted][18]

Recent efforts within Iraq, Afghanistan, Iran, Pakistan and Saudi Arabia to create, promote and implement secular constitutional roadmaps have been stymied by Islamic commissions established to review positive law *for compliance with Islamic law*. These partisan commissions have compromised the integrity and enforceability of positive law by declarations to the effect that no law contradicting

---

18 Ibid.

established provisions of Islam may be established.[19] However, the Qur'an is *notoriously vague* regarding the details of "Islamic Law," particularly after the death of Muhammad. In turn, this uncertainty has inexorably led to arbitrary and capricious interpretation and implementation by Islamic Clerics:

> "As long as the Prophet [Muhammad] lived among his people, there was no question as to the supreme interpretive agent for divine revelation. The problem that confronted the Muslim community immediately after Muhammad's death was how to interpret the Qur'an, particularly when verses are ambiguous or apparently contradictory, and what normative value, if any, to give the *sunna*, the sum total of Muhammad's prophethood in words and deeds."[20]

Regardless, however, of the religious context of Islamic Law, its precepts were subject to intense debate even within Islamic communities. Thus, rather than standing for natural law inherent in human rights, Islamic Law instead represents confusingly vague, and sometimes directly contradicting, religious edicts set forth within the Qur'an.[21]

---

19 Ibid.

20 Ibid.

21 The *Islam* article suggests that in the future, the solution to the inherently arbitrary and capricious nature of constitutionalism within the context of the Qur'an is to, first, resurrect and disseminate, "the early Mu'tazili emphasis on ethical objectivism, that is, that all human beings possess the rational faculty—as a God-given faculty—to discern right from wrong and to form moral conclusions on how to order their communal lives apart from reliance on one or another revelation. The second task is to develop a societal consensus that *ijtihad* is the birthright of all Muslims and that each Muslim generation has the right and the

Ancient Philosophers

Plato had similarly restrictive notions of the role of natural law in society.

> "According to Plato, only the philosopher kings are equipped and trained intellectually to comprehend the true forms.... These philosopher kings can grasp the Form of the Good, for instance, which is the fountainhead from which flow all true forms, including knowledge, truth, and beauty. But how are we to know who these philosopher kings are? How are we to distinguish them from charlatans? And why should the *polis* uncritically accept the supposedly sound judgments and determinations of those who cannot prove to us their purportedly superior faculties?"[22]

As pointed out,

> "There is no ideal city, no Platonic Utopia.... Plato's communistic fantasies have never been achieved. ... Plato seems to have continued to admire tyranny, despite his criticism of tyrants in The Laws, for elsewhere in that work he discusses how leaders ought to create an obedient disposition among the citizens. Commonplace though that proposition may sound, it suggests that the

---

obligation to understand the Qur'an and *sunna* in light of their own needs and their own circumstances."

22   Allen Mendenhall blog, https://allenmendenhallblog.com, The Literary Lawyer: A Forum for the Legal and Literary Communities, *Plato and Natural Law Theory* ("*Natural Law Theory*"), March 27, 2013.

State and its politicians should condition citizens to act for the good of the State. The problem is that the State is made up of those who live off the citizens, so unchecked obedience to the State means that the citizens ensure their perpetual subordination to those who exploit citizen labor. It is little wonder that the Platonic State devotes itself to educating the young, for the State must guarantee that there are future generations of uncritical followers to take advantage of."[23]

Aristotle (384-322 BCE) is perhaps the seminal ancient philosopher responsible for developing a philosophical theory of evaluating positive laws in the context of moral principles. Aristotle developed his theory in Book V of *Nicomanchean Ethics*.[24] It is well-known that Aristotle studied with Plato's Academy in Athens and was what amounts, in today's terms, to an "influencer" to the people of Athens and beyond. In *Nicomanchean Ethics*, Aristotle described law as promoting a harmonious and ethical lifestyle, which resulted in a "perfect community."[25] Aristotle saw compliance with law **as the pursuit of virtue:**

"And how the meanings of 'just' and 'unjust' which answer to these are to be distinguished is evident; for practically the majority of the acts commanded by the law are those which are prescribed from the point of view of

---

23 *Natural Law Theory*, Ibid.

24 *The Complete Works of Aristotle* (Princeton University Press, 1984), 1790-1, Jonathan Barnes (ed).

25 John Finnis, "Natural Law and Legal Reasoning" in Kenneth Himma and Brian Bix (eds), *Law and Morality* (Ashgate, 2005) pp. 3-4.

virtue taken as a whole; for the law bids us practice every virtue and forbids us to practice any vice. And the things that tend to produce virtue taken as a whole are those of the acts prescribed by the law which have been prescribed with a view to education for the common good. But with regard to the education of the individual as such, which makes him without qualification a good man, we must determine later whether this is the function of the political art or of another; for perhaps it is not the same to be a good man and a good citizen of any state taken at random."[26]

Aristotle spoke of the public using wisdom and reasoning to enhance their lives and to promote justice.[27] While modern commentators divide law between natural law and positive law, Aristotle used different terminology, drawing the distinction between immutable natural justice and variable conventional justice.

"**Of political justice** part is natural, part legal, **natural that which everywhere has the same force and does not exist by people's thinking this or that**; legal, that which is originally indifferent, but when it has been laid down is not indifferent, e.g., that a prisoner's ransom shall be a mina, or that a goat and not two sheep shall be sacrificed, and again all the laws that are passed for particular cases, e.g., that sacrifice shall be made in honour of Brasidas, and the provision of decrees. Now some think that all justice is of this sort, because **that which is by nature**

---

26 NICOMACHEAN ETHICS, Book V, Aristotle, Translated by W.D. Ross, p. 75.

27 J.A.K.; Thomson, *The Ethics of Aristotle* (Penguin Classics, 1953) Book V, 120-2.

is unchangeable and has everywhere the same force (as fire burns both here and in Persia), while they see change in the things recognized as just. This, however, is not true in this unqualified way, but is true in a sense; or rather, with the gods it is perhaps not true at all, while with us there is something that is just even by nature, yet all of it is changeable; but still **some is by nature, some not by nature. It is evident which sort of thing, among things capable of being otherwise, is by nature**, and which is not but is legal and conventional, assuming that both are equally changeable. … [T]he things which are just not by nature but by human enactment are not everywhere the same, since constitutions also are not the same, **though there is but one which is everywhere by nature the best.**"[28] (bold added for emphasis)

Thus, without attempting to categorize, define or even set forth examples, Aristotle clearly views justice (laws) as originating either by nature or by convention, or both. The justice originating by nature "is unchangeable and has everywhere the same force." The justice originating by convention, such as, "that a goat and not two sheep shall be sacrificed," is justice created by "human enactment" and thus, subject to change, "since constitutions also are not the same."

Fair enough, but this still begs the question of *specifically how* natural "justice" **is intrinsic to the human condition and immutable**; and *why* **is it inherent in life and unchanging?**

---

28 Aristotle, *NICOMACHEAN ETHICS, Book V*, at p. 83, Translated by W.D. Ross.

Contemporary Philosophical
Theories of Natural Law

Regarding the subject of natural law, "contemporary" theorists fall within two general schools of thought: (1) Neo-Thomism; and, (2) the Grisez, Finnis and Boyle Theory.[29]

> "The most important source of the neo-Thomist revival was Pope Leo XIII's 1879 encyclical letter *Aeterni patris*, in which Leo called for the rejuvenation of Christian philosophy and proposed St. Thomas Aquinas as its exemplar."[30]

Below, we will examine the notion of the Bible as a potential basis of natural law. The fair conclusion is that within Christianity, natural law amounts to the right of individuals to be free *to do as they are told* in conforming to Christian beliefs. As the ideas of Aquinas evolved, subsequent philosophers,

> "were Catholics and most were clerics; concern for the natural law was just a part of their concern for elaborating a comprehensive philosophy and theology."[31]

The *second* school of thought comprising contemporary natural law theory,

---

29 NATURAL LAW, NATURAL RIGHTS, AND AMERICAN CONSTITUTIONALISM, www.nlnrac.org/contemporary, *Contemporary Theories of Natural Law* ("*Contemporary Theories*"). This refers to the philosophers Germain Grisez, John Finnis and Joseph Boyle.

30 Ibid.

31 Ibid.

"is inspired by Aquinas, but is ultimately a novel philosophical enterprise that rejects central tenets of Aquinas's thought, and is noteworthy for its systematic character and engagement with practical moral questions. The theory emphasizes the priority of practical knowledge, as opposed to speculative knowledge of nature, in moral theory."[32]

However, the Grisez-Finnis-Boyal (or shortened: the "Grifinnboyl") moral philosophy has come under attack as being the result of a *crucial mistaken assumption,* as to,

"whether, in one of the key moves that is made early in the moral philosophy of the Grifinnboyl, that move may have been something of mistake; or if not a mistake, then at least a move fraught with consequences with which the Grifinnboyl themselves may not have clearly reckoned. Bluntly put, we believe their moral theory involves a crucial ambiguity concerning the focus of moral reasoning, namely, whether the moral focus must be said to be person-centered or person-neutral."[33]

Person-centered fosters and values individuality, independence, privacy, partnership, choice, dignity, respect, rights, equality (viewing [without judging] both sides of a moral quandary as equal)

---

32 Ibid.

33 JSTOR, www.jstor.org, "DOES THE GRISEZ-FINNIS-BOYLE MORAL PHILOSOPHY REST ON A MISTAKE? ("MISTAKE"), Henry Veatch and Joseph Rautenbert.

and diversity.[34] *Person-neutral,* in the philosophy of morality, on the other hand, means resolving a moral dilemma without regard to the interests of the particular actor, but rather, in a sort of forced lack of bias, following rules or social norms, for a vague concept of promotion of a "greater-good," regardless of how disagreeable the specific outcome may appear.

Moreover, the MISTAKE commentary, and the philosophy being critiqued therein, focuses not on natural human rights, but on *natural human duties* of one person to the next. This appears to have a parallel track as the Hindu religion's focus:

> "Hinduism tends to accord greater recognition to the rights that **others have** in relation to us as compared to the rights we have in relation to them."[35]

The contemporary focus on natural law *moral principles* (i.e., duties) for the utopian human to follow is captivating and valuable in its own right, but it brings us no closer to the origin of inalienable, inherent, natural human **rights** which are justifiably **enforceable** by an individual and by a society *against perpetrators of evil.* For those ignominious perpetrators of harm, all the philosophy in the world will not deter them from their predatory behavior. The old adage is proven true, time and time again: A leopard can't change its spots.[36]

---

34 Social Care Institute for Excellence, scie.org.uk Induction Standards for Northern Ireland, April, 2013.

35 University of Nottingham, Human Rights Law Centre, *The Religious Foundations of Human Rights: A Perspective from the Judeo-Christian Tradition and Hinduism* ("*Foundations*"), Commentary, p. 8, Dipti Patel 2005.

36 Jack's Handy List of Idioms, (JAFO PUBLISHING 2022), Jack Forbes.

Instead, the focus must be on the *actual basis* for natural rights, the *extent of such immutable baseline rights* and, of course, in order to retain their value, whether, to what extent and how such rights may be *enforced*.

CHAPTER TWO

Rights Against King and Country

T O ARRIVE AT a deep appreciation of the unimaginably rich texture of unalienable **human rights**, it is perhaps important to view the *historical foundations* of those ideas and beliefs. Are the rights, some rights, truly *inalienable*? Is there "a natural, universal and an eternal aspect" to human rights?[37] What *balance*, if any must be struck between governmental control and protection, and free competition for rights, privileges, goods and services, versus the "right" of humans to life, liberty and the pursuit of happiness? What begins as a simple concept suddenly becomes enormously complex. From the complex, can one detect an undercurrent of essential "human-ness," unwavering justice, endless compassion, passionate hope and enduring dreams? Can one also detect an **inherent baseline**, or *bottom line*, of inalienable human rights? Is *that* natural law?

Life, it turns out, is the same for all creatures, insofar as we strive to fulfill our purpose of existence, raising our young, engaging with others, producing our work and creating our cultural riches. This adventure of life is perhaps the essence of liberty and the pursuit of happiness. And for those who conspire to obstruct, destroy, limit,

---

37 *Foundations*, Ibid.

25

steal away, obscure, confuse, deprive, conflate and misrepresent those rights—for those *arch enemies of the People*—they will eventually find themselves destroyed and defeated along with all prior tyrants and tyrannical governments. Why? Because the zeal for freedom and liberty is an integral aspect of being human. The call to freedom, thrill and passion of existence, and associated *instinct for survival* can never be stamped out, because it is…*of our essence.* Regardless of setbacks, liberty will prevail victorious.

Developing Societies

For prehistoric man, the pressures and demands of occasional interaction with "strangers" would inevitably have created circumstances wherein certain "rights" would arise to protect oneself from the uncertainty of danger. These natural rights would represent resolution of positive and productive interaction versus the right of self-defense against other, potentially aggressive individuals or groups.

The **Code of Lipid-Ishtar** is a written codification of laws promulgated by Lipit-Ishtar (r. 1934 – 1924 BCE), the fifth king of Isin, an ancient city-state then-located in Lower Mesopotamia. The Code is written in the Sumerian language and was discovered in Nippur, Iraq.[38] Four tablet fragments established Lipit-Ishtar as the *earliest-known codifier of law.*[39] The Code was nearly two centuries older than the famed Code of Hammurabi (composed in 1755-

---

38 American Journal of Archaeology, Vol. 52, No. 3 (Jul. – Sep., 1948), pp. 425-450, *THE CODE OF LIPIT-ISHTAR* (*"Code of Lipit-Ishtar"*), Francis Rue Steele.

39 *LAW – A Treasure of Art and Literature* (*"LAW"*), (Hugh Lauter Levin Associates, Inc., Macmillan Publishing Company 1990), Sara Robbins, Editor, at p. 19.

1750 BCE) and provided a basis for study of, "the growth of legal concepts in Southern Mesopotamia."[40]

The Code had many provisions that provided a basic *quid-pro-quo* response to common problems of the era. For example, "If a man cut down a tree in the garden of [another] man, he shall pay one-half mina of silver."[41] But the Code also gives a fascinating insight into how the *interaction of citizens with slaves* was treated. On the one hand, the Code read:

> "If a man married a wife and she bore him children and those children are living, and a slave also bore children for her master [but] the father granted freedom to the slave and her children, the children of the slave shall not divide the estate with the children of their [former] master."[42]

However, the Code further provided:

> "If a man's wife has not borne him children but a harlot [from] the public square has borne him children, he shall provide grain, oil and clothing for that harlot; the children which the harlot has borne him shall be his heirs, and as long as his wife lives[,] the harlot shall not live in the house with the wife."

In this manner, the Code recognizes that:

---

40   *Id., Code of Lipit Ishtar,* p. 425.

41   *Id., LAW,* p. 19.

42   Ibid.

1. A master may grant freedom to his slave;

2. The children of a man and his wife will not be obligated to share any inheritance from their father with the children of the man and his slave;

3. But if there are no children borne to the man and his wife, and if the man and a "harlot" have children, not only must the man support the harlot with grain, oil and clothing, but also,

   (a) the children of the man and the harlot will be the heirs of the man; and,
   (b) the harlot may not live in the man's house until the wife dies.

Very clearly, the Code affirms a "property" right in men—the ability to grant freedom to (or in effect, "give away") a (female) slave, and *a right of freedom* for a slave (she may receive freedom, in the discretion of their Master). The Code also sets forth a rather sophisticated intestate succession "probate" law whereby *children of a Master and his slave* are **not** considered to be the inheritance-equal of (their half-sibling/children of their father) the progeny of the man and his wife. However, in the event the man and a "harlot [from] the public square" bear children but *the man does not have children from his wife*, then such ("illegitimate") children **do** have inheritance rights as heirs of their father, but their harlot mother **may not** live in the man's home, *until* the wife dies! Thus, even illegitimate children, of a man and a "harlot," have an established and legitimate legal stature as to (sometimes) being entitled to inheritance from their father. And, a harlot bearing children from one of her customers **also** has an established and legitimate stature

28

in the law, having the ability to live in her man's house, but only after the man's wife dies. This codified recognition of personal rights akin to liberty is the earliest written-legal code known to exist.

As societies formed through agrarian economies, and governments developed to implement a measure of order and protection for its citizens, "rights" developed. Eventually, these evolving rights were not only intended to keep aggression in check from other *individuals*, but also to keep *overreaching and oppression from governmental authorities* in check. With this, notions of personal autonomy, fair play and a search for prosperity, security, health and happiness arose, *as if* from nature.

The Code of Hammurabi, mentioned above, is a Babylonian legal text considered to be the longest and best-organized legal text from the ancient Near East. It was "proclaimed" (since by a single ruler) by the sixth king in the Babylonian dynasty, Hammurabi (r. 1792 to 1750 BCE). The Code of Hammurabi is composed of 282 rules, establishing standards for civil, commercial and criminal interactions and sanctions. It was carved into a four-ton slab of diorite, "looted by invaders and finally rediscovered in 1901 CE" by French mining engineer, Jacque de Morgan.[43] The edicts often proclaim varied standards of justice for Babylonian's three classes of society—propertied class, freedmen and slaves.[44]

The Code of Hammurabi also contains widespread protections for individuals against governmental abuses:

---

43 HISTORY, *Code of Hammurabi*, April 24, 2023. The stele of Hammurabi, had been broken into three pieces. It is believed to have been transported from Mesopotamia (now, Iraq) by king Shutruk-Nahhunte to Persia, at the Elamite capital of Susa, as spoils of war, in mid-12th century B.C.E.. Ibid.

44 For example, penalties for physician malpractice varied according to the victim's social status: "a doctor who killed a rich patient would have his hands cut off, while only financial restitution was required if the victim was a slave." Ibid.

"...[T]he code presents some of the earliest examples of the right to freedom of speech, the presumption of innocence, the right to present evidence, and the right to a fair trial by judges. To reinforce the rule of law and maintain the integrity of the judiciary, judges were held accountable according to a strict code of justice: If a judge renders a judgment, gives a verdict, or deposits a sealed opinion, after which he reverses his judgment, they shall charge and convict that judge ... and he shall give twelve-fold the claim of that judgment; moreover, they shall unseat him from his judgment in the assembly, and he shall never again sit in judgment with the judges. The Code of Hammurabi also provides certain protections for all classes in Babylonian society, including women, widows, orphans, the poor, and even slaves. Perhaps its most significant contribution can be found in its establishment of one particularly critical principle of the rule of law: **some laws are so fundamental that they apply to everyone, even the king.**"[45] (bold added for emphasis)

In 539 BCE, King Cyrus the Great of Persia conquered Babylon. In the wake of that victory, the King commissioned a **small clay cylinder** in the Babylonian language. It became known as the "Cyrus Cylinder" and endorsed *freedom of religion* **for newly conquered people**. The key component of the Cyrus Cylinder is that it allowed Babylonians to go about their business in peace. For Cyrus, *freedom*

---

45   Lauren, Paul Gordon, OXFORD HANDBOOK OF INTERNATIONAL HUMAN RIGHTS LAW, *Part II, Historical and Legal Sources, Chapter 7, The Foundations of Justice and Human Rights in Early Legal Texts and Thought,* (Oxford University Press 2013), Edited by Dinah Shelton.

of Religion was the freedom from the *governmental abuse* which the Babylonians would otherwise have received.

It is widely believed that these views influenced America's Thomas Jefferson in drafting the Declaration of Independence. But first, there was the *Magna Carta*.

Magna Carta

In the year 1215 CE, King John of England affixed his seal to the Magna Carta Liber Tatum, commonly known as simply, the "Magna Carta." This is widely believed to be the first official decree in the Common Era to broadly limit the power of the King. The document's name was Medieval Latin, meaning "Great Charter of Freedoms." This document was, in effect, a peace accord between a group of 25 Barons and the (unpopular) King. Think of the Magna Carta as an ancient form of settlement of a class action, with the Barons being the class and the King of England as the defendant. In 1217, the Magna Carta became a *portion of the peace treaty* at Lambeth. Thereafter, in 1297, the document was enacted into England's *statutory* law.

In the early 17th century, Sir Edward Coke referred to the document as evidence against the divine right of kings in England. Further research substantiated that the Magna Carta, in its *original* form, had been an effort to establish rights of barons and not of common people. Yet, the document continues to be revered as a monument to liberty.

The Magna Carta's limits, to the power of the King, have been described as follows:

> "Among the Magna Carta's provisions were clauses providing for a free church, reforming law and justice, and controlling the behavior of royal officials. One of the

31

charter's 63 clauses tasked the barons with choosing 25 representatives to serve as a 'form of security' ensuring the preservation of the rights and liberties that had been enumerated. Above all, the Magna Carta guaranteed that government, royal or otherwise, would be limited by the written law of the land."[46]

The UK Parliament proclaimed that the,

"Magna Carta...was **the first document to put into writing the principle that the king and his government was not above the law**. It sought to prevent the king from exploiting his power, and placed limits of royal authority by establishing law **as a power in itself**."[47] (bold added for emphasis)

Another way to express that sentiment is that the Magna Carta was an express recognition that governmental authority may not, under any circumstances, infringe upon certain basic human rights—*at least regarding the ruling class.* In *History Magna Carta,* it was said that,

"...the Magna Carta...was effectively the first written constitution in European history. ... The benefits of the charter were for centuries reserved for only the elite

---

46 Britannica, *Magna Carta England* [1215].

47 History, *Magna Carta*, October 21, 2021 ("*History Magna Carta*"). Of course, this claim fails to account for the human rights proclaimed in then-undiscovered ancient texts, such as in the Code of Hammurabi.

classes, while the majority of English citizens still lacked a voice in government."[48]

Two subsequent Acts of English legislation helped define, for all citizens, basic rights in England. The Petition of Right (1628) and the Habeas Corpus Act (1679), which affirmed, in Clause 39, that,

> "'no free man shall be...imprisoned or disseised [dispossessed]...except by the lawful judgment of his peers or by the law of the land.'"

And in Clause 40 that,

> "'To no one will we sell, to no one will we deny or delay right or justice'"

It took a while in the making, obviously. By these collective measures, England affirmed to every person within its borders the fundamental rights of habeas corpus, jury trial, speedy trial and due process of law. Were these rights—*natural* rights? Were they the result of bargaining between the people and government? A fair analysis would conclude that historically, the Magna Carta, and its related legislation 400-some years later, appear to have been *a bargained-for exchange.* But does that detract from their value in the study of human rights and natural law? The Magna Carta and its progeny stand as landmark **affirmations** of minimum human rights against government abuse, as advanced, promulgated and promoted first, by the elite classes, and second, by and for the common citizen.

---

48 Ibid.

America's Constitutional Foundation

The keystone document, marking the origin of justice in the United States, is the **Declaration of Independence**, executed July 4, 1776 by 56-men of the Second Continental Congress, in Philadelphia, Pennsylvania. The Declaration of Independence reflected these notions when it proclaimed:

> "[W]hen a long train of abuses and usurpations, pursuing invariably the same object evinces a design to reduce them under absolute Despotism, it is their right, it is their duty, to throw off such Government, and to provide new Guards for their future security."

The American forefathers thusly declared that the United States of America,

> "are and of Right ought to be Free and Independent States…Absolved from all Allegiance to the British Crown…."

The Declaration of Independence is so revered in the history of the United States of America that the original document is preserved and displayed at the National Archives in Washington DC. The *opening line of the second paragraph* is known verbatim *throughout the world* as the quintessential summary of natural, human rights:

> **"We hold these truths to be self-evident, that all men are created equal, that they are endowed by their Creator with certain unalienable Rights, that among these are Life, Liberty and the pursuit of Happiness."**

Several decades later, in 1863, these sentiments were echoed in another historic moment in the USA, by President Abraham Lincoln in what has become known as the Gettysburg Address, at the Gettysburg Battlefield, Pennsylvania:

> "Four score and seven years ago, our fathers brought forth on this continent a new nation, conceived in liberty and dedicated to the proposition that all men are created equal."

One hundred years later, Reverend Martin Luther King, Jr. proclaimed, at the March on Washington for Jobs and Freedom, in Washington DC:

> "I have a dream, that one day this nation will rise up and live out the true meaning of its creed: 'We hold these truths to be self-evident: that all men are created equal.'"

In 2015, President Barack Obama, in his Second Inaugural Address in Washington, DC, eloquently observed:

> "What makes us exceptional—what makes us American— is our allegiance to an idea articulated in a declaration made more than two centuries ago: [quoting the opening lines of the Declaration of Independence] Today we continue a never-ending journey to bridge the meaning of those words with the realities of our time."

And so easily, the meaning and challenge of understanding the nature of human rights is laid before us. Our four-page **Constitution**, on display at the National Archives in Washington DC, was signed and adopted into law by the Unanimous Consent, of the nine States present, on September 17, 1787. One of the signors was the first President of the United States, George Washington.

The Constitution served to define the foundation of the alliance of the original 13 States of the United States. It set up a tripartite government of equal, connected but independent parts: Executive, Congressional and Judicial. It sought to make a working framework for government by the People for the People, and with adequate checks and balances as a safeguard against tyranny. It set forth that,

> "This Constitution, and the Laws of the United States which shall be made in Pursuance thereof…shall be the supreme Law of the Land…"

These structures of justice, as amended from time to time, have boldly endured throughout the history of the USA—i.e. since 1776, for over 245 years!

On *September 25, 1789* a proposal was introduced in the First Congress of the United States for 12 amendments to the Constitution. Ten of such 12 amendments (Articles 3-12) were *ratified* by the requisite 3/4 of the State legislatures on December 15, 1791, just over four years following adoption of the U.S. Constitution. These first 10 Amendments to the Constitution have become known as the "U.S. Bill of Rights." The original of the Bill of Rights is on display in the Rotunda of the National Archives. In 1992, 203 years after its initial proposal, Article 2 was ratified as the 27th Amendment to the Constitution.

The Preamble to the Bill of Rights affirms that these Amendments resulted when,

> "Conventions of a number of the States, having at the time of their adopting the Constitution, expressed a desire, *in order to prevent misconstruction or abuse of its*

powers, that further declaratory and restrictive clauses should be added…" (italics added)

The Bill of Rights amounts to an *incredible monument to justice* and was, in its day, certainly the most sophisticated and exhaustive governmental articulation of rights ever expressly reserved to the People, as "unalienable" rights. This Bill of human rights is so important in the history of human rights that each Amendment deserves individual attention here.

1st **Amendment**: freedom of religion, freedom of speech and of the press, freedom to peaceably assemble and to petition the Government for redress of grievances.

2nd **Amendment**: right to a "well[-]regulated Militia" for "the security of a free State," and the "right of the people to keep and bear Arms."

3rd **Amendment**: right to be free in peacetime from the "quartering" of soldiers in any "house" without consent of the owner, and in time of war except as prescribed by law.

4th **Amendment**: right to be secure in their persons, houses, papers and effects, against unreasonable searches and seizures, and no warrants to be issued, "but upon probable cause, supported by Oath or affirmation, and particularly describing the place to be searched and the persons or things to be seized."

5th **Amendment**: freedom from Indictment, "for a capital, or otherwise infamous crime, unless on a presentment or indictment of a Grand Jury," "nor shall any person be subject for the same offence to be twice put in jeopardy of life or limb," "nor shall be compelled in any criminal case to be a witness against himself," nor, "deprived of life, liberty, or property, without due process of law," nor, "shall private property be taken for public use, without just compensation."

6th Amendment: In any criminal prosecution, the right to a speedy and public trial, by an impartial jury, and "to be informed of the nature and cause of the accusation," and "to be confronted with the witnesses against him," and "to have compulsory process for obtaining witnesses in his favor," and to have the right to "Counsel for his defence."

7th Amendment: Right to trial by jury in civil suits and as to the binding nature of factual findings by a jury.

8th Amendment: the right to reasonable bail, the right to be free of "excessive fines," and the right to be free from "cruel and unusual punishments."

Then, the often overlooked but *enormously* important,

9th Amendment: "The enumeration in the Constitution, of certain rights, shall not be construed to deny or disparage others retained by the people."

And, the,

10th Amendment: "The powers not delegated to the United States by the Constitution, nor prohibited by it to the States, are reserved to the States respectively or to the people."

The Bill of Rights has stood the test of time within the United States as a pillar of guidance in the realm of human rights.

United Nations Proclamations

In the United Nations Charter, all member states pledged themselves to jointly and separately take action to achieve, "universal respect for and observance of human rights and fundamental freedoms for all without distinction as to race, sex, language, or religion."

In 1948, the United Nations unanimously adopted[49] a roadmap of human rights in the **Universal Declaration of Human Rights** ("UDHR").[50] The UDHR embodies a *very specific listing* of rights. Think of this as detail extrapolated from an *international baseline of human rights*. The United States officially endorses and remains committed to the UDHR.

"In today's splintered world, it is hard to imagine that there might be a common denominator upon which all nations can agree. But international Human Rights Day reminds us that it wasn't so long ago that the world came together to do exactly that. On December 10, 1948, the United Nations unanimously adopted the Universal Declaration of Human Rights (UDHR), a set of rights to which all individuals are entitled."[51]

---

49   Eight nations abstained from the vote, but none dissented.

50   Adopted and Proclaimed in Paris, France, by United Nations General Assembly Resolution 217 A, December 10, 1948. This proclamation has been translated into over 500 languages and has inspired the adoption of in excess of seventy human rights treaties, at global and regional levels, all containing citations to the UDHR in their respective preambles.

51   https://br. usembassy.gov/united-states-remains-committed-to-universal-declaration-of-human-rights/ Robert Destro, EUA continuam comprometidos com a Declaracao Universal de Direitos Humanos, U.S. Department of State, published on *Folha de Sao Palo*, December 10, 2019

An astonishing collection of human rights,[52] the UDHR is both *eloquent and comprehensive* in its treatment of this subject, and cries out for close examination. There are **thirty (30)** Articles in the UDHR.

Article 1 proclaims the *natural origin* of these rights:

> "All human beings are born free and equal in dignity and rights. They are endowed with reason and conscience and should act towards one another in a spirit of brotherhood."

Article 2 affirms the across-the-board nature of these rights—that they may not be infringed by any form of suspect class discrimination:

> "Everyone is entitled to all the rights and freedoms set forth in this Declaration, without distinction of any kind, such as race, colour, sex, language, religion, political or other opinion, national or social origin, property, birth or other status. Furthermore, no distinction shall be made on the basis of the political, jurisdictional or international status of the country or territory to which a person belongs, whether it be independent, trust, non-self-governing or under any other limitation of sovereignty."

Article 3 offers a shorthand summary of the totality of human rights:

---

52 Albeit, perhaps largely overlooked by, and even unknown to, the average person, absent thorough investigation as to the origin and dynamics of contemporary human rights.

"Everyone has the right to life, liberty and security of person."

The reference to *security of person* is a *key component* to rights, since it arguably alludes to the *enforceability* of the right to life and liberty. Since the UDHR is referring to rights vis-à-vis governments and oppressive forces, "security" is not directed only towards security offered by the institution, but also security *against* the institution.

Article 4 assures freedom against slavery, involuntary servitude, the slave-trade (and, inferentially, unreasonable "false imprisonment" and prisoner "loan-outs" to private industry):

"No one shall be held in slavery or servitude; slavery and the slave trade shall be prohibited in all their forms."

Article 5 proscribes cruel and unusual punishment:

"No one shall be subjected to torture or to cruel, inhuman or degrading treatment or punishment."[53]

---

53 Exceptionally egregious examples of **Article 5 violations** occurred during the **Abu Ghraib prisoner abuse scandal**. The scandal arose upon discovery in 2004 of graphic photos evidencing the systemic mistreatment in 2003 of Iraqi detainees by U.S. Soldiers. The prison was located approximately 20 miles west of Baghdad on some 280 acres. Eleven US soldiers, including seven from Military Police, were later convicted of criminal offenses. The crimes were described by Secretary of Defense Donald Rumsfeld as being, "blatantly sadistic, cruel and inhuman." Extensive investigations by the U.S. Army and an independent commission revealed detainee-abuse including, among other things: forcibly arranging detainees in sexually explicit positions for photographing; forcing male detainees to wear women's underwear; forcing groups of male detainees to masturbate themselves while being photographed and videotaped; positioning a naked detainee on a box, with a sandbag on his head, and attaching wires to his

Article 6 affirms that these rights *follow* every person, wherever in the world they may go:

"Everyone has the right to recognition everywhere as a person before the law."

Article 7 assures that each person is entitled to "equal protection" of the law, in the sense of freedom from discrimination by receiving adverse disparate treatment:

"All are equal before the law and are entitled without any discrimination to equal protection of the law. All are entitled to equal protection against any discrimination in violation of this Declaration and against any incitement to such discrimination."

Article 8 purports to supply an (albeit *disturbingly vague*) institutional *forum* for enforcement of these rights:

"Everyone has the right to an effective remedy by the competent national tribunals for acts violating the fundamental rights granted him by the constitution or by law.

Article 9 provides for freedom from unreasonable seizure or forced exportation ("exile"):

---

fingers, toes and penis to simulate electric torture; and, a male Military Police guard having sex with a female detainee. CNN, *Iraq Prison Abuse Scandal Fast Facts*, March 10, 2023.

"No one shall be subjected to arbitrary arrest, detention or exile."

Article 10 asserts the right to a fair trial in a criminal prosecution:

"Everyone is entitled in full equality to a fair and public hearing by an independent and impartial tribunal, in the determination of his rights and obligations and of any criminal charge against him."

Article 11 assures rights in criminal prosecutions to a presumption of innocence, a fair and public trial, the guarantees necessary for defense, and a right against any *ex post facto* charge or sentence not in effect at the time of the alleged offense.

Article 12 represents a guarantee of a right to privacy and security against defamation, and a concomitant right of *legal enforcement* of such rights:

"No one shall be subjected to arbitrary interference with his privacy, family, home or correspondence, nor to attacks upon his honour and reputation. Everyone has the right to the protection of the law against such interference or attacks."

Article 13 establishes a universal right of travel inside and outside of any country:

"1. Everyone has the right to freedom of movement and residence within the borders of each state.

2.   Everyone has the right to leave any country, including his own, and to return to his country."

Article 14 confirms the right of persons to claim asylum from political persecution.

Article 15 assures the "right to a nationality," and to change one's nationality.

Article 16 proclaims a universal right to marriage, family and dissolution of marriage without discrimination:

"1.   Men and women of full age, without any limitation due to race, nationality or religion, have the right to marry and to found a family. They are entitled to equal rights as to marriage, during marriage and at its dissolution.

2.   Marriage shall be entered into only with the free and full consent of the intending spouses.

3.   The family is the natural and fundamental group unit of society and is entitled to protection by society and the State."

Article 17 establishes that each person has a "right to own property alone as well as in association with others," and to not be "arbitrarily deprived of his property."

Article 18 affirms "freedom of thought, conscience and religion":

"Everyone has the right to freedom of thought, conscience and religion; this right includes freedom to change his religion or belief, and freedom, either alone or in community with others and in public or private, to manifest his religion or belief in teaching, practice worship and observance."

Article 19 herald's freedom of thought and expression, "through any media":

"Everyone has the right to freedom of opinion and expression; this right includes freedom to hold opinions without interference and to seek, receive and impart information and ideas through any media and regardless of frontiers."

Article 20 guarantees freedom of peaceful assembly and association.

"1. Everyone has the right to freedom of peaceful assembly and association.

2. No one may be compelled to belong to an association."

Article 21 asserts a right to democracy and suffrage:

"1. Everyone has the right to take part in the government of his country, directly or through freely chosen representatives.

2. Everyone has the right of equal access to public service in his country.

3. The will of the people shall be the basis of the authority of government; this will shall be expressed in periodic and genuine elections which shall be by universal and equal suffrage and shall be held by secret vote or by equivalent free voting procedures."

Article 22 confirms the right of each person to "social security" and access to "economic, social and cultural rights indispensable for his dignity and…personality."

Article 23 affords everyone the right to work, against unemployment, "equal pay for equal work," to "an existence worthy of human dignity, and supplemented, if necessary, by other means of social protection," and a right to unionize.

Article 24 purports to assure a right to at least minimal, "rest and leisure, including reasonable limitation of working hours and periodic holidays with pay."

Article 25 asserts at least a minimum "standard of living," including, "food, clothing, housing and medical care and necessary social services, and the right to security in the event of unemployment, sickness, disability, widowhood, old age or other lack of livelihood in circumstances beyond his control." It further assures "special care and assistance" for motherhood and childhood, "whether born in or out of wedlock."

Article 26 affirms a right of compulsory education, "free at least in the elementary and fundamental stages," and parents shall "have a prior right to choose the kind of education that shall be given to their children."

Article 27 confirms cultural and intellectual property rights:

"1. Everyone has the right freely to participate in the cultural life of the community, to enjoy the arts and to share in scientific advancement and its benefits.

2. Everyone has the right to the protection of the moral and material interests resulting from any scientific, literary or artistic production of which he is the author."

Article 28 touts the right of all to, "a social and international order in which the rights and freedoms set forth in this Declaration can be fully realized."

Article 29 asserts duties of individuals and strict limitations against societal infringements upon rights:

"1. Everyone has duties to the community in which alone the free and full development of his personality is possible.

2. In the exercise of his rights and freedoms, everyone shall be subject only to such limitations as are determined by law solely for the purpose of securing due recognition and respect for the rights and freedoms of others and of meeting the just requirements of morality, public order and the general welfare in a democratic society.[54]

---

54 This particular proclamation is unfortunately and disturbingly *vague*, insofar as it suggests some sort of *general balancing* of "morality, public order and the

3. These rights and freedoms may in no case be exercised contrary to the purposes and principles of the United Nations."

And,

Article 30 affirms that no one may abrogate any rights set forth in the Declaration:

"Nothing in this Declaration may be interpreted as implying for any State, group or person any right to engage in any activity or to perform any act aimed at the destruction of any of the rights and freedoms set forth herein."

Overall, this is quite an articulate and comprehensive piece of international rights explication—*and written in 1948!* —over 75 years ago!

But where did these powerful notions of freedom, self-determination, liberty and the right to happiness *originally* arise, in their earliest, most primitive state? Surely, we had come a long way in the *expression* of human rights since the simplistic, so-called "10 Commandments",[55] to a *System* of Justice.

---

general welfare" against infringed upon individual rights. In this manner, the UDHR is *far behind* the level and specificity of constitutional protections afforded human rights within the State and federal governments of the USA. As seen *infra* in this book, the USA judicial system utilizes the very exacting *strict scrutiny test* in evaluating the lawfulness of any governmental infringement of "fundamental" human rights or discrimination against "suspect" classes.

55 The Ten Commandments, in any event, were essentially simplistic rules *against* certain activities (e.g., "Thou shall not steal" and "Thou shall not covet thy neighbor's goods"), rather than an affirmative statement of freedoms and personal rights.

But *why* is it that people abhor the proverbial Kangaroo Courts, lynch mobs and tyrannical despots? When did recognition of *essential, inherent natural law* actually commence? **Long before recorded time.**

CHAPTER THREE

The Beginnings
Prehistoric Times

PREHISTORIC TIME is generally considered to have lasted from 2.5 million years ago until some era of the Egyptian civilization. Three *archaeological periods* are involved: the Stone Age, the Bronze Age and the Iron Age. From around 300,000 BCE, now-extinct Neanderthals and Denisovans created stone and bone tools and blade weapons, jewelry such as marble rings and ivory pendants, and fire in stone hearths. In the Paleolithic period (2.5 million years ago to 10,000 BCE), humans created art which has been discovered and documented in recent times. The art ranged from paintings to stone, clay, antlers and bone figurines. In the latest glaciation period (peaking 18,000 years ago) of the "Quarternary" ice age (2.6 mya to the present) humans migrated into warmer climates. In the Neolithic period, from 8,000 BCE to 3,000 BCE, ancient humans gravitated from nomadic lifestyles as hunter/gatherers, to more consolidated living circumstances in an agrarian lifestyle. Humans began to settle into larger and larger communities, and empires such as the Egyptian Empire developed, flourished and lasted thousands of years. Culture, government and military strength were all developed.

It is during this clash of humans with humans and humans with governments that notions of human rights rose in prominence. Even during hunter-gatherer eras, itinerant groups had to differentiate between persons *within* their group, *others*—and persons *outside* of their group, *strangers*. The concept of "us" versus "them" compelled humans to consider concepts of humanity versus inhumanity, right and wrong relative to encounters with humans of competing interests and security. Even the limits, if any, of security and self-defense were in steady development.

It is widely reported in *modern* jurisprudence, that *self-defense is a natural law* which needs no statutory protection. Indeed, in an early California Court of Appeal case, *People v. Turpin*,[56] the Court affirmed a murder conviction and approved the trial court's jury instruction, on the law of self-defense, which had been read to the jury as follows:

> "'The right of self-defense, of a party violently assaulted by another to repel such attack, and fully protect himself, is a law of nature, it antedates all written enactments, and is fully recognized in the laws and legislation of all civilized people.'"

However, in a *historical* assessment of English "common law," the Court in *Sydnor v. State*[57] found that,

> "'The right to act in self-defense has been regarded as a natural right, taken all but for granted, but, as a legal

---

56 (1909) 10 Cal.App. 526.

57 (2001) 776 A.2d 669, 673-674, 365 Md. 205, 211-215.

defense to a charge of homicide, it was *not* part of early English common law."

Nevertheless, the **essence** of human rights—recognition of a right of self-defense and personal security—*would have developed* as a natural progression in *prehistoric human's response* to an, "us/others" versus "strangers," scenario. In their "attempts to structure a narrative of the evolution of human society and sociability," Anna Belfer-Chohen and Erella Hovers wrote,

> "Social 'connectivity' through time is currently considered as one of the major drivers of cultural transmission and cultural evolution ... The concepts of 'other' and 'stranger' have received little attention in the archaeological discourse, yet they are fundamental in the perception of social standing. ... We find that contrary to the null hypothesis the archaeological record implies earlier emergence of complex socio-cognitive categorization."[58]

In a fascinating bit of insight, Prehistoric Perspectives quotes from MEDITATION XVLL, Devotions upon Emergent Occasions:

> "'No man is an island entire of itself; every man is a piece of the continent, a part of the main.'"

This subtle observation may provide a necessary inference as to pre-historic humans. Once interaction, by oneself and others, with strangers occurs, the "others" become affected by the "strangers." No

---

58 Front. Psychol., *Prehistoric Perspectives on 'Others' and 'Strangers'* ("*Prehistoric Perspectives*"), January 21, 2020.

man is an island. Such interactions, and conflicts, were inevitable, even with hunter-gatherers.

> "At a group-level, when a number of individuals consider themselves as 'one,' vis-à-vis individuals or groups that do not belong to the 'one,' 'others' becomes a social cognitive construct. Still, there are degrees of social 'otherness' that can be perceived within and between groups. Hunter gatherer kinship terminologies [citation] make it psychologically possible to embrace non-kin members of one's residential or task group, with whom one shares common history and beliefs, in order to accept them as kin. ..."[59]

There were other reasons for inevitable interaction with outsiders, including,

> "the need to outcompete carnivores and gain safety through numbers. ... Encounters with individuals that did not belong to the same group would be less crucial for survival, and therefore would not be pre-scheduled or repetitive...[and] potential causes for inter-personal tensions would stem from economic interests, related to the availability, ownership and sharing of resources. Such encounters occurred between [meaning, "with"] 'strangers,' i.e., [with] individuals or groups that did not share common history, cultural traditions, or behavioral patterns."[60]

---

59 Ibid.

60 Ibid.

Through these interactions, humans developed relationships with others, but also developed **a right to be free from abuse** by those others *and by strangers*. The writers continued by pointing out that,

> "Notwithstanding any biological limitations on group size, humans acquired a cognitive flexibility that enabled them to first, enlarge the biological and social perception of kin and, secondly, to categorize their social world as one of stable ('kin'/'classificatory kin'/'others') and transient relationships ('strangers'). ... In late MP [Middle Pleistocene era--] in Eurasia may be the first time when 'strangers' become an element of the social structure, within networks of partial connectivity greatly contributing to the growth and evolution of human culture at large [citations]."[61]

Notions of complex social hierarchy, personal autonomy and security would inexorably arise in any group of "others," even more so in *transient relationships* of "others" with strangers. Thus, the inevitability of concepts akin to "human rights" of freedom, privacy, security, justice, expression and beliefs arose for prehistoric humans, naturally. In a crude sense, a sense of these "rights," *vis a vis* an interloper, was captured by Zechariah Chafee, Jr.:

> "Your right to swing your arms ends just where the other man's nose begins."[62]

---

61 Ibid.

62 *Freedom of Speech in Wartime*, Z Chafee, 32 Harvard Law Review 932, 957 (1919).

However, swinging one's arms, and other body parts, was only *the beginning* of the types of force developed and utilized for the notion of self-defense (and aggressive offense).

Weapons

Hand-held weaponry for hunting commenced the eventual escalation and innovation of weapons. Prior to recorded history,

> "the earliest stone tools … [were already] hundreds of thousands of years old, and the first arrowheads date to more than 60,000 years ago. Hunting tools—the spear-thrower (atlatl), the simple bow, the javelin, and the sling—had serious military potential, but the first known implements designed purposely as offensive weapons were maces dating from the Chalcolithic Period or early Bronze Age. The mace was a simple rock, shaped for the hand and intended to smash bone and flesh, to which a handle had been added to increase the velocity and force of the blow."[63]

Specialized technology for *communities* of humans included, of course, *fortress walls*:

> "The earliest evidence for a specialized technology of war dates from the period before knowledge of metalworking had been acquired. The **stone walls** of Jericho, which date from about 8000 BCE, represent the first technology that can be ascribed unequivocally to purely military purposes. These walls, at least 13 feet (4 metres [sic: meters]) in

---

63 Britannica, *Prehistory The earliest military weapons.*

THE BEGINNINGS PREHISTORIC TIMES

height and backed by a watchtower or redoubt some 28 feet tall, were clearly intended to protect the settlement and its water supply from human intruders."[64] (bold added for emphasis)

Fighting arts, including weaponry, arose to *unprecedented sophistication* in Asia.

"The fighting arts are as old as man himself. As a means of preparing an individual to defend himself and to wreak havoc on an enemy, in no other part of the world did they develop to the heights that they did in Asia. Beginning as hunting skills of prehistoric peoples, these arts developed with the experience gained when man pitted himself against man."[65]

Although fighting *systems* cannot be traced literally back to the evolution of humans, they are easily traceable thousands of years into the past:

"Elements of the Chinese martial arts, now popularly known in the West as Kung Fu, can be traced to the Neolithic Age approximately four thousand years ago. The earliest form of martial arts appears in the story in which the legendary Yellow Emperor, Huang Ti, fought and defeated his enemy, Chi You, by using classical Chinese wrestling methods. This incident occurred in the first half of the third millennium B.C. ... [D]uring

---

64 Ibid.

65 Draeger & Smith, *COMPREHENSIVE ASIAN FIGHTING ARTS*, (Kodansha Publishing 1981) at p. 7.

the Shang dynasty (c. 1523—c. 1027 V.C.) with the first evidence of oracle bone inscriptions and script itself, it again was asserted that wrestling existed.[66]

Fighting styles morphed into cultural traditions, which helped to pass techniques on from generation to generation.

"… [C]ertain fighting movements were developed into a type of folk dance performed by people wearing animal horns on their heads and butting into each other, then grabbing and throwing each other to the ground. This festive demonstration was designed to show strength and virility, as in two powerful bulls contending against one another. In this, the Age of Bronze, archaeological finds have proved that war chariots with horse in Harness were common. Spears, arrows, knives and needles were made from bronze, indicating the advancement of fighting and hunting tactics."[67]

In the Chou dynasty (c. 1027—256 BCE), records are abundant that archery and charioteering were popular and practiced, as was hand-to-hand combat:

"The classic Book of Odes, a compilation of some three hundred poems circa 700 B.C., celebrates great moments of Chinese ceremony or ritual. Fighting with the fists,

---

66 Chow & Spangler, *KUNG FU History, Philosophy and Technique* (*"Kung Fu"*), (Action Pursuit Group 1980) at p. 2.

67 Ibid.

Ch'uan p'o, is mentioned in at least one line, 'Without the fist, there is no bravery.'"[68]

A sort of ancient mercenary resource of warriors (with their own code of justice) developed in China during the second half of the Chou dynasty (770—221 B.C.). Drawing on demand by feudal lords for armies of fighters for wars between neighboring feudal states, countless peasants, artisans and merchants volunteered:

> "Sensing employment and adventure, they became professional men, better known as knights-errant. They roamed from state to state offering their services to beleaguered lords. Most of the knights-errant, according to [historian] Ssu-ma, were skilled in military arts with special emphasis placed on swordsmanship. From this piece of information, it can be determined that fighting arts were widely practiced by the common people, especially those who were or wished to become knights-errant."[69]

Confucius lived from 551—479 BCE, and is widely considered to be the foremost source of Chinese philosophy. Within the many schools of philosophical thought to follow Confucius was the most influential—Taoism (pronounced *Dowism*). Taoism was anarchistic and professed that,

---

68 Id. at p. 3.

69 Ibid.

"'The more restrictions and prohibitions there are in the law books, the more thieves and bandits there will be.'"[70]

The Taoist sought to remove him/herself from the constraints of society:

"'Te,' or 'the Power,' is the manifestation of Tao in substantiality or corporeity, the most important element in any existence, created by the interaction of Yin and Yang. This means that every object or substance possesses positive and negative elements with itself. ... Herein lies a major East-West difference in philosophical attitudes. The Westerner, *a la* Shakespeare's *Hamlet*, would say, 'To be or not to be? That is the question.' The Taoist sage, on the other hand, would say, 'To be and not to be. That is the answer!'"[71]

The principal Taoist writer, Chuang Tzu, 365—290 B.C., heralded un-assumed, unstrained action. Thus, the power of a warrior comes from *doing nothing which is forced or unnatural*.[72] Moreover, the Chinese fighter was anything but a reckless force, but rather, he (or she) acted based upon a strong code of conduct and concern for justice.

"Despite having the capability of crushing an assailant's body, a true Chinese master, steeped in Taoist philosophy, would never dishonor his art by reducing himself to work

---

70   Id. at p. 15.

71   Id., p. 17.

72   Id., p. 20.

such base, senseless aggression. He would say, 'To rejoice in the conquest is to rejoice in murder.'"[73]

From stone maces, to archery and martial arts, copper mace heads in the 3rd millennium BCE, bronze and iron, steel, chariots, swordsmanship, fire power, including explosive bombs and, zipping through time, to the present:

"Magneto Hydrodynamic Explosive Munition (MAHEM)

The MAHEM weapons system by DARPA uses a magnetic flux generator to fire a projectile without the traditional use of chemical explosives creating a more efficient and precise launch system. This projectile weapons system also uses molten metal to penetrate enemy armoured vehicles increasing lethality and effectiveness on the battlefield."[74]

The technological progression of weaponry for self-defense is limited only by time, resources and ingenuity. Fighting skills and weaponry constitute *physical manifestations* of the human instinct and struggle for survival, and the evolutionary means of self-defense (and defense of others and of property[75]). Human rights likewise evolve to respond to the complexities of contemporary life.

---

73 Ibid.

74 Pocket-lint, *61 interesting and incredibly futuristic weapons and modern fighting vehicles,* June 9, 2021. www.pocket-lint.com.

75 *See,* Forbes, Jack, *Stand Your Ground, TO KILL, OR NOT TO KILL, The Legal Limits of Safety* ("*Stand Your Ground*"), (JAFO Publishing 2015), Scenarios 9 and 10 at pp. 81-101.

Natural law right of self-preservation

The evolution of self-defense is on-going. It has progressed from crude, hand-to-hand combat to national campaigns by world powers for "strategic stability" and "managing escalation in the midst of limited war." The *underlying base principle*, however, is a simple one:

> Each *person*—and by extension to communities of persons—each *sovereign nation*, has the natural law right to preserve liberty and protect oneself physically, culturally, and spiritually from outside aggression, interference and the use of force.

That is the fundamental basis for what we now refer to as "human rights." Indeed, in the United States, our System of Justice goes to *great lengths* to promote and implement these concepts of freedom from unwanted aggression, physical assault, theft and annoyance. But how have *religious beliefs* affected the development of human rights?

CHAPTER FOUR

Religious Influence

SINCE TIME IMMEMORIAL, the world and its various nations and cultures have known, and largely embraced, competing religions of one kind or another. Each of the religions seem to inexplicably contend that it happens to be the *final word on truth*. Christianity, for example, evolved (with some help from Constantine and various forgers of Biblical scriptures) from a belief in Jesus as a *metaphorical* character in history to a belief in Jesus as an *actual* historical "Son of God."[76] Each religion naturally develops its own, unique formula for explaining the unknown and unknowable and delving into the origins of life, and for that matter, the *origins of everything*.

Organized religions have literally taken on lives of their own. Perhaps, through the millennia, religious notions of the essence of

---

76 The play, *Deconstructing the Code* [Forbes, Jack, *Deconstructing the Code*, (JAFO Publishing 2017)], is a story, based on historical facts, "of love, lost meaning, treachery, distrust, creative expression, blatant forgery, book burnings and the chance discovery of priceless writings of antiquity." [back cover description] It chronicles the perverse manipulation of the Christian religion from its origins to the present day.

life and of ideals to be achieved have helped shape what are now considered to constitute inalienable human rights.

Ancient Egypt

In one of the earliest civilizations in recorded history, the Egyptians practiced a religion characterized by many gods (polytheism) which co-existed with mankind and controlled existence from afar. These deities were characters in mythology/stories which described and gave meaning to the universe as they understood it. They believed in an afterlife, taking many forms according to the social stature of the decedent. They believed that in an underworld known as the Duat, there was a single entrance which could be accessed by travel through the tomb of the deceased. They believed in eternal life. And, they believed in reincarnation—specifically of the soul. Souls were presented to Osiris, who determined the relative virtue of the decedent's soul. Those favorably determined, received from Osiris a rewarding and peaceful afterlife. The deeds of a deceased were reflected in afterlife texts and spells which were placed within tombs, pyramids, and coffins of the decedent. An ancient book known as the **Book of the Dead** catalogues spells and texts created to help the deceased find their way safely to Duat. Mummification was implemented in order that the bodies of the dead would be preserved and reborn in the afterlife. Once the judging was concluded, Souls arrived at the Hall of Ma'at, where the purity and goodness of the deceased would act as the *force du jure* of whether they would enter the Kingdom of Osiris.

Egyptian law developed over thousands of years. Fundamental concepts of law and order were established in Egypt as early as the Predynastic Period (c. 6000 – c. 3150 BCE) and continued to thrive until Egypt was conquered by Rome in 30 BCE. Essentially, Egyptian law was based on a view of right and wrong, adhering (eventually) to codified laws and court precedents based on the concept of Ma'at (harmony). Ma'at embodied truth, balance, justice and order everywhere in the universe. In order to enter the afterlife, one needed to be at peace with oneself, others and the gods, and to live a life characterized by consideration, thoughtfulness and balance. The laws were created and administered in order to foster and encourage people to live according to these principles of harmony.

The Pharaoh, was the political and religious leader of Egypt, and was considered to be *a living god*. Though he made the laws and appointed the highest legal official, the Vizier, as the supreme jurist in Egypt, the Pharaoh and his family were considered *exempt* from all laws. Penalties for violating laws against murder, rape, false testimony, tomb-robbing and substantial theft were grave and often family members were punished along with the offender. The most serious punishments reportedly included excision of the offender's nose, ears, tongue, ears, penis, testicles, hands or feet, depending on the crime. Thieves were commonly administered amputation of the nose, hands or feet. Banishment or branding with a mark of shame could be administered. Capital punishment could be by burning alive, drowning in a basket in the Nile River, decapitation, or impalement on a stake. Punishment for rape would be castration or penis amputation. Punishment for murder would be that the offender was beaten and then fed to crocodiles on the Nile River, burned alive or otherwise executed in harshly creative ways.

As to human rights, Pharaoh Bocchoris reportedly banned imprisonment for debt. On the other hand, persons accused of crime were *presumed guilty* until and unless proven innocent. It was assumed that no one would be brought before the court and charged with a crime unless they were guilty. Accordingly, witnesses were commonly *beaten* to assure that they were telling the truth. Even persons *acquitted* of crimes were nevertheless saddled with the label of having been a "suspect." *Case precedents* from at least as early the Early Dynastic Period (c. 3150 – c. 2613 BCE) were referred to within the early years of the Old Kingdom (c. 2613 – c. 2181 BCE). Precedents from the Old Kingdom were, in turn, used in adjudicating cases in the Middle Kingdom period (c. 2040 – c. 1782 BCE) and so on.

With the exception of slaves and the Pharaoh and his court, all persons in ancient Egypt were treated as equals under the law. Men and women could hold and own property, including slaves. Both sexes could request and receive a divorce although women were favored in receiving the children. Persons could designate to whom their property would pass upon their deaths. Men and women could testify with equal weight. There were courts/places to adjudicate disputes, although in the early periods of ancient Egypt, *priests acted as the judges and conferred with the gods* to assist them in making decisions. Thus, in addition to freedom from debtor's prison (and except for slaves), *the sexes were deemed equal* as to competency to testify, to have a paying job, and as to property rights, inheritance rights, and access to divorce. These entitlements and penalties, however, were not *per se* considered as preexisting, inalienable rights of Egyptians, except insofar as the *origin* of the laws was the Kingdom of Osiris, through the living-god Pharaoh.

Bearing false witness was deemed one of the most heinous crimes, since legal proceedings were said to be implemented on behalf of the gods. Law was said to have been a product of the gods on "the First Occasion" (the instant of creation). A false verdict was a serious problem for this concept, and so persons accused and convicted of giving false witness could expect punishment by amputation or drowning.

Although divorce was available by either party to a marriage, *infidelity* became a serious crime once brought to the attention of a local magistrate by either the married couple or outsiders. Punishment for an unfaithful wife could be by the cutting off of her nose, or death. Punishment for an unfaithful husband could be up to 1,000 strikes of a cane, but not the death penalty.

Women were permitted to play, and played, prominent roles in the governance of Egypt. However, since Pharaohs were considered to be *living gods*, they could not marry mortals. Pharaoh Hatshepsut commenced rule in around 1,500 BCE and married her half-brother, Thutmose. A beautiful Nefertiti later became Queen when she married Pharaoh Amenhotep IV. During his rule, Egyptians were devoted to only one god. Cleopatra became Queen of Egypt at age 18 and later had a relationship with Caesar when he visited Alexandria, Egypt. They had a son, and Caesar helped Cleopatra to resume power in Egypt, now as a Pharaoh. Following Caesar's murder in Rome, Cleopatra developed a relationship with Marc Anthony, also a leader of Rome. They had two children and together ruled two enormous empires. After his death by suicide upon defeat in combat, Cleopatra committed suicide by poisonous snake.

Despite this attention to detail in creating substantial equality, Egypt considered *slaves to have lesser rights*. As primarily prisoners of war, "slaves" were more like quasi-owned servants during that period. They could marry, own land and themselves employ servants. Many slaves worked on household tasks, were gardeners, entertainers or assistants in business affairs. The sale of children into slavery was also a practice within Egypt and from other nations. And the children of slaves also became slaves as an operation of law.

This troubling dichotomy between the civil rights of most citizens of Egypt, versus a sort of officially sanctioned, permanent, indentured servitude class of persons, indicates that in Egypt, **notions of equality were anything but absolute, innate human rights**. Instead, "equality" consisted of **an accumulation of *rights of convenience* to perpetuate a complex society** consistent with treating the royal family as gods, exempt from all laws, and privileged with fabulous wealth and indulgence. Ordinary citizens, on the other hand, were rewarded with a modicum of prosperity, security and the promise of an afterlife, but only so long as they lived their lives "harmoniously" and with respect to the Pharaoh and the gods. This manner of *invidious societal manipulation*— providing apparent rewards for conformity to religious precepts and harsh punishment for diversion from the righteous—was later adopted as the predominant *modus operandi* in a subsequent religion: Christianity.

Christianity

The Bible is an edited collection of original, modified and even *forged*[77] scriptures in the "New Testament" and of miscellaneous scriptures "before Christ" of the "Old Testament." There are primitive laws, duties and warnings referred to within the Bible, such as the so-called "Ten Commandments" (purportedly a set of laws directly from God him/herself—that sounds familiar, doesn't it?).

But is there evidence within the Bible of any *personal freedoms and individual "rights"* as against others and as against authorities, such as governments or religious authorities?

Some claim that human rights are inherent in Christian beliefs, derived from being "created" in "God's image," and the "state of grace" giving all humans inherent worth. Jesus Christ, it is written, granted to believers their *freedom*:

> "It is for freedom that Christ has set us free. Stand firm, then, and do not let yourselves be burdened again by a yoke of slavery." Galatians 5:1

---

77 Pagels, Elaine, *Beyond Belief, The Secret Gospel of Thomas*, pp. 30-73, (Vintage Books 2004); and, Freke & Gandy, *The Jesus Mysteries*, pp. 237-239, (Three Rivers Press, Random House 1999).

At least an aspect of that freedom is *freedom from eternal damnation as sinners*:

> "For one who has died has been set free from sin."
> Romans 6:7

In a sense, the *strawman*-threat is "eternal damnation" for sinners, and the purported freedom-solution is absolution from the unspeakable horrors of that terrible, *false-hypothetical* fate. Along the same lines:

> "For the law of the Spirit of life has set you free in Christ
> Jesus from the law of sin and death." Romans 8:2

Thus, the "freedom" is in the nature of a *spiritual or conceptual* freedom:

> "For you were called to freedom, brothers. Only do not
> use your freedom as an opportunity for the flesh, but
> through love serve one another." 4 Galatians 5:13

The freedom which is yours *lives within the Spirt*:

> "Now the Lord is the Spirit, and where the Spirit of the
> Lord is, there is freedom." 2 Corinthians 3:17

This freedom arrives from understanding the "truth," and truth must be understood as being *Christian beliefs*:

> "And you will know the truth, and the truth will set you
> free." John 8:32

The Bible tells believers to,

"Fear God. Honor the emperor." 1 Peter 2:17.

It warns to not use freedom, as a "cover-up for evil" but rather for, "living as servants of God." 1 Peter 2:16.

Thus, the Biblical theme keeps circling back to "freedom" as being the freedom and obligation **to *adhere to Christian beliefs*** and to **spread the Word**. Some would argue this kind of "freedom" seems suspiciously like ***submission to indoctrination***. If you submit to Christian beliefs (indoctrination) then you avert proverbial damnation and will experience both nirvana (freedom) and the compulsion to "love the brotherhood" and spread the word. 1 Peter 2:16.

Moreover, in Christianity, one should spread the word to the *brokenhearted, captives and prisoners* alike:

> "The Spirit of the Lord God is upon me, because the Lord has anointed me to bring good news to the afflicted; He has sent me to bind up the brokenhearted, to proclaim liberty to captives and freedom to prisoners." Isaiah 61:1

Christian salvation comes directly *from God Himself*:

> "Out of my distress I called on the Lord; the Lord answered me and set me free." Psalm 118:5

Ultimately, however, such freedom represents *non-negotiable, conscripted devotion*:

> "You have been set free from sin and have become slaves to righteousness." Romans 6:18

Believers even become, "slaves of God," the reward for which is "sanctification" and immortality:

> "But now that you have been set free from sin and have become slaves of God, the fruit you get leads to sanctification and its end, eternal life." Romans 6:22

In this sense, the righteous follower *succeeds* as,

> "a slave of Christ." 1 Corinthians 7:22.

Worldly sin and death magically *transmute* to freedom in Christ Jesus:

> "For the law of the Spirit of life has set you free in Christ Jesus from the law of sin and death." Romans 8:2

Unless one happens to be *blinded* by ubiquitous Christian dogma and indoctrination, **the bottom line is readily apparent**: "freedom" as referred to within Christianity is freedom from responsibility for, or attraction to, "misbehavior" violative of core Christian dogma. In effect, one becomes "free" of "bondage to corruption" as to *participation* in worldly pleasures, by submission to the Word of God:

> "That the creation itself [i.e., humans] will be set free from its bondage to corruption and obtain the freedom of the glory of the children of God." Romans 8:21

Christ "Himself" foregoes all freedom in order to serve others—with a purpose of *converting more believers*:

"For though I am free from all, I have made myself a servant to all, that I might win more of them." 1 Corinthians 9:19

The freedom achieved through belief creates a sort-of *vested-immunity* from the harsh laws of the Bible's Old Testament:

"And by him everyone who believes is freed from everything from which you could not be freed by the law of Moses." Acts 13:39

The *fear of death*, and of *the devil* who has the power of death and damnation, *will be freed by Christ*:

"...[S]o that by his death he might break the power of him who holds the power of death—that is, the devil— and free those who all their lives were held in slavery by their fear of death." Hebrews 2:14-15

Unfortunately, the *Christian version of freedom* is that **you are free *to do as you are told*,** or to suffer the *alternative* of **eternal, agonizing damnation.** Not such a cheerful mission statement in this religion. Thus, the promise of freedom, in the Christian sense, is not a *human right*, so much as a *blatant and unrepentant form* of *extortion* for everyone to fulfill an obligation and commensurate commitment to intractable, institutional, Christian religion indoctrination.

Hindu Religion

Similarly, as pointed out by Dipti Patel, in Hinduism,

"[t]here is more emphasis on the concept of **human duties** as opposed to human rights."[78] (bold added for emphasis)

In *Foundations* [*see*, fn. 35, *supra*] Ms. Patel ties natural law in Hinduism to the concept of dharma, a central concept of Hindu thought:

"The word is derived from the root *dhr* and means to uphold, sustain and nourish. It is a comprehensive term, which includes duty, morality, ritual, law, order and justice. ... The concept of *dharma* also refers to the structure of reality."[79]

Hindu society is steeped in class (caste) structure and social regulation. *Peaceful coexistence* in Hindu culture is considered to be dependent upon, "the mutual obligations of the individual and society."[80] In terms of the *religious precepts* of Hinduism, then, although there are duties, there are few if any enforceable "rights" distinct from the duties.[81] Ms. Patel concludes,

"Therefore, human rights are not inherent but rather **to be worked towards** by the fulfilment of **duties**. ... Hinduism

---

78 *Foundations*, p. 6.

79 Ibid.

80 Id., p. 7.

81 An exception pointed out in *Foundations* is raised in the Mahabharata, a Hindu text which affords believers the right to "gird themselves up and kill a cruel king, who does not protect his subjects, who extracts taxes and simply robs them of their wealth." *Mahabharata*, 61.32-33. Id., p. 8.

tends to accord greater recognition to the rights that **others have** in relation to us as compared to the rights we have in relation to them. [footnote deleted]"[82] (bold added for emphasis)

There is an important distinction between what *duties* a person owes to others, and what *rights* a person has against mistreatment and denial of privileges by others against that person. For example, a parent may have a *legal duty* to care for and provide sustenance to his or her child. If the parent is neglectful in the *discharge* of that duty, there would be potential, adverse legal consequences such as criminal prosecution or losing custody of the child. Duties are "enforced" against the person bearing responsibility to perform the duties, by the threat or implementation of cultural or legal adverse consequences.

On the other hand, if that same parent may retain and care for his or her child versus an officious interloper or kidnapper of the child, then that is the human right. Thus, there may be *human rights* of both parent and child, and a *parental duty*. Each are enforceable, by the power of law, through restraining orders, injunctive relief, custody orders, arrest and prosecution. But in positive law and in religions, the mere existence of a "duty" does not necessarily include a corresponding *and enforceable* "right" for the individual.

Thus, in the Hindu religion, many societal benefits to the individual are believed dependent upon that individual's *contributions to others and contributions to social welfare*. This would be distinguished from societal benefits inuring to individuals pursuant to preexisting, essential human *rights*, inherent in natural law.

In a related sense, then, an important issue is whether **perceived *"rights"*** are in any manner **enforceable** by law, moral

---

82 Ibid.

precepts, religion or culture against governmental misconduct and wrongdoer abuse and violence. Without enforceability, a so-called human "right" becomes merely a tool for placating the masses into a false sense of security, an illusory notion of freedom, and a weapon of oppression.

At the close of the 17th Century, in the Bay Colony of Salem, Massachusetts, the right to a fair trial proved to be anything but an enforceable right.

Bay Colony—Salem, Massachusetts

In the harsh winter of 1691-1692, at the Bay Colony of Salem, Massachusetts, the Puritan religion thrived. Its pious believers lived an austere lifestyle, in the image of their Lord. Life seemed pure and simple—that is, until it became overwhelmed in the midst of suspicion and fear of witches. Here's how the carnage began.

A Reverend Samuel Parris employed a "colored" domestic servant, Tibuta (more likely, his slave), who had been raised in Barbados. Tibuta enjoyed telling stories of supernatural witches, spells and curses to some of the local children. Some of the children began to believe in the lurid stories as fact and furthermore began to believe that the supernatural was actually having an effect *on them*. After a long winter, an unspecified illness appeared to sweep through this colony, causing Elizabeth Parris and Abigail Williams, the Reverend's daughter and niece to,

> "...fall into convulsions, scream inhumanly, and engage in other extraordinary behavior."[83]

---

83 Bednarski, Joyce, *Witchcraft and Sorcery*, "The Salem Witch-Scare Viewed Sociologically" ("*Witch-Scare*"), (Penguin Books 1982), at p. 191.

The curious and distressing condition seemed to spread to several other children who exhibited fits, contortions of their bodies and speaking in gibberish. Adults in the colony were frantic to find a solution. After the Reverend's prayer sessions proved ineffective (*what a surprise!*), the town physician, Dr. Griggs, was consulted but was unable to attribute the children's affliction to any medical condition known to him.

Modern historians and medical practitioners, incidentally, have suggested that at least some of the children likely suffered symptoms caused by the ingestion of ergot fungus-infected rye, or alternatively, by mass hysteria from stresses inherent in the persistent threat from nearby Indians and by the harsh winters of Salem.[84]

But Dr. Griggs chose to diagnose the children as having been touched by the "Evil Hand," which translated meant they were the victims of "witchcraft!" Three suspected "witches"—Tibuta, a homeless woman, Sarah Good, and a nonconformist, Sarah Osborne—were arrested and charged with witchcraft. In June, 1692, the **Salem Witch Trials** began. By the end of the scourge, 24 villagers had died of the illness, and through September, 1692, hundreds had been accused and jailed.[85] 19 men and women were convicted of witchcraft and *hanged* (none of whom were "burned at the stake"), two died in prison, and another man was "pressed" to death, by a pile of stones, for *failure to admit* to witchcraft.

A servant girl of Dr. Griggs, Elizabeth Hubbard, was a witness who testified "against 29 people, 17 of whom were arrested, 13 were hanged and two died in jail."[86] During the trials,

---

84 Legends of America, *The Afflicted Girls of Salem Village* ("*The Afflicted*"), Kathy Weiser 2020, www.legendsofamerica.com.

85 *Witch-Scare*, p. 194.

86 *The Afflicted*, p. 2.

"Several witnesses came forward and testified against
Elizabeth's character, stating that she was a religious deviant,
a girl with a vivid and powerful imagination, was known to
speak untruths, and often denied the Sabbath day."[87]

Other accusers, such as the orphaned Mercy Lewis, are seen as
having *fabricated* symptoms and accusations, with some support
from others, in order to target their enemies in the village.[88] In March
1692, twelve-year-old Ann Putnam, Jr. claimed to be afflicted from
the witchcraft. She was a friend of both Elizabeth Parris and Abigail
Williams and played a central role in testifying against 19 people
accused of witchcraft, 11 of whom were hanged.[89] Fourteen years later,
and blaming her perjury on both her "childhood" and the work of
"Satan," Ann Putnam *admitted that she had lied* at the trials and that
she now believed the accused to have been "innocent persons."[90]

The Salem tragedy, viewed in the hindsight of history, offers up
valuable epiphanies. Fear of the unknown, false "medical" diagnoses,
conspiracies to harm enemies, religious fervor, mob mentality, sham
trials with primitive experience in safeguarding the rights of the accused,
and authoritarian edicts against nonconformity *can readily conspire
to abandon justice for unmitigated suspicion and prejudice.* Human
rights can be subverted and ignored in favor of an almost predictable
absolution against Satan and his *witchcraft handiwork.*

In the face of tragedy at the Bay Colony village, reason and respect
for natural rights fell victim to *immutable and emphatically dogmatic*

---

87   Ibid.

88   Ibid.

89   Ibid.

90   Ibid.

religious beliefs and perverse concepts of social expediency. The unthinkable can evolve to the reality, and if religious convictions can result in a wholesale abandonment of basic human rights, *what effect might all-out* **warfare** *have*?

CHAPTER FIVE

All's Fair in War?

THE OLD ADAGE, "All's fair in love and war" is catchy and even somewhat accurate. In battles for love interest, many a friendship has been destroyed, and lives have been lost. And in war, never was an idiom so popular as, "The ends justify the means." One only has to recall Hiroshima and Nagasaki to illustrate this principle. But *do* the ends, always justify the means? To put it another way, are the (often *unreliable*) results of torture, murder and mayhem worth the deep and enduring cost to society?

In the United States we have decided, and the 4th Amendment to the Constitution so provides, that here, people shall be free from unreasonable searches and seizures. The penalty for violation of this principle, in a criminal prosecution, is that the evidence derived from the incident shall not be admissible in evidence against the person whose interests are violated.[91] The people have formally reserved to themselves a *fundamental right*—freedom from unreasonable searches and seizures—which tips the balance in favor of liberty at the expense of criminal law enforcement. Also, there is the

---

91 *See, e.g., Terry v. Ohio* (1968) 392 U.S. 1.

constitutional protection against cruel and unusual punishment.[92] However, exceptions have arisen.

National Security Interests and Fog of War

"National security interests" is the phrase in English which captures the concept of *self-defense for a **nation***. In this sense, national security interests constitute, optimally, self-defense for human rights *of the aggregate* of a nation's inhabitants. Nations, such as the United States, search for *effective geo-political/military strategies* in order to protect themselves, and their allies, from foreign (and domestic) aggressors:

> "One of the earliest and most influential concepts associated with these efforts was Herman Kahn's 'escalation ladder,' which defined 44 'rungs' on a metaphorical ladder of escalating conflict. The rungs ranged from 'sub-crisis maneuvering' to civilization-destroying nuclear exchanges. In between were two dozen distinct levels of escalation beyond the threshold of nuclear use, including such 'limited' attacks as non-lethal demonstrative detonations, tactical strikes on military forces, and small-scale attacks on civilians."[93]

Kahn's theory of an effective global strategy to protect national security interests became highly popular.

---

92 U.S. Constitution, 8th Amendment.

93 WAR ON THE ROCKS, *The False Allure of Escalation Dominance*, Michael Fitzsimmons, November 16, 2017.

ALL'S FAIR IN WAR?

"In this context, Kahn also introduced the term 'escalation dominance,' which became shorthand for one school of thought in deterrence and nuclear strategy. The idea posits the ability of a state to maintain such a markedly superior position over a rival, across a range of escalation rungs, that its rival will always see further escalation as a losing bet. Such dominance, the thinking goes, serves as the most effective possible deterrent to conflict, as well as the most reliable means for managing escalation if deterrence fails. As Colin Gray and Keith Payne put it in their famous 'Victory is Possible' article in 1980, 'an adequate U.S. deterrent posture is one that denies the Soviet Union any plausible hope of success at any level of strategic conflict.' Beyond U.S.-Soviet competition, analysts have continued to apply the concept to such contemporary strategic challenges as the India-Pakistan rivalry, a potential Taiwan Strait crisis, and even Middle Eastern terrorism."[94]

But securing national interests, even for arguably the strongest military power in the world (the United States), is anything but a simple task. The escalation dominance strategy has several weaknesses, including:

"*Asymmetric stakes*. As already noted, one of the key sources of escalation risk is the asymmetry of interests between prospective combatants. The most plausible scenarios of escalation involve core, vital interests of the challengers juxtaposed with American extended deterrence commitments to allies and partners. For

---

94 Ibid.

instance, the United States seeks to deter a Chinese attack on Taiwan. But under extreme circumstances, Chinese leaders may well see the survival of their regime riding on a military victory, while U.S. stakes in protecting Taiwan lie in more abstract goals of maintaining stability, order, and deterrent credibility. Will the United States really engage in nuclear war over Taiwan? Or, in a NATO-Russia conflict, risk trading Virginia Beach for Vilnius?"[95]

Escalation dominance might be better termed, "**Simplistic Overconfidence.**"

"Such potential imbalance of interests is a long-standing problem of extended deterrence. Thomas Schelling famously observed that escalation may take the form of a 'competition in risk taking,' and therefore may be governed at least as much by 'balance of resolve' as by balance of capabilities. This poses a challenge for any escalation management strategy, but is especially problematic for escalation dominance, which relies heavily on superiority in capabilities. While theoretically plausible, *establishing "dominant" resolve* as well as dominant capabilities *is a difficult standard* to meet in a conflict where a capable, nuclear-armed rival has already gambled great stakes."[96] (italics added for emphasis)

---

95 Ibid.

96 Issues, according to this cited essay, include conventional balance of strengths, the influence of new technologies to bypass Kahn's initial ladder of 44 escalation "rungs," and peacetime provocation in the sense that *escalation dominance* in peacetime constitutes, in and of itself, a palpable form of provocation.

One solution, however, is not to abandon the notion of escalation dominance altogether, but rather,

> "...to extend the concept of strategic stability beyond its classic conception of avoiding general war and into the realm of managing escalation in the midst of limited war."[97]

In any event, the desire of nations to adopt successful policies, for their respective national security interests, is an increasingly complex task. These *adaptive policies* reflect a vitally important component of enforceable human rights and "natural law."

For a period of time in the United States, a balance against torture tipped, regarding **waterboarding**, under the guise of national security.[98] Waterboarding has enormous, long-lasting and well-documented adverse consequences for the victim:

> "Waterboarding is a form of torture in which water is poured over a cloth covering the face and breathing passages of an immobilized captive, causing the person to experience the sensation of drowning. ... Torturers pour water onto the face over the breathing passages, causing an almost immediate gag reflex and creating a drowning sensation for the captive. Normally, water is poured intermittently to prevent death. However, if the water is poured uninterruptedly it will lead to death by asphyxia, also called dry drowning. Waterboarding can cause extreme pain, damage to lungs, brain damage from oxygen deprivation, other physical injuries including

---

97   Ibid.

98   CBS NEWS, *Cheny Defends U.S. Use of Waterboarding*, February 8, 2008; Los Angeles Times, *Waterboarding is legal, White House says*, February 7, 2008.

broken bones due to struggling against restraints, and lasting psychological damage. Adverse physical effects can last for months, and psychological effects for years."[99]

The practice of waterboarding sacrificed humane techniques of interrogation in order to "enhance" that interrogation and to arguably generate quicker and fuller informational results.[100] Later, the U.S. Congress declared waterboarding to be unconstitutional in all circumstances.

> "President Obama signed an executive order in 2009 banning the use of torture by any government agency. Last year, Congress codified that ban into law in the National Defense Authorization Act. So, if waterboarding is considered torture, it would take an act of Congress to allow its use as an interrogation technique, since that's now forbidden under current U.S. law. Only those interrogation techniques outlined in the Army Field Manual are considered legal — and those techniques do not include waterboarding.
>
> But if waterboarding is not considered torture, a president could argue he or she has the legal right to order it — much as George W. Bush did during his administration.

The Short Answer

> For [Sen. Ted] Cruz, it's torture only if excruciating pain 'equivalent to losing organs and systems' has been inflicted.

---

99 WIKIPEDIA, *Waterboarding*.

100 Long ago, this rationale was rejected by the U.S. Supreme Court in the landmark decision of *Brown v. Mississippi* (1936) 297 U.S. 278; *see infra*.

That is not the standard used by international organizations whose definitions of torture have been endorsed by the U.S. There is a wide legal and diplomatic consensus that waterboarding is torture, and therefore illegal.

The Long Answer

Cruz's contention that waterboarding 'does not meet the generally recognized definition of torture' largely echoes the rationale used by the Bush administration to get around the existing legal strictures surrounding torture. But the argument made in the 2002 'Bybee Memo' — named for Jay Bybee, who at the time headed the White House Office of Legal Counsel — has been repudiated even by members of that administration.

Waterboarding is, in fact, widely considered to meet the definition of torture in the United Nations Convention Against Torture, ratified in 1990 by the U.S. Senate. 'Torture,' it says, 'means *any act by which severe pain or suffering, whether physical or mental*, is intentionally inflicted on a person for such purpose as obtaining from him or her information of a confession' and when it is done with the consent of anyone acting in an official capacity. The International Committee of the Red Cross also considers waterboarding [to constitute] torture. And the U.S. executed half a dozen Japanese generals after World War II found guilty of torturing American prisoners of war with techniques that included water torture."[101] (italics added for emphasis)

As can be seen from the waterboarding example, there can be *shifting-sands* of tolerance for incursions on civil rights, human rights and natural law, in the name of national security.

The **Fog of War** is another example of tolerance for outrageous loss of innocent life which is both anticipated and acceptable, albeit with remorse. We know that innocents will suffer or die in war. We expect that somewhere or somehow it will happen. We regret the occurrence, yet recognize, it is inevitable. We are remorseful, but we carry on with the war, and with wars, because we believe collateral loss cannot be averted. And at times, this rationale is perfectly valid.

In the fog of war, innocent men, women and children will suffer, but the "greater good" is that the war effort will be successful. Individual rights, human rights, are sacrificed in the name of national security or national interests, and most (except, of course, the victims) can tolerate that explanation. An uneasy balance between societal and individual interests has been struck.

By definition, neither National Security nor the fog of war negates natural law, the natural human *rights* which are *at stake*. If anything, those human rights are magnified since *it requires a war* or *the threat of war* to justify a compromise of those rights—nation versus nation (or nation versus terrorists)—before the inevitability of "collateral damage" can be grudgingly acceptable.

However, some actions committed, even during wartime, are **never** acceptable under *any* circumstances. Some actions are so repulsive, unnecessary, "inhumane," and horrific that the international community views these acts to constitute **war crimes**.

---

101 SPECIAL SERIES Fact Check, *Fact-Check: Could The Next President Bring Back Waterboarding?*, February 13, 2016.

Ironically, the nature of war crimes itself is *highly pertinent* in exposing the **absolute minimum standards of *inviolable human rights*,** below which neither tolerance, justification, fog of war nor other collateral damage explanations will be tolerated. Understanding a selection of particularly prominent war crimes illuminates actions which are deemed to *per se constitute irrefutable violations of unalienable, natural rights of humans.*

The Holocaust and Nuremberg

Adolf Hitler, and his despicable Nazi political framework, conquered many other nations and sought to exterminate persons of Jewish descent. Before being stopped by the Allies in World War II, the Nazis had murdered millions of Jewish men, women and children, along with additional political opponents, hundreds of thousands Polish and Russian prisoners of war, and countless members of minorities such as gays and gypsies.

Following the war, Nazi party members were prosecuted for *war crimes* in what has become known as the **Nuremberg Trials.** Drafted by the International Law Commission of the United Nations, Nuremberg principles were developed to codify and proscribe that conduct which constitutes *prosecutable, war crime offenses.* **Seven War Crimes principles emerged:**

I.   Any person who commits an act which constitutes a crime under international law is responsible therefor and liable to punishment.

II.   The fact that *internal* law does not impose a penalty for an act which constitutes a crime under international law does not relieve the person who committed the act from responsibility under international law.

III.   The fact that a person who committed an act which constitutes a crime under international law, acted as *Head of State or responsible government official*, does not relieve him from responsibility under international law.

IV.   The fact that a person acted *pursuant to order* of his Government or of a superior does not relieve him from responsibility under international law provided a moral choice was in fact possible to him.

V.   Any person charged with a crime under international law has the right to a fair trial on the facts and law.

VI.   The crimes hereinafter set out are punishable as crimes under international law:

    (i)   Crimes against peace;

    (ii)   Planning, preparation, initiation or waging of a war of aggression or a war in violation of international treaties, agreements or assurances; and,

    (iii)   Participation in a common plan or conspiracy for the accomplishment of any of the acts mentioned under (i).

(a) War crimes:

Violations of the laws or customs of war which include, but are not limited to, murder, ill-treatment or deportation to slave labor or of any other purpose of civilian population of or in occupied territory; murder or ill-treatment of prisoners of war or persons on the Seas, killing of hostages, plunder of public or private property, wanton destruction of cities, towns, or villages, or devastation not justified by military necessity.

(b) Crimes against humanity:

Murder, extermination, enslavement, deportation and other inhumane acts done against any civilian population, or persecutions on political, racial or religious grounds, when such acts are done or such persecutions are carried on in execution of or in connection with any crime against peace or any war crime. Leaders, organizers, instigators and accomplices participating in the formulation or execution of a common plan or conspiracy to commit any of the foregoing crimes are responsible for all acts performed by any persons in execution of such plan.

VII.   Complicity in the commission of a crime against peace, a war crime, or a crime against humanity as set forth in Principle VI is a crime under international law.

Subsequently, the 1998 Rome Statute of the International Criminal Court was created, granting a **defense** to prosecution when all of the following three conditions are met:

(1) the person was under a legal obligation to obey orders of a Government or the superior in question;

(2) the person did not know that the order was unlawful; and,

(3) the order itself was not "manifestly unlawful."

The Statute then gave, as an example of a *manifestly unlawful* order: "orders to commit genocide or crimes against humanity."

Thus, international prohibitions which set the bar for absolute and inviolate human rights include freedom from governmental murder, extermination, genocide, enslavement (or, "other inhumane acts"), killing of hostages, plunder of private or public property, destruction and devastation of municipalities not justified by military necessity, and persecutions on "political, racial or religious grounds." In the U.S. Constitution, a shorthand (albeit, exceedingly general in description) version of the foregoing would be to guarantee, "life, liberty and the pursuit of happiness."

The Nuremberg principles formed a set of institutionally enforceable, rights of self-defense against atrocities. Few would seriously contend that the right to be free from these horrendous acts, did not constitute natural law—i.e., *inherent* human rights.

The Tokyo Trial

At the International Military Tribunal for the Far East 1946, commonly known as the Tokyo Trial or the Tokyo War Crimes Tribunal, leaders of the Empire of Japan were tried for crimes against peace, war crimes and crimes against humanity. The proceedings took place from April 29, 1946 through November 12, 1948, the judges for which were provided by eleven countries, including, notably, the United States, the Soviet Union, Australia, China, the Philippines and the United Kingdom. Twenty-Eight Japanese military and political leaders responded to fifty-five charges of war crimes committed against POWs, civilian internees and occupied territory inhabitants.[102]

> "Unlike the Nuremberg trials, the charge of crimes against peace was a prerequisite to prosecution—only those individuals whose crimes included crimes against peace could be prosecuted by the Tribunal."[103]

The indictment, mainly the work of the British associate prosecutor, Arthur S. Comyns-Carr, was lodged with the Court

---

102 National WWII Museum, New Orleans, *Overview ("Overview")*, www. nationalww2museum.org.

103 Encyclopedia.com, Tokyo Trial, *The Indictment ("Indictment")*.

during a preliminary proceeding on April 29, 1946.[104] It charged the defendants with participating in and promoting a battle plan which,

> "contemplated and carried out murdering, maiming and ill-treating prisoners of war [and] civilian internees, forcing them to labor under inhuman conditions, plundering public and private property, wantonly destroying cities, towns and villages beyond any justification of military necessity, [sanctioning and perpetrating] mass murder, rape, pillage, brigandage, torture and other barbaric cruelties upon the helpless civilian population of over-run countries."[105]

At the Tokyo Trial, prosecutors relied upon the concept of command responsibility and eschewed any obligation to prove a chain of "criminal orders." Instead, the prosecution was obligated to prove:

(1) that war crimes were systemic or widespread;
(2) that the person had actual or constructive knowledge that the troops were committing atrocities; and,
(3) that the person had the power or authority to stop the crimes.

Defense claims of *ex post facto laws*, unfair evidentiary rulings and the lack of legal precedent to criminally proscribe omissions, all fell on deaf ears. The international *outrage* over Japanese war atrocities was so profound as to *itself* create the basis for convictions

---

104   Ibid.

105   *Basic Facts on the Nanjing Massacre and the Tokyo War Crimes Trial*, THE TOKYO WAR CRIMES TRIALS, THE INDICTMENT, https://humanum.arts. cuhk.edu.hk/NanjingMassacre/NMNJ.html.

and punishment. Following the defense resting, the Tribunal took fifteen months to reach its judgment and file its 1,781-page opinion. All but three defendants (two died and one was unfit to stand trial) were convicted and received sentences ranging from seven years of imprisonment to execution.[106]

While Emperor Hirohito was controversially granted exemption, or implicit immunity, from the Tribunal's proceedings, Judge William Web of Australia wrote a concurring opinion, arguing that Hirohito bears legal responsibility for the charged war crimes since as a constitutional monarch, he received and accepted, "ministerial and other advice for war" and that,

> "no ruler can commit the crime of launching aggressive war and then validly claim to be excused for doing so because his life would otherwise have been in danger. ... It will remain that the men who advised the commission of a crime, if it be one, are in no worse position than the man who directs the crime [to] be committed."

Vladimir Putin would be well-advised to take note of this judicial sentiment.

The Tokyo Trial reflected profound international outrage against acts constituting war crimes, and against the men who directed such atrocities to be perpetrated. The trial exemplifies *judicial enforcement of human rights against* purveyors of war crimes, including those human rights violations which are manifestly unlawful. At times, however, such war crimes relentlessly and inexorably ***evolve* from *war strategies***.

---

106 *Overview.*

The My Lai Massacre

On March 16, 1968, during the heart of America's involvement in the Vietnam War, between 347 and 504 unarmed South Vietnamese civilians in My Lai and My Khe of South Vietnam were mass-murdered by U.S. Troops under the command of Lieutenant William Calley, Jr.. The incident later became known as the My Lai Massacre. The victims included men, women and children. Women and children as young as 12-years of age were gang-raped and their bodies mutilated. The incident, and its deliberate cover-up by the United States, contributed significantly to the domestic anti-war sentiment and campaign within the United States.

One anecdotal account of killings was by PFC Dennis Konti:

> "A lot of women had thrown themselves on top of the children to protect them and the children were alive at first. Then, the children who were old enough to walk got up and Calley began to shoot the children."[107]

One soldier testified that they were convinced that the village inhabitants were booby-trapped with grenades and were ready to attack the soldiers. Soldiers pushed 70 to 80 men, women and children Vietnamese into a ditch and shot and killed them all.[108]

Another soldier, PFC Michael Bernhardt testified that,

> "'I walked and saw these guys doing strange things... 'Setting fire to the hootches and huts and waiting for people to come out and then shooting them' ...gathering

---

107 WIKIPEDIA, *My Lai massacre.*

108 Ibid.

people in groups and shooting them...piles of people all through the village...I saw them shoot an M79 (grenade launcher) into a group of people who were still alive. But it was mostly done with a machine gun. They were shooting women and children just like anybody else. We met no resistance and I only saw three captured weapons. We had no casualties... I don't remember seeing one military-age male in the entire place, dead or alive."[109]

Twenty-six soldiers were charged with various criminal offenses. Only Lt. Calley was convicted. A Life sentence was originally imposed but Lt. Calley was *released from house arrest after only 3 ½-years imprisonment*! Secretary of the Army, Howard Callaway, stated in 1976 in a New York Times interview that Lt. Calley's sentence was reduced on the basis that he had honestly believed that the mass killings were part of his orders to eliminate Vietnamese in order to enhance the body-count of suspected Vietnamese enemies.[110]

Assuming that Lt. Calley was not a mass murderer, he may have actually believed that slaughtering hundreds of innocent men, women and children served the war interests of the United States. However, does subjective "good faith" in any way absolve an individual from the consequences of a "manifestly unlawful" order to commit genocide? No, it would not—at least not according to the rules promulgated by the 1998 Rome Statute of the International Criminal Court, *supra*. Even under principles applied in the Tokyo and Nuremberg trials, a good faith belief that genocide, plunder, rape and mutilation of civilians was a lawful order, would constitute neither a defense nor even a mitigating factor in sentencing.

---

109 The Plain Dealer, *Eyewitness accounts of the My Lai massacre*, Seymour M. Hersh, November 20, 1969.

110 https://glosbe.com/en/en/Howard%20Callaway.

Yet, the United States chose to *turn a blind eye* to the egregious crimes against humanity perpetrated by Lt. Calley. But why? Why would the United States, the veritable *bastion of freedoms and human rights*, in effect *absolve* Lt. Calley from his horrendous war crimes?

Unfortunately, the My Lai Massacre was simply the inevitable *tip of the proverbial iceberg* in atrocities perpetrated by the American government during the Vietnam war. J. Houston Gordon was appointed as a military appellate attorney representing Lt. Calley in the aftermath of Calley's conviction. He reveals that the My Lai Massacre involved,

> "Nearly 300 soldiers, civilian advisors, military and CIA intelligence operatives, ARVN troops, and South Vietnamese Special Police [who] participated. ... The only person convicted for the atrocities of that day was 25-year-old, 5-foot-3, 109 pound, 2d. Lt. William L. Calley, Jr."[111]

Attorney Gordon described the first of two conclusions drawn by him from the case:

> "First, America's war in Vietnam was fought for the wrong reason, at the wrong time, in the wrong place, against the wrong enemy and in the wrong way. The aspirations of America's WWII friends, Ho Chi Minh

---

111 Commercial Appeal, *50 YEARS AFTER MY LAI: What I learned representing Lt. Calley*, J. Houston Gordon, J.D., March 9, 2018, https://www.commercialappeal.com/story/opinion/contributors/2018/03/09/50-years-after-my-lai-what-learned-representing-lt-calley/401063002/.

NATURAL LAW AND INALIENABLE HUMAN RIGHTS

and his revolutionaries, who fought side-by-side with us against the Japanese, were ignored."[112]

Gordon explains:

"When America's political and military leaders committed our nation's treasure and the lives of her children to the war in Vietnam, they knew nothing about Vietnamese history, language, culture, society, religions or leaders. Worse, they refused to learn.

Their deliberate ignorance, coupled with hubris, fear, insecurity, self-promotion, deceit, and continuing lies set the stage for the 12-year debacle that followed. Like lemmings led to the sea, we were caught up in and betrayed by their arrogance and continuing deception.

...

There never was a 'democratically elected government in South Vietnam', only a dictatorship propped up by American power. Its corrupt officials forcibly removed millions of South Vietnamese peasants from their lands into fenced-in 'refugee camps.'[113]

Attorney Gordon then drops the *real bombshell*—that Lt. Calley's participation in the My Lai atrocities was *part of a much broader, U.S. government-sanctioned **war plan** of atrocities*:

---

112 Ibid.

113 Ibid.

"My second conclusion: The massacre in My Lai was no aberration. Rather, it went off as planned — the result of false 'intelligence,' misguided policies, and intentionally nihilistic combat strategies and tactics.

In 1964, General William Westmoreland, MACV/ AFVN Commander, adopted a war of attrition strategy; emphasizing body counts, psychological warfare and technological weapons superiority.

In 1966, President Johnson, not seeing Westmoreland's promised progress in the war, issued **National Security Memorandum 192**, appointing Robert Komer as his man to be in charge of the 'other war,' the so-called 'pacification' effort in Vietnam led by America's 'shadow warriors' to whom **the laws of war did not apply**."[114] (bold added for emphasis)

Repeatedly through history, we see that governments are disturbingly willing to ignore human rights and natural law under the guise of national security interests. National Security Memorandum 192 is simply an *ugly, prime example* of this despicable proclivity. Gordon continued:

"Their operations [those of the Komer's 'shadow warriors'] were quickly merged with those of the regular combat troops, where the laws of war did apply. By March of 1968, the coordination of Komer's CORDS/ ICEX/Phoenix covert operatives with MACV's combat and psywar forces was 'fully operational.'

---

114   Ibid.

Upon the consummation of this unholy marriage, new, classified MACV directives were issued. South Vietnamese peasants supporting the Viet Cong were redesignated as 'Viet Cong Infrastructure (VCI).' 'Elimination of the VCI,' killing all 'Viet Cong sympathizers,' 'leveling of villages,' expanding 'free fire zones,' and a 'sterile depersonalized murder program' became the modus operandi for American combat units and their ICEX/ Phoenix/CORDS adjuncts.

Planned eradication, annihilation, indiscriminate bombing, napalming, destruction of villages, making large areas of South Vietnam uninhabitable, and mass slaughter of South Vietnamese civilians all became commonplace. My Lai was inevitable."[115]

An acquaintance of mine, we will call him Bill S., now deceased, was a Navy SEAL in the Vietnam War during the President Johnson era. One day, decades later, he described to me that a tactic which he commonly utilized, to reduce traffic along the Ho Chi Minh Trail, was to **booby-trap bicycles to explode** when they were ridden. I asked how he could make sure the bicycle bombs killed only Viet Kong and not women and children. His stoic reply was that,

"It didn't matter. Once they learned bikes would explode, the Kong stopped using bikes."[116]

---

115 Ibid.

116 On another occasion, decades after the Vietnam War, Bill S. accidentally ran over a heavily inebriated fellow who, late one night, happened to walk unexpectedly across a downtown street directly in front of his car. Bill later

In law, if a contractual right is not legally enforceable, it is characterized as "illusory." Likewise, to the extent human rights have no "teeth" for their violation and enforcement, they become meaningless against aggressors. A failure in *enforcement* of human rights grossly undermines the force and effect of the *rights themselves*. Limiting punishment of Lt. Calley to 3 ½-years is not only patently insufficient in the context of his conduct at My Lai, but it tends to negate any *realistic disincentive* for similar human rights violations in war time. Worse yet is that governmental officials, including President Richard Nixon and President Lyndon Johnson were never prosecuted for their war crimes in perpetrating and lying to the American people about America's war of atrocities in Vietnam.

Chilean Dictator Augusto Pinochet

General Augusto Pinochet came into power in Chile after CIA-backed[117] revolutionaries killed the elected Socialist President Allende in a coup on September 11, 1973. Pinochet's rule lasted from 1973 to 1990.

"At least 3,095 people were killed during Pinochet's dictatorship, according to government figures, and tens

commented to me that, "As I was sitting on the curb, waiting for police to arrive, I thought to myself, 'I've never killed someone with a car before.'"

117 "From the moment of his [Salvador Allende's] election in 1970, the Nixon administration mounted a covert campaign against him. Henry Kissinger, then Nixon's National Security adviser, declared: 'I don't see why we need to stand idly by and watch a country go Communist due to the irresponsibility of its own people.'" (Countercurrents.org, *The Atrocities of Augusto Pinochet and the United States*, Roger Burbach, December 17, 2006).

of thousands more were tortured or jailed for political reasons."[118]

Dr. Kenneth P. Serbin, an expert in the Chilean government and its repressive system under Pinochet's reign of terror, wrote:

"Under dictator General Augusto Pinochet[,] the Chilean military tortured some 4,500 people at Villa Grimaldi. A guide shows visitors the spot where military vehicles drove over the legs of prisoners. Mock-ups of wooden boxes that held as many as six prisoners each, the swimming pool into which detainees were dunked, and a replica of the tower used as a torture chamber and extermination center are all on display. The Muro de los Nombres lists the names of the 226 people killed or 'disappeared' by the military at the villa."[119]

Dr. Serbin elaborated:

"Prolonged detention affected people's lives forever… 'Some people were ferociously tortured. Others were, let us say, less tortured, but they were always expecting to be treated ferociously.' She says, adding that most prisoners lost their jobs, often because employers used their absence from work as a pretext for firing them. Imprisonment especially affected the poor, who could not fall back on a profession, as could doctors and others who went into

118   CBS NEWS, *Bloody secrets of Chile's darkest days spilling out* ("*Bloody Secrets*"), December 30, 2015.

119   RELIGION ONLINE, www.religion-online.org, *Behind Pinochet's Reign of Terror* ("*Reign of Terror*"), Kenneth P. Serbin reviews two books by John Dinges.

exile and resumed their work with the help of foreign colleagues."[120]

Villa Grimaldi was not an isolated occurrence during Pinochet's regime, and the Commission on torture and Political Prisoners, headed by Sergio Valech, made some *gripping* revelations:

"One of the commission's most shocking findings was the discovery of a veritable archipelago of variations on Villa Grimaldi. Human rights organizations assumed that Pinochet's security forces had set up 350 such centers—jails, stadiums, concentration camps and other places separate from the regular police system. The commission's final report listed at least 1,300 [centers for torture]."[121]

A commission member, Elizabeth Lira, clarified that the torture, murder and oppression under Pinochet was neither isolated to nor the result of a few deranged military officers:

"'The story they tell that it was just a captain or a lieutenant who got angry and wanted to do his job well offends our intelligence. These are things that you cannot improvise. You cannot have 1,300 centers throughout a country like this one if there is no coordination, if there is no financing,' Lira notes, adding that to date no one has studied the costs of Pinochet's system. Intelligence-gathering on thousands of people and the movement of

---

120 Ibid.

121 Ibid.

prisoners around the country required extensive resources and personnel including specialists in repression, many of whom studied at the U.S.-run School of the Americas, she says."[122]

Although some 1,373 former and current military leaders faced trial in Chile, only,

"344 have been convicted, and most of them were sentenced to house arrest or some other form of non-jail punishment."[123]

The official investigations were hampered by massive undertakings *obstructing justice*:

"Former Supreme Court President Sergio Munoz, who oversaw special judges handling hundreds of dictatorship cases, says members of the military have gone to great lengths to remain silent about the crimes. He hit roadblocks in some investigations and often there was 'deficient cooperation among institutions,' Munoz told the Associated Press."[124]

The atrocities of the Pinochet regime were hideous.

"One former Chilean soldier said he shot 10 people in the head and then blew up their bodies with dynamite.

---

122 Ibid.

123 *Bloody Secrets.*

124 Ibid.

Another said his platoon drenched two teens with gasoline and set them on fire."[125]

The human rights abuses under Pinochet were systemic and brutal:

"According to the Rettig Report, the violations of human rights committed between 1973 and 1989 did not occur in a context of war, as the armed forces claimed. Rather, they were committed against defenseless people for political reasons. The report established three stages of repression. **First**, between September and December 1973, repression was not systematically implemented; massive detentions occurred throughout the country, prisoners were interned in concentration camps, political prisoners and peasants involved in the process of agrarian reform were executed, and a 'social cleaning' of young people in urban squatter settlements took place. During this period, executions were a product of the so-called war councils, in which defense lawyers had no real power and corpses were hidden, thrown into the sea, or dynamited. Valdivia | Terrorism and Political Violence 187. A **second** phase corresponded to the period between 1974 and 1977, during which the regime developed *a systematic policy of repression in order to exterminate* those whom it deemed a political threat, applying on a massive scale the method of forced disappearance. The goal was to kill and hide

---

125   Ibid.

the bodies of the dead in order to destroy the supposed enemy."[126] (bold added for emphasis)

A *secretive military agency* designed and implemented this virtual *terror-train* throughout Chile.

"The principal military institution that implemented this political repression was the DINA, created by decree with numerous secret powers and resources, which acted throughout the entire country and engaged in operations outside the country (like the assassination of Allende's ex–foreign minister Orlando Letelier in Washington, DC in 1976), and depended directly on the 'president' of the military junta, General Augusto Pinochet. These years produced the greatest number of disappearances. Victims were detained in the DINA's clandestine centers, where they were blindfolded and submitted to physical and psychological torture, which included rape, especially, though not exclusively, of female prisoners. Torture often resulted in death. Finally, the Rettig Report defined a **third** stage corresponding to the years 1977 through 1989, identified with DINA's successor, the National Information Center (CNI, Centro Nacional de Inteligencia). This period began with a brief repressive lull, owing to the international pressure following the assassination of Orlando Letelier, but the CNI and other repressive organs did not take long to revert to a familiar pattern of violence, resulting in the deaths of prominent

---

126 Radical History Review, Duke University Press, Project MUSE, *Terrorism and Political Violence during the Pinochet Years: Chile, 1973-1989 ("Terrorism"),* Issue 85, Winter 2003, pp. 187-188, Veronica Valdivia Ortiz de Zarate.

opponents of the military regime, like union leader Tucapel Jiménez. A similar fate awaited the mass protests unleashed in 1983, where many Chileans fighting against dictatorial rule fell under police or military bullets."[127] (bold added for emphasis)

Interrogation torture was an ever-present fact of life in Pinochet's Chile:

"The first time Lelia Pérez felt the sear of a cattle prod it was at the hands of a Chilean soldier. She was a 16-year-old high school student, used as a guinea pig to help Pinochet's security services hone their skills in torture. They didn't even bother to ask any questions.

'They would teach them how to interrogate, how to apply the electricity, where and for how long. When they were torturing me, I went into my own world – it was as if I was looking down on myself – like it wasn't happening to me. It was brutal,' she said.

Lelia told Amnesty International how she was arrested along with 10 of her classmates and taken to the Estadio Chile (now called Victor Jara after the singer who was imprisoned there). There detainees were kept in the stands, with their hands tied, with soldiers constantly pointing machine guns at them.

---

127 Ibid.

'You would quickly loose [sic: lose] sense of time as lights were constantly on. The only way we knew if it was day or night was by the food the guards were eating,' she said.

While they watched, special booths were constructed. It was in these that the worst of the torture took place. Lelia spent five days in Estadio Chile. Finally[,] she was released with no explanation, pushed out onto the streets late at night.

'I was forced to wear the clothes of people we had seen being killed. There was a curfew and the few people around just walked away from us. The street was full of brothels and the sex workers took me in. They bathed me and gave me clothes. I went in the stadium as a 16-year-old and left as a 60-year-old.'"[128]

After enrolling at Universidad Técnica del Estado, noted for its political activism, to study history, Lelia was *once again arrested* by the Pinochet political police and transported to the infamous Villa Grimaldi.

""They took us to an interrogation room where they had a metal bunk-bed. There was another detainee on the top and my partner was tied to the side. They were interrogating all three of us at the same time, taking turns to electrocute us one after the other. The interrogation session lasted through the night to the next morning.'

---

128 AMNESTY INTERNATIONAL, *Life under Pinochet: "They were taking turns to electrocute us one after the other"* (*"Life under Pinochet"*), September 11, 2013.

In Villa Grimaldi detainees would be electrocuted, waterboarded, had their heads forced into buckets of urine and excrement, suffocated with bags, hanged by their feet or hands and beaten. Many women were raped and for some detainees, punishment was death.

For detainees, the dark, damped cell they were held in was the only world that existed and, in time, a sense of community emerged.

'After an interrogation you would be thrown back your cell. They would shut the door and then first thing you would experience is someone coming closer, they would hold you, help you lie down, take the blindfold off, and put some water on your lips. The electric shocks would make you stream with sweat and you'd get extremely dehydrated – so very, very thirsty,'

It is estimated that 4,500 people crossed Villa Grimaldi's doors. Many never made it out and of those, hundreds are still missing.

Lelia spent the best part of a year in Villa Grimaldi. She was then transferred to a labour camp where she was held for another 12 months before she was forced to leave the country in late 1976."[129]

But no institutionalized human rights violations would be complete without *the institutions to cover them up* and to absolve the perpetrators from prosecution, guilt and punishment.

---

129 Ibid.

"The [Rettig Commission] report also stated that the judiciary did not react with appropriate energy, an attitude which aggravated the systematic violation of human rights, leaving victims defenseless and granting 'the agents of repression a growing certainty of impunity for their criminal actions.'"[130]

The United States was complicit with Pinochet's gruesome regime:

"John Dinges puts the Pinochet regime into an international perspective and signals again the need for atonement for the many versions of Villa Grimaldi that the U.S. quietly ignored during the highly repressive Latin American dictatorships of the 1970s. Dinges argues that the United States had detailed information about terrorist assassination plots on its own soil and elsewhere in the Americas but did nothing to stop them. Instead of saving lives, it preferred to coddle Pinochet and other dictators because they were allies in the fight against world communism."[131]

In the overthrow of Allende and establishment of Pinochet as a dictator, *political* considerations were seen by the United States and by the Pinochet regime *as overcoming any interests comprising even the most basic of human rights*. This dangerous road of means-to-an-end justification and natural law suppression is an all-too-common theme within the contemporary international landscape.

---

130 *Terrorism*, Id. at 188.

131 *Reign of Terror*, Ibid.

Chemical and Biological Warfare

Chemical warfare is one of the clearest violations of natural rights. One might compare it to nuclear weapons, taking into account similarities in the widespread and hideous catastrophic consequences.

Long ago, in 256 CE, Sassanian Persian forces attacked Roman forces at Dura Europos. Reportedly, the Persians excavated a tunnel at the base of the city barrier and ignited sulfur crystals and bitumen to create a deadly gas which rose into a tunnel above, annihilating the Roman defenders.[132]

In World War I, on April 22, 1915, Germans unleashed a yellow-green fog of gas on Algerian and French soldiers in trenches near the Belgian town of Ypres. The fog was chlorine gas released from 6,000 pressurized cylinders.

> "The effect was immediate: Thousands of soldiers choked and clutched at their throats, unable to breathe, before falling dead; thousands more fled in panic, opening a four-mile gap in the allied lines. ... The effects of the attack were horrific, causing 'a burning sensation in the head, red-hot needles in the lungs, the throat seized as by a strangler,' as one soldier later described it. More than 5,000 soldiers were killed in this first gas attack, while thousands more, stumbling to the rear and frothing at the mouth, suffered the debilitating aftereffects for decades."[133]

---

132 Smithsonian MAGAZINE, *One of the First Known Chemical Attacks Took Place 1,700 Years Ago in Syria*, Rachel Nuer, September 6, 2013.

133 Politico Magazine, *Why the World Banned Chemical Weapons* (*"Why the World"*), Mark Perry, April 13, 2017, www.politico.com And *see*, The Jerusalem

Winston Churchill was notoriously *in favor* of using,

> "'poisoned gas against uncivilized tribes. ... It is not necessary to use only the most-deadly gasses: gasses can be used which cause great inconvenience and would spread a lively terror and yet would leave no serious permanent effects on most of those affected.'"[134]

In more modern times, Egypt used chemical weapons in the civil war in Yemen between 1963 and 1967, yet steadfastly denied its use.[135] Likewise, from 1979 through 1981, the Soviet Union is believed to have used chemical attacks (poison gas) against civilians in the course of its Afghan war.[136]

Despite Iraqi denials, between May 1981 and March 1984, Iran charged Iraq with some forty instances of the use of chemical weapons.[137] Iraq developed two variations of chemical weaponry.

> "During the Iran-Iraq War, Iraq developed the ability to produce, store, and use chemical weapons. These included H-series blister and G-series nerve agents.

Post, *Chemical warfare in the Middle East: A brief history* ("*Brief History*"), Alex Joffe, December 17, 2012, "The bloody golden age of chemical weapons...began in late 1914, when the Germans attacked British forces in France using chlorine gas, which formed hydrochloric acid that dissolved the victims' lungs."

134   Ibid.

135   Ibid.

136   *Brief History*, Ibid.; New York Times, *U.S. Accuses Soviet of Poisoning 3,000*, Richard Halloran, March 9, 1982.

137   Venter, Al J., *Iran's Nuclear Option, Tehran's Quest for the Atom Bomb* ("Nuclear Option"), p. 56, and *see* 247, (Casemate 2005).

Iraq built these agents into various offensive munitions including rockets, artillery shells, aerial bombs, and warheads on the Al Hussein Scud missile variant. There is also good evidence that Iraqi fighter-attack aircraft dropped mustard and tabun-filled five hundred-pound bombs and half-ton bombs containing mustard gas on Iranian targets."[138]

Iran *responded in kind* with its own CW development program and advanced capabilities:

"John Pike's GlobalSecurity.org also deals with the subject. His website states that 'Iran is currently able to employ chemical weapons and is progressing in its development of a large self-supporting CW infrastructure.' This activity, he points out, is taking place in spite of Tehran having ratified the new Chemical Weapons Convention, under which it is obligated to eliminate its chemical weapons assets over a period of years. [Para.] 'Nevertheless, it continues to upgrade and expand its chemical warfare production infrastructure and munitions arsenal. The magnitude of this effort suggests that the Iranian leadership intends to maintain a robust CW capability.'"[139]

In 1988, the then Majlis Speaker, Ali Akbar Hashemi Rafsanjani made a revealing proclamation that,

---

138 Id., p. 63.

139 Id., p. 239.

"'Chemical and biological weapons are the poor man's atomic bombs and can easily be produced. ... We should at least consider them for our defense. Although the use of such weapons is inhuman, the war taught us that international laws are only scraps of paper.'"[140]

After becoming President of Iran, Rafsanjani doubled down:

"'We should fully equip ourselves in the defensive and offensive use of chemical, bacteriological and radiological weapons.'"[141]

Whether from military deficiencies, or from the horrifying collateral damage on innocent civilian lives, on April 29, 1997, the United Nations Chemical Weapons Convention created the Organization for the Prohibition of Chemical Weapons (OPCW). According to the UN:

"The OPCW mission is to implement the provisions of the CWC and to ensure a credible, transparent regime to verify the destruction of chemical weapons, to prevent their re-emergence in any member State; to provide protection and assistance against chemical weapons; to encourage international cooperation in the peaceful uses of chemistry, and to achieve universal membership of the OPCW."[142]

---

140 Id., p. 256.

141 Ibid.

142 United Nations, Office for Disarmament Affairs, *Chemical Weapons.*

The nerve gas, sarin, was used in April 2017 by Syria, as its SU-22 jets dropped bombs filled with sarin gas on the town of Khan Shaykhun.

> "The attack killed dozens of Syrian civilians, including 11 children. The effects of the sarin, a deadly nerve agent, were similar to those of 1915: The victims choked and vomited as their lungs constricted, then suffered through tormenting muscle spasms and eventual death."[143]

But **militaries** respond to chemical warfare with *countermeasures*, such as gas-impermeable suits and gas masks. Accordingly, deadly or debilitating chemicals are deemed inefficient in modern warfare.[144] Primarily, CWs are effective in murdering civilians.

Currently, 188 nations, representing around 98% of the global population, are members of the CWC. Nevertheless, according to a United Nations study,

> "On 1 February 2019, Syria [again] dropped chemical barrel bombs on its own people 'as part of [a] barbaric siege', followed by a chemical attack, which burned the skin of its victims, he said, pointing out that these facts underscored the 'audacity of the Assad regime', which steadfastly denies the truth and portrays itself as victim.... Syria has used chemical weapons an estimated 50 times since the start of the conflict, he added."[145]

---

143 *Why the World. And see, Brief History.*

144 Ibid.

145 United Nations Web TV, Security Council, *The situation in the Middle East (Syrian chemical weapons programme)* ["*The Situation*"], December 8, 2021.

The grisly consequences to combatants and collateral damage of chemical and biological weaponry on civilian noncombatants apparently is widely, albeit often secretly, *ignored* as somehow being *incidental* to the greater "good." Even the United States succumbed to this false logic when it covertly and indirectly contributed to **weaponized, biological-agent research** in Wuhan, China, which program led to the Covid-19 global fiasco of 2019-2020.

The Covid-19 Global Pandemic

It appears that World Leaders are caught in a recurring spiral of suspicion, greed, deceit and subterfuge when it comes to the development, storage and use of chemical and biologic weapons. This web of deception is reminiscent of the "Prisoner's Dilemma" game theory scenario invented in 1950 by Merrill Flood and Melvin Dresher at the RAND Corporation, with the "prisoner" aspect added by Albert W. Tucker.[146] Essentially, this modestly well-known conundrum involves two prisoners, ostensibly loyal to each other, who make simultaneous, final decisions (without knowing in advance the decision of the other prisoner) whether to cooperate with the prosecution.[147] Deceiving the other party will work to one's advantage in Prisoner's Dilemma, so long as the other party

---

146 Wikipedia, *Prisoner's dilemma.*

147 There are four possible outcomes: (1) A and B each betray the other and each of them will serve two years in the joint; (2) A betrays B but B does not cooperate with the prosecution, in which case A will be set free and B will serve three years in the joint; (3) B betrays A but A does not cooperate with the prosecution, in which case B will be set free and A will serve three years in the joint; and (4) A and B both remain silent and both of them will only serve only one year in prison on a lesser charge. What is not taken into account in this "dilemma" is the subsequent *retribution* to be expected against a prisoner in the event he or she elects to testify for the prosecution.

does not *also* choose to deceive and testify for the prosecution. In what is known as "Iterated Prisoner's Dilemma," the same players repeatedly engage in the game (or world political activity). So long as the number of ultimate iterations is *unknown*, cooperation, by each player refusing to testify against the other, appears to be the strategy which naturally emerges. However, in the real-world version of biological and chemical weaponry, leaders of the world **do not *actually* cooperate** and instead adopt the alternate strategy of saying one thing, convincingly, and secretly preparing to do the opposite.[148] In turn, this duplicity/deception results in a continuing spiral of human rights violations.

From documents released under Freedom of Information mandates, the United States has now been exposed as having **funded** coronavirus research in China. This appears to contradict Dr. Anthony Fauci's repeated assertion (apparently without any accountability whatsoever), under oath, to Congress that the National Institutes of Health ("NIH") did *not* fund gain-of-function research[149] in Wuhan.[150] Widespread media accounts confirm that the NIH *admits* that the United States government *funded* gain-

---

148 This is likely the result of the *stakes* of "trust" in others, as to chemical and biological weaponry development, being so potentially *catastrophic*—not a paltry-few-years in prison, but rather, *existential extermination* at the hands of a nation, or terrorist group, who betrays that trust.

149 "Gain-of-function research involves genetically altering an organism to enhance its biological functions. For example, in viruses, one could manipulate *how contagious or severe* a virus might be." MSN, KCBS Radio San Francisco, *Wuhan lab documents show US-funded coronavirus bat research, contradicting Fauci* ("*Wuhan Documents*"), Seth Lemon, September 7, 2021 (italics added for emphasis).

150 Ibid.

of-function research on bat coronaviruses at China's Wuhan lab—notwithstanding Fauci's repeated denials.[151]

The NIH threw the blame of this funding on EcoHealth Alliance (EcoHealth), a New York City-based nonprofit which purportedly, "funneled US funds to the Wuhan lab."[152] Moreover, NIH principal deputy director, Lawrence A. Tabak claims that,

> "the bat coronaviruses studied under the NIH grant could not have become COVID-19 because the 'sequences of the viruses are genetically very distant.'"[153]

Of a $3.1 million NIH grant to EcoHealth, $599,000 was directed to the Wuhan Institute of Virology for bat coronavirus research.[154] The grant proposal from EcoHealth specified the inherent risks of such research:

> "'Fieldwork involves the highest risk of exposure to SARS or other CoVs [coronaviruses], while working in caves with high bat density overhead and the potential for fecal dust to be inhaled.'"[155]

According to trusted medical sources, as of April 17, 2022, deaths attributable (or at least, *ascribed*) to Covid-19, in the United States

---

151 New York Post, *NIH admits US funded gain-of-function in Wuhan – despite Fauci's denials* ("*NIH Admits*"), Emily Crane, October 21, 2021.

152 Ibid.

153 Ibid.

154 Ibid.

155 Ibid.

alone, surpassed 988,000 men, women and children, at a death- rate of 1.2% of cases. Other examples include Brazil, where the deaths have been in excess of 662,000 at a rate of 2.2% of cases. In Italy, over 161,000 deaths at the rate of 1.0% of cases. In the UK, over 172,000 deaths at 0.8% of cases. In Russia, over 365,000 deaths at a death rate of 2.1% of cases. In Australia, where repressive lockdowns and forced vaccinations have become notorious, there were 6,779 deaths at a 0.1% of cases death rate. The deaths and human misery from the Covid-19 pandemic have been staggering.[156] The economic havoc foisted on the world has been unprecedented.

> "Estimates indicate the COVID-19 pandemic reduced global economic growth in 2020 to an annualized rate of around -3.2%, with a recovery of 4.2% to 6.0% projected for 2021 and a slightly slower rate projected for 2022. Global trade is estimated to have fallen by 5.3% in 2020, but was projected to have grown by 10.8% in 2021, followed by a projected growth rate of 4.7% in 2022. The length of the health crisis is affecting the global economy more than any typical economic recession, [and] repercussions could be long-lasting and far-reaching. ... Meanwhile, supply shortages reflect lingering disruptions to labor markets, production and supply chain bottlenecks, and shipping and transportation constraints."[157]

---

156   JOHNS HOPKINS UNIVERSITY OF MEDICINE, Coronavirus Resource Center, "Mortality Analyses," April 17, 2022.

157   Congressional Research Service, *Global Economic Effects of COVID-19: Overview*, James K. Jackson, February 14, 2022.

The annualized Consumer Price Index in the United States showed 12-month inflation, through the first quarter of 2022, to have been substantial:

> "In March, the Consumer Price Index for All Urban Consumers rose 1.2 percent, seasonally adjusted, **and rose 8.5 percent over the last 12 months**, not seasonally adjusted. The index for all items less food and energy increased 0.3 percent in March (SA); up 6.5 percent over the year (NSA)."[158] (bold added for emphasis)

By late 2023, and following draconian measures by the Federal Reserve Bank[159] and resulting widespread financial suffering, figures for annualized inflation have fallen to less severe levels (albeit, of course, not wiping out *prior* inflation):

> "The Consumer Price Index for All Urban Consumers (CPI-U) increased 0.1 percent in November on a seasonally adjusted basis, after being unchanged in

---

158   U.S. BUREAU OF LABOR STATISTICS, "Consumer Price Index," April 12, 2022.

159   New York Times, *The Fed May Finally Be Winning the War on Inflation. But at What Cost?*, Michael Steinberger, January 10, 2023. Inflation began spiking in the first quarter of 2021 and ran at about 8% annualized year-after-year. The Federal Reserve Bank aggressively increased the Federal Funds interest rate so far that it heavily impacted the middle class in America and caused a virtual halt to the real estate market. *And see*, Associated Press, The San Diego Union-Tribune, *The average long-term US mortgage rate dips below 7% to its lowest level since early August*, Alex Veiga, December 14, 2023 ("Still, the average rate on a 30-year home loan remains sharply higher than just two years ago, when it was 3.12%. The large gap between rates now and then is contributing to the low inventory of homes for sale by discouraging homeowners who locked in rock-bottom rates two years ago from selling.")

October, the U.S. Bureau of Labor Statistics reported today. Over the last 12 months, the all items index increased 3.1 percent before seasonal adjustment."[160]

If, as an international community, we have learned *anything* from the Covid-19 debacle, it is that serious violations of human rights and natural law have the potential of *devastating and long-ranging, adverse global consequences.*

Russia's 2022 Invasion of Ukraine

In an age where it seems impossible to imagine one country invading another peaceful, sovereign nation, Russia has proved to the world that such invasions are not only possible, but also, entirely feasible. President of Russia, Vladimir Putin, directed the Russian military to invade Ukraine in the early morning hours of February 23, 2022. The fighting continues to date, without a clear Russian victory. President Putin announced in December 2023 that Russia's goals in the Ukraine remain unchanged, and that the war will continue unless and until Kiev agrees to an agreement consistent with Russia's goals of "demilitarization" and "neutral status."[161]

In the process, Ukraine has been decimated from Russian bombings, and Russia's military forces have also taken a beating with significant numbers of men, machines and aircraft destroyed. The death toll is rising, and on both sides the human toll has taken other forms as well:

---

160   U.S. BUREAU OF LABOR STATISTICS, "Consumer Price Index— *NOVEMBER 2023*," December 12, 2023.

161   CNBC, *Putin says goals in Ukraine have 'not changed' and war will continue until Kyiv agrees a deal*, Holly Ellyatt, Jenni Reid, December 14, 2023.

"More than 7 million people have been displaced within Ukraine, according to the United Nations, and an additional 4.5 million have fled abroad. … But finding a way out was a challenge. A bus from Kherson to Odesa, a key stop on the journey to Romania, usually cost $10 and took [meaning: would normally take] four hours. Miller [an American who had been in Ukraine taking care of his grandmother] had to pay a taxi driver $600, and the ride took 12 hours. The danger of staying in Ukraine's besieged cities was emphasized by Friday's missile strike at a train station in the eastern city of Kramatorsk that killed at least 57 and left more than 100 wounded. The station was crowded with civilians fleeing the Donbas. Ukraine and its Western allies blamed Russia for the deadly strike. Moscow denied carrying out the attack. [Ukrainian President, Volodymyr] Zelensky vowed that those responsible for the railway strike would be discovered and would face war-crimes charges. …"[162]

Devastation and human suffering in Ukraine have resulted in international attention and concern:

"Since Russia's full-scale invasion in 2022, its war against Ukraine has had a disastrous impact on civilian life, killing thousands of civilians, injuring many thousands more, and destroying civilian property and infrastructure. Russian forces committed a litany of violations of international humanitarian law, including indiscriminate and disproportionate bombing and

---

162 Los Angeles Times, *Ukrainians flee as Russian troops converge on the east and south*, Nabih Bulos, Carolyn Cole and Kate Linthicum, April 10, 2022.

shelling of civilian areas that hit homes and healthcare and educational facilities. Some of these attacks should be investigated as war crimes. In areas they occupied, Russian or Russian-affiliated forces committed apparent war crimes, including torture, summary executions, sexual violence, enforced disappearances, and looting of cultural property. Those who attempted to flee areas of fighting faced terrifying ordeals and numerous obstacles; in some cases, Russian forces forcibly transferred significant numbers of Ukrainians to Russia or Russian-occupied areas of Ukraine and subjected many to abusive security screenings. Russian forces' countrywide, repeated attacks on Ukraine's energy and other critical infrastructure appeared aimed at terrorizing civilians and making their life unsustainable, which is a war crime."[163]

Putin's Russia, on the other hand, has its own version of the need to rein-in Ukraine through a forced political outcome:

"The Russian political elite contends that Russia should be a superpower in a multipolar world, recognized as such by the international community. However, this elite also argues that Russia is strategically on the defensive due to a hostile West. Russia, the Russian identity, and Russia's territorial integrity are under permanent threat, according to this view, and this threat must be addressed. The threat is not only military in the form of NATO's eastward expansion—it is also reflected in the spillover of the West's culture, values, ideology, and political system

---

163   Human Rights Watch, *Russia-Ukraine War*, https://www.hrw.org/tag/russia-ukraine-war.

into Russia. It is precisely this, elites argue, that poses an existential threat to Russia. Indeed, the emergence of an affluent, politically active, liberal-oriented social middle class may threaten Russia as an authoritarian-run, conservative autocracy. To counter this, the Russian political elite seeks to end the perceived American-led Western hegemony and replace it with a multipolar world order.

From the Russian perspective, the Ukraine invasion is a necessary offensive move within a strategic defensive posture. A prosperous, Western-oriented Ukraine that is a member of the EU may offer the Russian population a dangerous glimpse of an alternative political system and thereby fuel dissatisfaction with Russia's political and economic system. Furthermore, Ukrainian entry into NATO and the EU would lead to a political-strategic loss of face for the Russian regime at home and abroad and therefore represents a military-strategic vulnerability for Russia's defense."[164]

Notwithstanding the foregoing, self-serving view by Russian "elites" as to the sanctity of Russian's "authoritarian-run, conservative autocracy," the invasion of a democratic and peaceful sovereign nation (albeit with its own problems of corruption), attacks upon civilian transportation, and possible prisoner of war atrocities on both sides—constitute blatant war crimes and human rights violations—*today, right now*. Despite all of the proclamations and treaties, historical understanding of natural law and "inalienable"

---

164 Modern War Institute at West Point, *WHAT IS RUSSIA'S THEORY OF VICTORY IN UKRAINE*, Marnix Provoost, March 31, 2023.

rights, there remain continuing human rights violations on both a small and global scale.

On December 6, 2023, the U.S. Justice Department announced[165] that the United States has indicted four Russian military officers[166] for alleged commission of War Crimes against an American in the course of the Russian invasion of Ukraine.[167]

> "The four Russians are identified as members of the Russian armed forces or its proxy units. Two are described as commanding officers. ...[They] are accused of kidnapping an American man from his home in a Ukrainian village in 2022. [It is alleged in the indictment that the]... American was beaten and interrogated while being held for 10 days at a Russian military compound, before eventually being evacuated with his wife, who's Ukrainian, U.S. authorities said."[168]

This purportedly is the first time the United States has pursued charges pursuant to a nearly 30-year-old federal statute making it a crime to subject an American to torture or inhumane treatment during a war. The four Russian defendants are still at large, with prospects of capturing and extraditing them deemed poor at best.

---

165 Associated Press, *US files war crime charges against Russians accused of torturing an American in the Ukraine invasion*, Lindsay Whitehurst and Eric Tucker, December 6, 2023.

166 Ibid. The Russian defendants are named as Suren Seiranovich Mkrtchyan and Dmitry Budnik, commanding officers in Russia's armed forces, and two lower-ranking officers identified by their first names only.

167 Ibid.

168 Ibid.

Is there a **natural trigger or tendency towards abusing other human beings**, and if so, what if anything can be done about that *enduring human proclivity*?

Torture

Over the millennium, heinous mistreatment of humans has flourished under the twisted imaginations of captors over captives. There seems, literally, to be *no limit* to the callous and unspeakable brutality which has been practiced against captives in the name of retribution, interrogation, sexual obsession, compulsion to give false confessions, deterrence, compliance and terror.[169] Drawings in *The History of Torture* expose ancient techniques such as: placing a bound victim in a basket filled with wasps; an "iron maiden" in which the captive is slowly crushed to death; a steel "necklace," in which the inner band contains sharp arrowheads; the classic thumbscrew; the "scavenger's daughter," a device to keep a captive constrained in a leaning-forward seated position; the "liar rack," involving a five-sided rail over which a victim was "seated" with weights pulling down on his limbs while the rack was slowly turned; a "ducking stool," in which captives were forcibly dunked completely in water for varying lengths of time; pully systems where prisoners are hung by their thumbs; an early form of water-boarding, where the victim is nearly drowned with water dripping into a rag stuffed into his or her mouth, as their bones are broken on a rack; crude pits where captives were roasted alive; and a large, spiked barrel in which an unwilling passenger is sealed and rolled down a long hill. Examples of other hideous methods of inflicting harm and drawing out a painful death are virtually endless in mankind's ignominious past.

---

169 Mannix, Daniel P., *The History of Torture*, (Sutton Publishing Limited 2003).

Occasionally, in the Middle Ages, there were those who questioned the morality, if not the effectiveness, of government-sponsored torture. Many of these outspoken critics found themselves the object of that which they condemned. But there was one Jurist from Milan who had seen enough questionable confessions that he decided to run a crude and brutal sociological experiment of his own.

> "A Milanese judge became suspicious of confessions obtained under torture and finally decided on an efficient if rough method of testing their truth. He killed his mule and then [falsely] accused one of his servants. The man confessed under torture and refused to retract his statement even on the gallows for fear of new punishments. The judge promptly abolished the use of [confessions obtained by] torture in his court."[170]

In more contemporary times, it appears the Russians and Chinese governments have literally cornered the market on a form of "brain-washing" that goes well beyond infliction of pain, and enters into the realm of permanently manipulating the captive's sense of self, memories and allegiance. In this regard,

> "The Russian technique differs hardly at all from the Chinese. It depends on the use of solitary [confinement], tiredness (no sleep), exposure to alternating heat and cold, uncertainty, threats to family, starvation, offer of rewards, and hopelessness."[171]

---

170 Id. at pp. 133-134.

171 Id. at p. 210.

These techniques are not limited to hours, days or weeks of such treatment, but reportedly have lasted *for years on end* to break and control the captive and to squeeze every ounce of information and cooperation available from them over time.

In the United States, the U.S. Constitution, Fifth Amendment right to due process of law and to the privilege against self-incrimination renders confessions or admissions against interest, obtained through coercion, *inadmissible* in evidence. In the matter of *Brown v. Mississippi*, the U.S. Supreme Court established, once and for all, that confessions resulting from the use of physical force violate the Due Process Clause. There, defendants Ellington, Brown and Shields (all black tenant farmers) had been convicted *and sentenced to death* in Mississippi for the murder of Raymond Stewart (a white planter). The convictions were based solely on *confessions obtained through violence*:

> "... defendants were made to strip and they were laid over chairs and their backs were cut to pieces with a leather strap with buckles on it, and they were likewise made by the said deputy definitely to understand that the whipping would be continued unless and until they confessed, and not only confessed, but confessed in every matter of detail as demanded by those present; and in this manner, the defendants confessed the crime, and, as the whippings progressed and were repeated, they changed or adjusted their confession in all particulars of detail so as to conform to the demands of their torturers. When the confessions had been obtained in the exact form and contents as desired by the mob, they left with the parting admonition and warning that, if the defendants changed their story at any time in any respect from that last stated, the perpetrators of the outrage would [again] administer

126

the same or equally effective treatment. Further details of the brutal treatment to which these helpless prisoners were subjected need not be pursued. It is sufficient to say that in pertinent respects the transcript reads more like pages torn from some medieval account than a record made within the confines of a modern civilization which aspires to an enlightened constitutional government."[172]

Upon this record, the Supreme Court held:

"It would be difficult to conceive of methods more revolting to the sense of justice than those taken to procure the confessions of these petitioners, and the use of the confessions thus obtained as the basis for conviction and sentence was a clear denial of due process ... In the instant case, the trial court was fully advised by the undisputed evidence of the way in which the confessions had been procured ... The court thus denied a federal right fully established and specially set up and claimed, and the judgment must be reversed."[173]

Moreover, even a credible *threat* of force or violence has been held to be sufficient to render a confession coerced and thus, inadmissible in evidence. In *Payne v. Arkansas* (1958) 356 U.S. 560, 561 the Supreme Court held that when an officer told the accused that he would protect him from the angry mob outside *if he confessed*, the ensuing confession was coerced. Then, in *Blackburn v. Alabama* (1960) 361 U.S. 199, 206, the Court observed that:

---

172   *Brown v. Mississippi* (1936) 297 U.S. 278.

173   Ibid.

"[C]oercion can be mental as well as physical, and . . . the blood of the accused is not the only hallmark of an unconstitutional inquisition."

Nevertheless, man's inhumanity to man continues to be alive and well. For the many reasons mentioned above, captors continue to be willing *to dehumanize and perpetrate atrocities* upon their victims in order to suit the captor's governmental, religious or personal agendas.

What can be done to strive for a future where not only are laws, abhorrent to torture, in place, but perpetration of torture is *no longer tolerated* by the world community at large? How can international torturers and killers be held *accountable*?

CHAPTER SIX

The Role of Positive Law and the Judiciary in Natural Law

NATURAL LAW long-preexisted the U.S. Constitution. Indeed, as developed earlier in this book, natural law, for humans, is *inherent* in humanity itself. That is to say, natural law exists *independently from* and even *superior to* "positive" law created by institutions and societies. **Positive law** may augment natural law and may even render it more specific in enumeration of certain aspects of human rights, but positive law *can never*, by definition, *supersede* natural law. Think of **natural law** as constituting the unwritten, *naturally* existing, ***minimum*** **standards** of human decency, liberty and freedom. And yet, regulations, statutes, constitutions and judicial opinions have served to confirm the existence of, implement and give form to "natural law."

Origin of the Right to Act in Self-preservation is in Natural Law

In *Osland v. Star Fish & Oyster Co.* (5ᵗʰ Cir. 1939) 107 F.2d 113, the court reviewed a demurrer sustained by a District Court without leave to amend. The Appellant had filed an action for damages arising from him being struck, "by a jar of burning gasoline hurled through the companion way by the appellee's cook, a member of the crew." Appellant seaman was severely burned. The Court rejected the contention on demurrer that the cook was not acting within the scope of his authority when he hurled the gasoline through the companion way. The Court observed:

> "The defect in this argument is that, in attempting to get rid of the explosive, **the cook was acting under the natural law of self-preservation**. [However, i]f in so doing his aim was bid [sic: bad] or his judgment faulty, neither he nor his employer may be held responsible for his action."[174] (bold added for emphasis)

Thereafter, the Court reversed the District Court's granting of the demurrer, holding that the "origin of the danger" in the first place, to wit: the presence of the burning gasoline aboard the vessel and consequent injury to appellant, was properly pleaded as *negligence* by the cook and his employer.

> "His negligence was not in casting the explosive from him, but in using material so combustible to kindle the fire."[175]

Osland articulated, in real life circumstances, an understanding that acts of self-preservation are, as a general rule, protected by natural law. But natural law does not serve as a defense to every act of violence. For example, natural law would not protect a murderer

---

174   107 F.2d at 114.

175   Ibid.

from taking the life of a victim who fights back after being attacked in the first instance with deadly force.[176]

Scope of Natural Law

So, just how are we to know when the right of self-preservation (in all of its permutations and combinations) creates an entitlement and when the right of self-presentation gives way to other countervailing considerations? Understanding the boundaries of "natural law," is *similar* to asking the question,

> "What is the length of a piece of string?"

Even when recognized, the question ultimately becomes, just *how inviolate* are the principles of natural law? Under *what circumstances* may fundamental rights of life, liberty and the pursuit of happiness be *lawfully violated*? What corresponding *duties* are created by natural law?

The various answers depend upon many variables, culturally and factually. The courts in the United States have struggled to respond to these questions, concerning day-to-day affairs.

Natural Law as 'Absolutism" and an *Abolishment* of Democracy

Some commentators argue that claims of and beliefs in natural law are merely invoking a moral or religious "high ground" to unfairly and arbitrarily defeat their opponents. One such commentator remarked:

---

176   *See, Legal Limits of Safety, supra,* **Scenario Twelve** Wrongdoers pp. 107-112.

"Supreme Court Justice Oliver Wendell Holmes emphasized the danger of invoking divine morality when he wrote, in a 1917 opinion, 'The [common] law is not a brooding omnipresence in the sky.'"[177]

From the point of view of these objectors, there is a sort of **absolutism** which contends that legislation and constitutions constitute the *only* rights which inure to the people. The argument goes that the judiciary should have no power to "create" any other purported "rights" out of whole cloth—including out of vague notions of "natural law." U.S. Supreme Court nominee (now, Justice) Clarence Thomas was chastised for acknowledging that although the Constitution is "[t]he positive law," it is not the *only* supreme law since,

"We look at natural law beliefs of the Founders as a background to our Constitution."[178]

Absolutism commentators attempt to discredit the notion of natural law by pointing to Thomas Jefferson's Declaration of Independence document:

---

177 *The Atlantic*, January 27, 2014, *When Judges Believe in "Natural Law,"* Anthony Murray. Unfortunately for Mr. Murray, the Holmes comment was in a **Dissent**. "The fight he was losing was Southern Pacific Co. v. Jensen, which held that the general common law of admiralty preempted contrary state law, even though no federal statute or constitutional provision spoke to the question at issue. [fn omitted]" *SAINT LOUIS UNIVERSITY LAW JOURNAL*, Vol. 43:1349, "THE LAST BROODING OMNIPRESENCE: ERIE RAILROAD CO. v. TOMPKINS AND THE UNCONSTITUTIONALITY OF PREEMPTIVE FEDERAL MARITIME LAW," Ernest A. Young.

178 Ibid. *When Judges Believe in "Natural Law."*

"... Jefferson cited every possible source of the rights the new country was claiming. They came from 'powers of the earth,' from 'laws of nature and of nature's God'; they were 'self[-]evident,' and 'endowed by [a] Creator. By investing the rights with a divine origin, the Declaration elevated them. These were not mere political rights. They were higher, transcendent rights that were 'unalienable.' If the rights were God-given, they could neither be denied nor withdrawn by the target of the Declaration, Britain's King George III."[179]

Utilizing this **strawman basis of critique**, the commentator concluded:

"If natural law were regarded as simply a religious creed, it would not conflict with the positive laws embedded in our Constitution and laws. The threat lies in the use of natural law by courts in judicial decisions. Invoking it in construing the Constitution and statutes raises an obvious question: **If natural law exists, what is in it?** Is it a blank slate on which anyone may write subjective beliefs? Does it include religious dogmas? If so, of what religions?"[180] (Bold added for emphasis)

Anthony Murray, in *The Atlantic* piece, concludes, based on the above-described **false premise** as to the origin of natural law, that,

---

179 ibid.

180 Ibid.

"...[I]n the [American] courtroom the only commandments that matter are the Constitution and the laws enacted pursuant to it. A government that tries to invoke divine law ceases to be of, by, and for the people. ... 'Democracy requires the nourishment of dialog and dissent, **while religious faith puts its trust in an ultimate divine authority above all human deliberation.**' The moment a judge turns to natural law, democracy vanishes."[181] (Bold added for emphasis)

This might be a rational criticism of the existence and use of natural law as a foundation for human rights *but for the fact* that **natural law is neither dependent upon nor derived from** *religions* **or "moral precepts" of any kind.** As developed elsewhere in this book, natural law is instead **inherent in the human condition** as a *manifestation of self-defense* against others and against institutions, in protection of the rights to freedom and liberty.

This natural law right of self-defense even *imposes*, upon certain others, **manifest duties** to care for and protect persons who are otherwise *defenseless* and in vital need of such protection. For instance, *Blackstone* described **manifest parental duties** to children as follows:

"The duty of parents to provide for the maintenance of their children **is a principle of natural law;** an obligation...laid on them not only by nature herself, but by their own proper action bringing them into the

---

181 Ibid. Interestingly (to me), this *misleading* analysis is by a lawyer then practicing at Loeb & Loeb LLP in "civil and criminal law," former president of the State Bar of California and former part owner of the Long Beach Barracudas in Long Beach, California—my home town, and a team, the games of which I enjoyed attending, which played at Blair Field in Long Beach years ago.

world." 1 *Blackstone, Commentaries* 435. (bold added for emphasis)

When viewed in this **naturalistic light**, it is clearly feasible to both visualize and articulate the absolute and historical parameters of natural law. And as to the complaint that natural law is overly subjective, ambiguous and susceptible to multiple interpretations,[182] I would simply observe that it is no more so than American guarantees of due process of law, and of life, liberty, the pursuit of happiness. Similar to the U.S. Constitution in this regard, **natural law is an *evolving standard***, subject to factual and cultural progressions which have historically occurred.

Moreover, as sure as "Justice will out," the Courts themselves have played and will continue to play a key role in shaping application of natural law. In the judicial context, think of the process as answering the question,

"How do you sculpt an elephant?"

The answer:

"You cut away everything that is not an elephant."

The Courts Step In

In a commentary, Felix Morley, educator and journalist and Pulitzer Prize winner, stated:

---

182 *See, Federalist Society Review*, Volume 22, "What Happened to Natural Law in American Jurisprudence?", Kody Cooper, December 13, 2021, Part III; and, Banner, Stuart, *THE DECLINE OF NATURAL LAW: HOW AMERICAN LAWYERS ONCE USED NATURAL LAW AND WHY THEY STOPPED*, (Oxford University Press 2021).

"Our whole system of government is based on the assumption that there are **certain absolute values**, referred to in the Declaration of Independence as 'the Laws of Nature and of Nature's God.'... **Our form of government** is based upon abstract ideas; is **founded on a belief in natural rights**."[183] (Bold added for emphasis)

Author, George J. Marlin, wrote:

"America needs the natural law if our democratic form of government is to survive. For it is the natural law that assures that government will be for the people and not the people for the government. It assures that the citizenry as well as those who control the daily operations of government will be subject to law. It assures that there is a distinction between good and evil. It assures that the murderer's taste for taking human life is treated differently than the physician's taste for preserving it. [fn. deleted] The natural law assures that every man maintains his inalienable rights to life, liberty, and property.

This does not mean that the members of civil society cannot possess positive legal rights. Natural law simply places a limit on the extent of experimentation in government."[184]

---

183 Barron's, p. 3, *Affirmation of Materialism*, Felix Morley, June 18, 1951.

184 Marlin, George J. *THE POLITICIAN'S GUIDE to Assisted Suicide, Cloning, and Other Current Controversies*, Chapter 8, "The Need for Natural Law," (Morley Inst. 1998).

No less than the U.S. Constitution's **Ninth Amendment** *itself* proclaims (and admits) that **rights retained by the people exist** *beyond* those specifically granted in the Constitution. The Ninth Amendment reads:

> "The enumeration in the Constitution, of certain rights, shall not be construed to deny or disparage **others retained by the people**." (bold added for emphasis)

Institutions and societies continue to acknowledge and expound upon details and application of natural law. Such proclamations have contributed to a deeper understanding of the parameters of human rights.

The electorate in California, by Proposition 7,[185] arguably *memorialized* the existence and legitimacy of natural law (and of one of its cornerstones, the right of privacy) as follows:

> "**All people** *are by nature* **free and independent and have** *inalienable* **rights.** Among these are enjoying and defending **life and liberty, acquiring, possessing, and protecting property**, and **pursuing and obtaining safety, happiness and privacy**."[186] (bold and italics added for emphasis)

Natural law is not only a fact of life, **it is a fact of life** *around the world*, and is the **fountainhead of** *hope* **for oppressed people** everywhere. Natural law necessarily transcends the borders of America. While the United States may have a positive law structure

---

185 Added to California law on November 5, 1974.

186 Article 1 Section 1, California Constitution.

to *mimic and elaborate upon* the substance of natural law, not all nations, and their peoples, are so fortunate. For those persons and nations, the existence, substance and credibility of natural law is *particularly germane.*

It would be grievously ethnocentric to view natural law as living or dying according merely to American jurisprudence. However, in order to confirm the *credibility* of natural law as creating inalienable human rights, it is worth sampling how **various American judicial opinions** deal with the subject—of natural law. However, not all courts are willing to recognize natural law.[187]

Judicial resistance

For example, in *United States v. Lynch,*[188] the Court was faced with an appeal by defendants of a District Court's permanent injunction against the defendants from violating the Freedom of Access to Clinic Entrances Act, 18 U.S.C.S. Section 248 ("FACE"). Defendants did not contend that the statute was unconstitutional. Instead, **defendants' sole contention on appeal** was that,

> "...the FACE statute protects [meaning: *facilitates*] the taking of innocent human life [*i.e.*, unborn children], and is therefore contrary to natural law and accordingly null and void."

The District Court had considered this defense, and stated:

> **"'I don't recognize my authority to refuse to issue an injunction under natural law,'** and 'I don't have the

---

187 Court opinions on actual controversies are known as judicial "Opinions," or simply, "case law."

188 (2nd Cir. 1996) 104 F.3d 357 (not certified for publication).

right to act my own private conscience.'" (bold added for emphasis)

Accordingly, the Court *Affirmed* the District Court's ruling, stating,

> "Under Supreme Court precedent, well-settled constitutional principles, and the rule of stare decisis, **we decline to invalidate a federal statute (on its face or as applied) on the basis of natural law principles.**" (bold added for emphasis)

Notwithstanding the *Lynch* case and similar judicial ideology, judicial interpretation of the U.S. Constitution **widely incorporates** notions of natural law, including as to due process of law.

Historical development of due process of law
In the early U.S. Supreme Court case of *Calder v. Bull*, Justice Samuel Chase expounded on the theme:

> "The purposes for which men enter into society will determine the nature and terms of the **social compact**. ... An act of the legislature (for I cannot call it a law) contrary to the great first principles of the social compact, cannot be considered a rightful exercise of legislative authority."[189] (Bold added for emphasis)

Justice Chase elaborated as examples, "a law that makes a man a judge in his own cause, or a law that takes property from A and gives it to B." The first example pertains to "procedural due process;" and

---

189 (1798) 3 U.S. 386.

the second example implicates "substantive due process of law"—each based on the Fifth and Fourteenth Amendment. There is a **natural law origin** of the concept of **due process of law**.[190] The Fifth Amendment to the United States Constitution provides:

> "**No person shall be** held to answer for a capital, or otherwise infamous crime, unless on a presentment or indictment of a Grand Jury, except in cases arising in the land or naval forces, or in the Militia, when in actual service in time of War or public danger; nor shall any person be subject for the same offence to be twice put in jeopardy of life or limb; nor shall be compelled in any criminal case to be a witness against himself, nor be **deprived of life, liberty, or property, without due process of law**; nor shall private property be taken for public use, without just compensation." (bold added for emphasis)

Procedural Due Process and Equal Protection of the Law

Initially, Due Process was viewed as *procedural* **due process**. Procedural due process protects individuals from unfairness in procedures of governmental bodies—so-called State Actors or State Action. It requires mechanisms for decisions which afford timely and adequately specific notice, the opportunity to be heard, and the right to produce relevant evidence, in a fair and impartial adjudicatory forum, at levels appropriate to the rights at stake.[191]

---

190 *See also,* Grant, J.A.C., *The Natural Law Background of Due Process,* 31 Colum. L. Rev. 56 (1931).

191 *Hagar v. Reclamation Dist.* (1884) 111 U.S. 701, 708.

In *Yick Wo v. Hopkins*,[192] the U.S. Supreme Court considered a case involving the constitutionality of ordinances made by a municipal corporation to regulate the carrying on of public laundries in wooden buildings. Petitioners (persons of Chinese descent) were charged, convicted and imprisoned for violating the ordinances.

The Court discussed the ordinance as to whether and to what extent it **conferred upon municipal authorities a form of *arbitrary power***, at their own unlimited discretion, to give or withhold consent as to persons or places, without regard to the competency of the persons applying, or the propriety of the place selected, for the carrying on of the business. Justice Matthews delivered the **landmark** Opinion of the Court, explaining:

> "The Fourteenth Amendment to the Constitution is not confined to the protection of citizens. It says: 'Nor shall any State deprive any person of life, liberty, or property **without due process of law**; nor deny to any person within its jurisdiction the equal protection of the laws.' These provisions are universal in their application to all persons within the territorial jurisdiction, without regard to any differences of race, of color, or of nationality, and the equal protection of the laws is a pledge of the protection of equal laws."[193] (bold added for emphasis)

Upon holding that Chinese laborers were within the class of persons protected by the Fourteenth Amendment, the Court then ruled that the *Yick Wo* parties **were protected, in their pursuit of**

---

192   (1886) 118 U.S. 356.

193   Id. at 369.

business interests, against *arbitrary discrimination* evidenced in the administration of the San Francisco ordinance. *Yick Wo* held:

"When we consider the nature and the theory of our institutions of government, the principles upon which they are supposed to rest, and review the history of their development, we are constrained to conclude that **they do not mean to leave room for the play and action of purely personal and arbitrary power**. ... [S]overeignty itself remains with the people, by whom and for whom all government exists and acts. And the law is the definition and limitation of power. ... But the **fundamental rights to life, liberty, and the pursuit of happiness**, considered as individual possessions, are secured by those maxims of constitutional law which are the monuments showing the victorious progress of the race in securing to men the blessings of civilization under the reign of just and equal laws, so that, in the famous language of the Massachusetts Bill of Rights, the government of the commonwealth 'may be a government of laws, and not of men.' For the very idea that one man may be compelled to hold his life, or the means of living, or any material right essential to the enjoyment of life **at the mere [arbitrary] will of another** seems to be intolerable in any country where freedom prevails, as being the essence of slavery itself."[194] (bold added for emphasis)

---

194   Id. at 369-370.

The Court then proceeded to apply an **equal protection**[195] **of the law analysis** to resolve the case in favor of the Chinese Petitioners:

> "Though the law itself be fair on its face and impartial in appearance, yet, **if it is applied and administered by public authority with an evil eye and an unequal hand**, so as practically to make unjust and illegal discriminations between persons in similar circumstances, material to their rights, the denial of equal justice is still within the prohibition of the Constitution. ... The present cases, as shown by the facts disclosed in the record, are within this class. It appears that both petitioners have complied with every requisite deemed by the law or by the public officers charged with its administration necessary for the protection of neighboring property from fire or as a precaution against injury to the public health. No reason whatever, except the will of the supervisors, is assigned why they should not be permitted to carry on, in the accustomed manner, their harmless and useful occupation, on which they depend for a livelihood. And while this consent of the supervisors is withheld from them and from two hundred others who have also petitioned, all of whom happen to be Chinese subjects, eighty others, not Chinese subjects, are permitted to carry on the same business under similar conditions. **The**

---

195 Equal protection of the law requires that any State Action treat similar persons similarly and without discrimination not otherwise permitted by law. In the case of discrimination disfavoring "suspect classes" such as age, race, ethnicity and gender, any such discrimination must, to be lawful, be justified by "strict scrutiny" under a "compelling interest" test. In *Bolling v. Sharpe* (1954) 347 U.S. 497, the Supreme Court held that the Due Process Clause of the Fifth Amendment requires equal protection under the laws of the federal government.

fact of this discrimination is admitted. No reason for it is shown, and the conclusion cannot be resisted that no reason for it exists except hostility to the race and nationality to which the petitioners belong, and which, in the eye of the law, is not justified. The discrimination is, therefore, illegal, and the public administration which enforces it is a denial of the equal protection of the laws and a violation of the Fourteenth Amendment of the Constitution. The imprisonment of the petitioners is, therefore, illegal, and they must be discharged."[196] (bold added for emphasis)

In *Yick Wo*, although the ordinance was *on its face neutral* as to race and national origin,[197] circumstantial *evidence of invidious discrimination on racial and national origin grounds* was **overwhelming and beyond rational dispute.** A neutral reason neither offered by Respondents, nor believable. Thus, the *Yick Wo* Court's holding was that despite the facially neutral administrative rules, actual discrimination in *application* of those rules denied the Petitioners and the other Chinese persons equal protection of the laws under the Fifth and Fourteenth Amendments of the Constitution. The U.S. Constitution, Bill of Rights and judicial rulings gave *form and substance* to the concept of freedom of discrimination based upon manifestly unjust classifications such as racial and national origin. However, these inalienable rights *preexisted and were independent of* such positive law, as part of a universal natural law.

But in *Yick Wo*, it was not merely a matter of people being treated *differently*, without justification. At the *heart* of the *Yick Wo*

---

196 Id. at 373-374.

197 Albeit, such ordinance was without otherwise adequate *standards* for the legitimate exercise of administrative discretion.

decision is the Court's conclusion that petitioners were harmed by *de facto* **arbitrary governmental decisions** adversely affecting their chosen livelihoods. The **lack of adequately specific, *substantive* standards** for approval or denial of the licenses to operate laundries in wooden buildings invited an arbitrary and capricious exercise of administrative "discretion." A vague and uncertain law denies substantive due process of law under what has become known in American Jurisprudence as the "void-for-vagueness doctrine."

Substantive Due Process of Law

A California Court of Appeal, in *Parker v. State*,[198] described in detail the void-for-vagueness doctrine. Part of this doctrine lies in the nature of *procedural* due process (regarding adequate *notice* within a statute), and part lies in the nature of *substantive* due process (regarding the *risk of arbitrary and capricious enforcement* of an excessively vague law). The *Parker* Court wrote:

> "'The requirement of a reasonable degree of certainty in legislation, especially in the criminal law, is a well[-] established element of the guarantee of due process of law.' (*People v. Superior Court* (*Caswell*) (1988) 46 Cal.3d 381, 389 (*Caswell*), quoting *In re Newbern* (1960) 53 Cal.2d 786, 792.) This is the foundation of the void-for-vagueness doctrine. The doctrine arises from due process protections under the United States and California Constitutions. (*Ibid.*; U.S. Const., 5th & 14th Amends.; Cal. Const., art. I, § 7.) 'The vagueness may be from uncertainty in regard to persons within the scope of the [statute] . . . or in regard to the applicable tests to

---

198   (2013, Fifth Dist.) 221 Cal.App.4th 340.

ascertain guilt.' (*Winters v. New York* (1948) 333 U.S. 507, 515-516.)

A commonly cited formulation of the doctrine is stated in *Connally [v. General Constr. Co.* (1926) 269 U.S. 385]. There, a criminal statute punishing contractors who paid their workers less than the "'current rate of per diem wages in the locality where the work is performed'" was found unconstitutionally vague on its face. (*Connally, supra,* 269 U.S. at 393.) The court held that 'a statute which either forbids or requires the doing of an act in terms so vague that men of common intelligence must necessarily guess at its meaning and differ as to its application violates the first essential of due process of law.' (*Id.* at 391.)

In California, criminal statutes must satisfy two requirements to withstand a facial vagueness challenge under the due process clause. 'First, a statute must be sufficiently definite to provide adequate notice of the conduct proscribed.' (*Caswell, supra,* 46 Cal.3d at 389.) **'Second, a statute must provide sufficiently definite guidelines for the police in order to prevent arbitrary and discriminatory enforcement.'** (*Id.* at 390.)

These basic requirements are distilled from several decades of jurisprudence. (See *Caswell, supra,* 46 Cal.3d at pp. 389-390.) As stated in *Grayned v. City of Rockford* (1972) 408 U.S. 104 (*Grayned*), '[v]ague laws offend several important values. First, because we assume that man is free to steer between lawful and unlawful conduct, we insist that laws give the person of ordinary intelligence a reasonable opportunity to know what is prohibited, so that he may act accordingly. Vague laws may trap the innocent by not providing fair warning.' (*Id.* at p. 108.)

'Second, if **arbitrary and discriminatory enforcement is to be prevented**, laws must provide **explicit standards for those who apply them**. A vague law impermissibly delegates basic policy matters to policemen, judges, and juries for resolution on an *ad hoc* **and subjective basis**, with the attendant **dangers of arbitrary and discriminatory application**. Third... [u]ncertain meanings inevitably lead citizens to steer far wider of the unlawful zone . . . than if the boundaries of the forbidden areas were clearly marked.' (*Grayned, supra,* 408 U.S. at pp. 108-109, footnotes and internal quotation marks omitted.)" [bold added for emphasis]

Arbitrary and wrongfully discriminatory enforcement of laws is, at its core, a violation of life, liberty and the pursuit of happiness and is clearly an unacceptable and egregious violation of natural law. In *any* society, police, Judges, administrators and politicians must not single-out persons with whom they have some personal animosity and then use the force of law against them for capricious and harmful purposes. Even if there were no void-for-vagueness doctrine implicit within a constitutional provision guaranteeing due process of law, the **underlying misconduct would *still violate* natural law** as being repugnant to life, liberty and the pursuit of happiness.

In the United States, the development of *substantive* **due process** followed an *uneven path*.[199] In *Pierce v. Society of Sisters*,[200] the Supreme Court held that an Oregon law prohibiting parochial school education was unconstitutional:

> "The fundamental theory of **liberty** upon which all governments in this union repose[,] excludes any general power of the state to standardize its children by forcing them to accept instruction from public teachers only. The child is not the mere creature of the state; those who nurture him and direct his destiny have the right, **coupled with the high duty**, to recognize and prepare him for his additional obligations."[201] (bold added for emphasis)

The *Pierce* Court based its ruling on substantive due process grounds, explaining that, "rights guaranteed by the Constitution may not be abridged by legislation which has no reasonable relation to some purpose within the competency of the state."[202]

Similarly, in *Meyer v. Nebraska* (1923) 262 U.S. 390, the Supreme Court held a Nebraska law to be unconstitutional which *proscribed* teaching *in the German language*. The Court held, on substantive due process grounds,[203] that "the statute as applied is arbitrary and

---

199   *See*, Touro University Jacob D. Fuchsberg Law Center, Touro Law Review, Vo. 15, No. 4, Article 15, *Substantive Due Process*, Erwin Chemerinsky, 1999.

200   (1925) 268 U.S. 510.

201   Id. at 535.

202   Ibid.

203   *Meyer*, 262 U.S. at 399.

without reasonable relation to any end within the competency of the state."[204] The Court explained:

> "…[T]he state may do much…in order to improve the quality of its citizens, physically, mentally and morally… **but the individual has certain fundamental rights which must be respected**. The protection of the Constitution extends to all, to those who speak other languages as well as those born with English on the tongue. Perhaps it would be highly advantageous if all had ready understanding of our ordinary speech, but this cannot be coerced by methods which conflict with the Constitution—a desirable and [sic: end] cannot be promoted by prohibited means."[205] (bold added for emphasis)

By enforcing a **judicial right of constitutional oversight** of governmental actions and enactments, *through the lens of substantive (and even, procedural) "due process,"* the Court is recognizing the existence, legitimacy and enforceability of **natural law**—inherent law—as memorialized in part in federal and State constitutions as "due process of law."[206] Professor Chemerinsky argues that,

---

204 Id. at 403.

205 Id. at 401.

206 The U.S. Supreme Court has struggled with this apparent close association between natural law, on the one hand, and due process of law, on the other hand. In *Rochin v. California* (1952) 342 U.S. 165, the court confronted the question of what limitations the due process clause of the Fourteenth Amendment imposes on the conduct of state criminal proceedings? Justice Frankfurter, writing for the majority, stated, "Even though the concept of due process of law is not final and fixed, these limits are derived from considerations…deeply rooted in reason," 342 U.S. at 170. He clarified, "Due Process of law thus conceived is not to be derided as resort to a revival of 'natural law.'" 342 U.S. at 171.

"The reality is that substantive due process can be used [by the courts to protect the public] any time the government takes away life, liberty or property."[207]

This is consistent with the concept of natural law as a fundamental right of self-defense of the individual against tyranny and other dangers—protecting the individual or their dependents against arbitrary and capricious acts in contravention of one's life, liberty and the pursuit of happiness (including ownership of property).

"We have emphasized time and again that '[t]he touchstone of due process is protection of the individual against the arbitrary action of government.' *Wolff v. McDonnell*, 418 U.S. 539, 558 (1974), whether the fault lies in a denial of fundamental procedural fairness..., or in the exercise of power without any reasonable justification in the service of a legitimate governmental objective..."[208]

But the point to be garnered here is not the extent to which the U.S. Constitution protects human rights. The point is that natural law exists for humans *regardless* of what any constitution, statute, proclamation or Court of law states, whether labeled as "due process of law" or otherwise.

The Length of a Piece of String

In 1764, James Otis argued that positive laws and governments have arisen,

---

207 *Substantive Due Process*, Id. at 8.

208 *Sacramento v. Lewis* (1998) 523 U.S. 833, 845.

"from the necessities of our nature, and has an everlasting foundation in the unchangeable will of God, the Author of nature, whose laws never vary...[and] there can be no prescriptions old enough to supersede the law of nature and the grant of Almighty God, who has given to all **a natural right to be free**."[209] (bold added for emphasis)

There are many interesting iterations on the theme of how American Courts view principles of natural law and the human rights which they embody.

Trial by Jury

In 1795, the U.S. Supreme Court reasoned, in *Vanhorne's Lessee v. Dorrance*:

"...[T]he right of **trial by jury** is a fundamental law, made sacred by the Constitution... [and] the right of acquiring and possessing property, and having it protected, is one of the **natural, inherent rights of man**."[210] (bold added for emphasis)

Right of privacy

A U.S. Supreme Court case *suspiciously close* to a natural law analysis is *Griswold v. Connecticut*.[211] In *Griswold*, the Court was faced with a set of State laws forbidding both the use of any contraceptive device or medicine, and the aiding and abetting of

---

209   Otis, James, *The Rights of the British Colonies Asserted and Proved* (pamphlet), (1764).

210   (1795) 2 U.S. 304.

211   (1965) 381 U.S. 479.

any other person to use any such device or medicine. Appellant Griswold was the executive director of a Planned Parenthood clinic and Appellant Buxton was the Medical Director of its New Haven Center. Appellants were found guilty as accessories, fined $100 each and then appealed based on a claim that the statutes so applied violated the Fourteenth Amendment.

The Court, in *Griswold*, pointed to the *absence* of any mention, in the Constitution or Bill of Rights, to freedom of association, the right to educate a child in a school of the parents' choice, and the right to study any particular subject or in a foreign language. Citing the holdings of *Pierce* and *Meyer, supra,* the Court observed,

> "Yet the First Amendment has been *construed* to include certain of those rights."[212] (italics added for emphasis)

The Court further pointed out,

> "In *NAACP v. Alabama* [(1958)], 357 U.S. 449 we protected the 'freedom to associate and privacy in one's associations,' noting that freedom of association was a peripheral First Amendment right. ... In other words, the First Amendment has a penumbra where privacy is protected from governmental intrusion. ... The foregoing cases suggest that specific guarantees in the Bill of Rights have penumbras, formed by emanations from those guarantees that help give them life and substance. Various guarantees create zones of privacy."[213]

---

212   Id. at 482.

213   Id. at 483.

The Court remarked that the case,

> "... concerns a law which, in forbidding the use of
> contraceptives rather than regulating their manufacture
> or sale, seeks to achieve its goals by means having a
> **maximum destructive impact upon that relationship**.
> Such a law cannot stand in light of the familiar principle,
> so often applied by this Court, that a 'governmental
> purpose to control or prevent activities constitutionally
> subject to state regulation **may not be achieved by means
> which sweep unnecessarily broadly** and thereby invade
> the area of protected freedoms.'"[214] (bold added for
> emphasis)

The Court (and the Concurring Opinion of Justice Goldberg,
Justice Brennan and the Chief Justice) concluded that Connecticut's
birth-control law **unconstitutionally intruded upon the right of
marital privacy.** Accordingly, the Court *Reversed* the lower appellate
Courts which had affirmed Appellants' convictions. Explaining the
rationale for its holding, the Court *looked back*, to **before** the Bill
of Rights:

> "We deal with **a right of privacy older than the Bill of
> Rights** – older than our political parties, older than our
> school system. Marriage is a coming together for better or
> for worse, hopefully enduring, and intimate to the degree
> of being sacred. It is an association that promotes a way of
> life, not causes; a harmony in living, not political faiths; a
> bilateral loyalty, not commercial or social projects. Yet it

---

214   Id. at 485.

is an association for as noble a purpose as any involved in our prior decisions."[215] (bold added for emphasis)

The **right of marital privacy** is nowhere mentioned in the Constitution, and yet it was held to be, "older than the Bill of Rights," "sacred," a "harmony in living" and "a bilateral loyalty." While the Court based this jump on the idea of a "penumbra" from various cited Amendments to the Constitution,[216] it may as well have stated, *or admitted*, that it was **applying natural law to reveal the inherent fundamental right of privacy in human lives.**

Infringement of "fundamental" rights and discrimination against "suspect" classes

In the United States, a "compelling state interest" becomes a required element of the "strict scrutiny test" applicable both to incursion of any right considered to be "fundamental" in nature, *or* to discrimination against any person within a "suspect" class.[217]

This form of analysis in American jurisprudence had its *origins* in *Skinner v. Oklahoma*,[218] in which the Supreme Court subjected to "strict scrutiny" a state statute providing for **compulsory sterilization of habitual criminals**, since the subject law affected, "one of the most basic civil rights"[219] pursuant to the due process

---

215 Id. at 486.

216 Including, notably, the Ninth Amendment to the Constitution.

217 *See,* Free Speech Center, *THE FIRST AMENDMENT ENCYCLOPEDIA,* "Compelling State Interest," last updated, Robert Steiner, September 19, 2023, https://firstamendment.mtsu.edu/article/compelling-state-interest.

218 (1942) 316 U.S. 535.

219 Id. at 541.

clause and equal protection of the law clause of the Fourteenth Amendment to the U.S. Constitution. The *Skinner* Court wrote:

> "Marriage and procreation are fundamental to the very existence and survival of the race. The power to sterilize, if exercised, may have subtle, farreaching [sic: far-reaching] and devastating effects."[220]

In *striking down the statute*, the Court referenced an enhanced test for the legality of laws infringing fundamental rights:

> "We mention these matters not to reexamine the scope of the police power of the States. We advert to them merely in emphasis of our view that **strict scrutiny of the classification** which a State makes in a sterilization law **is essential**, lest unwittingly or otherwise invidious discriminations are made against groups or types of individuals in violation of the constitutional guaranty of just and equal laws."[221] (bold added for emphasis)

Strict scrutiny has become the *highest standard of review*[222] which the courts use to determine the constitutionality of laws adversely impacting fundamental rights and also what are known as "suspect" classes such as race, religion, national origin, and age. To pass strict scrutiny, the law or "state action" must both **further a**

---

220 Ibid.

221 Ibid.

222 The *lesser* standards, where neither fundamental rights nor suspect classifications are in play, are the "rational basis" test and the "intermediate scrutiny" test (employed, for example, on commercial speech and state action pertaining to classifications based on sex).

compelling governmental interest and **be narrowly tailored and the least restrictive means** to achieve that interest.

For example, in *Loving v. Virginia*,[223] applying the strict scrutiny test, the Supreme Court invalidated a law banning *interracial marriage*. There, in June 1958, two residents of Virginia, a black woman and a white man married (together, the "Lovings") in the District of Columbia pursuant to its laws. After returning to Virginia, a grand jury in the Circuit Court of Caroline County, Virginia, issued an Indictment charging the Lovings with violating Virginia's ban on interracial marriages. The defendants pled guilty, moved back to D.C. and filed motions challenging the basis of their convictions. The Court in *Loving* wrote:

> "... [T]he State does not contend in its argument before this Court that its powers to regulate marriage are unlimited notwithstanding the commands of the Fourteenth Amendment. ... [T]he State contends that, because its miscegenation statutes punish equally both the white and the Negro participants in an interracial marriage, these statutes, despite their reliance on racial classifications, do not constitute an invidious discrimination based upon race. ... Because we reject the notion that the mere 'equal application' of a statute containing racial classifications is enough to remove the classifications from the Fourteenth Amendment's proscription of all invidious racial discriminations, we do not accept the State's contention that these statutes should

---

223   (1967) 388 U.S. 1.

be upheld if there is any possible basis for concluding that they serve a rational purpose."[224]

Loving then *struck down* the Virginia miscegenation statutes, holding:

"Over the years, this Court has consistently repudiated '(d)istinctions between citizens solely because of their ancestry' as being 'odious to a free people whose institutions are founded upon the doctrine of equality.' *Hirabayashi v. United States*, 320 U.S. 81, ... (1943). At the very least, the Equal Protection Clause demands that racial classifications, especially suspect in criminal statutes, be subjected to the 'most rigid scrutiny,' *Korematsu v. United States*, 323 U.S. 214, 216, ..., and, if they are ever to be upheld, they must be shown to be **necessary to the accomplishment** of some permissible state objective, independent of the racial discrimination.... [Here, there] is patently no legitimate overriding purpose independent of invidious racial discrimination which justifies this classification. .... [**Moreover, these] statutes also deprive the Lovings of liberty without due process of law in violation of the Due Process Clause of the Fourteenth Amendment.** The freedom to marry has long been recognized as one of the vital personal rights essential to the orderly pursuit of happiness by free men. **Marriage is one of the 'basic civil rights of man,' fundamental**

---

224   Id. at 13-14.

to our very existence and survival. *Skinner v. State of Oklahoma....*"[225] (bold added for emphasis)

Here, the *Loving* court literally snatched the "freedom to marry" *out of thin air* in declaring it to be a fundamental right deserving of the utmost judicial scrutiny—the strict scrutiny test. Remarking that, "Marriage is one of the 'basic civil rights of man,' fundamental to our very existence and survival," *Loving* implicitly drew the fundamental right to marriage from the doctrine of natural law.[226]

California case law

California[227] caselaw is *replete* with references, in a wide variety of contexts, to natural law as the basis for human rights and associated duties.

In *People v. Batchelder,*[228] the California Supreme Court reviewed the conviction of Batchelder on manslaughter charges. The defendant and others arrived at an island to collect eggs, but were confronted by armed guards who stated their principles had the exclusive rights to the island. Batchelder and his party were ordered to leave, but refused and came on shore. The guards opened fire and one of them was killed by shots fired by Batchelder. At trial, the court refused to give jury instructions on self-defense. In *reversing*

---

225 Id. at 17-20.

226 Then, by stating that the statute in question must act in such a manner as to be "necessary" in accomplishing "some permissible state objective," *Loving* implicitly utilized the *compelling state interest test*. In this manner, *Loving* distinguished the standard of review away from merely inquiring as to whether a "rational basis" for the statute hypothetically existed.

227 California is one of 50 "States" within the United States of America.

228 (1864) 27 Cal. 69.

the conviction and ordering a new trial, the Court reasoned as follows:

> "While courts and juries should be extremely cautious how they excuse the slayer of his fellow upon the pretext that the act was the result of a necessity, they should be equally careful not to find the accused guilty if it appears that the homicide was committed in the necessary defense of himself, **or in the defense of those whom he is bound by natural law to protect and defend.**"[229] (bold added for emphasis)

Then, in *Lux v. Haggin*,[230] the California Supreme Court faced the issue of whether a private corporation may divert the waters of a watercourse and thereby deprive the riparian proprietor of all use of the same, without compensation made and tendered to such proprietor. The Court held that owners of land by or through which a watercourse naturally and usually flows have a *right of property* in the stream.

> "'...[N]o nation can possibly assert that it is unable to enjoy the fullest use of the sea without the exclusion of others, so no nation can have any just ground for excluding others from an advantage which all may enjoy, together with equally full utility to each. This legal doctrine is thus admirably summed up by a German civilian: "The great sea is a thing, the use of which is inexhaustible; consequently, as no one can acquire the

---

229   Id. at 72.

230   (1886) 69 Cal. 255.

dominion of things, the utility of which is unbounded and inexhaustible, no one (even were it possible in fact) can subject the great sea to his dominion **without violating natural law**. And the same must be understood of several nations, who cannot, for the same reasons, divide the dominion of the great seas among them. Consequently, **no nation can, without infringement of natural law, subject to its dominion the great sea.**'" (Bowyer's Com. On the Modern Civil Law, p. 64, citing the Pandects, Grotius, Puffendorf, Bynkershoek, Wolf's Jus. Gent.)"[231] (bold added for emphasis)

Davis v. Franson[232] presented a case over a car accident where plaintiffs were injured but the trial court verdict was in favor of the defendant. Due to amnesia, defendant had no memory of the accident itself. The Court held that the trial court properly instructed the jury on the presumption—in such a case and where no other eye witnesses were located—that the defendant is entitled to a *statutory presumption of due care*, unless rebutted. The Court of Appeals wrote:

> "This presumption is one which may be invoked for the benefit of ... [the amnesiac party] when unable to produce any eyewitnesses to a collision, **and is based upon the sound foundation of the natural law of self-preservation.**"[233] (bold added for emphasis)

---

231 Id. at 318.

232 (1956) 141 Cal.App.2d 263.

233 Id. at 270.

Then, in *Serrano v. Priest*,[234] the California Supreme Court considered the constitutionality of a public-school finance system based upon local property taxes alone. The *Serrano* Court ruled that such a system did not withstand strict scrutiny because there was no compelling state interest furthered by the system, which discriminated against the poor and violated the equal protection clause. The Judgment below, upholding the constitutionality of the finance system, was *Reversed*, as the Court reasoned as follows:

> "By our holding today, we further the cherished idea of American education that in a democratic society free public schools shall make available to all children equally the abundant gifts of learning. This was the credo of Horace Mann, which has been the heritage and the inspiration of this country. 'I believe,' he wrote, 'in the existence of **a great, immortal immutable principle of natural law, or natural ethics;—a principle antecedent to all human institutions, and incapable of being abrogated by any ordinance of man.** . . . which proves the ***absolute right* to an education** of every human being that comes into the world, and which, of course, proves the correlative duty of every government to see that the means of that education are provided for all. . . .' . . . (Old South Leaflets V, No. 109 (1846) pp. 177-180 [citation omitted]."[235] (bold added for emphasis)

---

234   (1971) 5 Cal.3d 584.

235   Id. at 619.

White v. Davis,[236] a 1975 California Supreme Court Decision, is the first appellate ruling regarding the State's newly enacted privacy clause in its Constitution. There, taxpayers sued to enjoin LAPD from inserting undercover agents as students at UCLA to develop "police dossiers" on students, which dossiers had no particular relation to any specific, targeted illegal activities. The Court reversed a trial court's ruling dismissing the action. In doing so, the Court held that the police action unlawfully abridged freedom of expression and association, and also that it violated the privacy clause of California's Constitution.[237] *White* wrote:

> "...[T]he amendment does not purport to prohibit all incursion into individual privacy but rather that any such intervention must be justified by a compelling interest... [and that] **the constitutional provision**, in itself, '**creates** a legal and enforceable **right of privacy** for every Californian.'"[238] (bold added for emphasis)

Thus, the Court *fell short* of acknowledging that a right of privacy was *inherent* in natural law itself, and seems to assert that the right of privacy was instead *created* by amendment to the California Constitution. Importantly, however, the *White* decision explained that in order to excuse a governmental incursion on, or limitation of, the right of privacy, it "must be justified by a compelling interest."

---

236   (1975) 12 Cal.3d 757.

237   *White*, 533 P.2d at 232-234.

238   Id. at 234.

In this manner, the court gave some further definition to, or shape of, the right of privacy and its boundaries.[239]

In *Kasler v. Lockyer*,[240] the California Supreme Court held that a penal statute does *not* violate constitutional separation of powers by restrictions on a class of semiautomatic firearms characterized as "assault weapons." Justice Brown **concurred** with the majority opinion, while still recognizing natural law as "logically linked" to "the natural right of self-defense":

> "The founding generation certainly viewed **bearing arms as an individual right based upon both English common law and natural law, a right logically linked to the natural right of self-defense**. Blackstone described self-defense as the primary law of nature, 'which could not be taken away by the law of society.' (2 Jones' Blackstone (1976) p. 4)."[241] (bold added for emphasis)

Referring to the duty of governments to protect and preserve what is known as "public trust property," such as wildlife, the Court

---

239   *Cf., People v. Privitera* (1979) 573 P.2d 919. There, the California Supreme Court considered the issue of whether the State constitution's privacy clause supported a **constitutional right of access to drugs** (in that case, purported cancer drugs) which had not been approved by the government for treatment of diseases. *Privitera* **upheld** the appellant's conviction for unlawful distribution of drugs, ruling that there was no "intent," in the enactment of a constitutional right to privacy, to create "a right of access to drugs of unproven efficacy." As illustrated by the *Privitera* holding, courts sometimes bypass consideration of whether a "right" is *inherent and fundamental* in the sense of *natural law* concepts, and instead pursue a question of "legislative intent" as to the intended scope of the legislative enactment.

240   (2000) 23 Cal.4th 472.

241   Id. at 505.

of Appeals, in *Center for Biological Diversity, Inc. v. FPL Group, Inc,*[242] wrote:

> **"The public trust doctrine**...has been described as 'a transcendental legal principle. While its articulation can be found in European civil and English common law and its reflection noted in United States statutory and constitutional law, **its roots are in natural law.**'"[243] (bold added for emphasis)

Statutory natural law reference in Louisiana
In the State of Louisiana, the Louisiana Code, Article 21 provides:

> "In all civil matters, where there is no express law, the judge is bound to proceed and decide according to equity. **To decide equitably, an appeal is to be made to natural law and reason, or received usages, where positive law is silent.**" (bold added for emphasis)

In the Louisiana case of *Grigsby v. Coastal Marine Service, Inc.*,[244] a federal Court of Appeal reviewed a finding in the trial court that, despite the absence of negligence, the owner of a barge was liable for damages in a wrongful death action concerning the death of a Good Samaritan seaman in attempting a rescue. On appeal, the court framed the issue:

---

242   (2008) 166 Cal.App.4th 1349.

243   *Center for Biological Diversity*, 166 Cal.App.4th at 1360, fn. 11.

244   (5th Cir. 1969) 412 F.2d 1011.

"The issue here turns on the construction of the term 'fault'. Does Article 2315 encompass an action based on non-negligent unseaworthiness?"

The Court found no Louisiana decision on point, but stated,

"When there is no express codal or statutory provision dealing with particular situations, Article 21 provides guidance for the courts: 'In all civil matters, where there is no express law, the judge is bound to proceed and decide according to equity. **To decide equitably, an appeal is to be made to natural law and reason, or received usages, where positive law is silent.**'"[245] (bold added for emphasis)

Citing, *Miller v. Holstein* (1840) 16 La. 395, 406, the Court held, under natural law principles, that "fault," so as to create legal responsibility for damages, is not limited to negligence, but also encompasses,

"'...breach of obligation. Any breach of warranty or obligation is fault within the meaning of this statute whether imposed by law, by contract or by statute. Unseaworthiness is such a breach.'"[246]

In *R.J. Reynolds Tobacco Co. v. Hudson*,[247] the issue was: At what point in time would a one-year limitation of actions statute

---

245 Id. at 1025.

246 Id. at 1029.

247 (5th Cir. 1963) 314 F.2d 776.

commence? The statutes pertaining to the limitation of action were somewhat vague and there was *no caselaw on the subject* in the jurisdiction.[248] The federal Court of Appeal expressly referred, *inter alia*, to Article 21 and held that,

> "Pulling all of the loose threads together, as well as we can, we hold that the prescription commenced to run from the time the disease manifested itself to the point when Hudson knew, or should have known, that the damages he sustained, which were the subject of his suit, resulted from smoking the defendant's tobacco products. When this took place is a jury question. We believe that this holding is more consistent with the language and spirit of the Code, the Louisiana cases (such as they are), analogous decisions from other jurisdictions, and with good sense than the more limited view the defendant takes..."[249]

Federal Circuit Court of Appeals Opinions

Likewise, federal Circuit Court of Appeals caselaw commonly recognize, in a wide variety of contexts, natural law as the basis for human rights and associated duties.

U.S. Constitution, generally

Ali Hamza etc. v. United States[250] dealt with the military prosecution of appellant for conspiracy to commit war crimes,

---

248   Id. at 779-780.

249   Id. at 786.

250   (D.C. Cir. 2014) 767 F.3d 1.

providing material support for terrorism and solicitation of others to commit war crimes. Justice Rogers, Circuit Judge for the District of Columbia concurred and dissented in the judgment of the Court. Justice Rogers observed:

> "As one drafter explained: 'The **law of nature**, when applied to states or political societies, **receives a new name, that of the law of nations.**' JAMES WILSON, OF THE LAW OF NATIONS, in 1 THE WORKS OF JAMES WILSON 148 (Robert Green McCloskey, ed., Harvard Univ. Press 1967) (1804)."[251] (bold added for emphasis)

Justice Rogers noted,

> "The philosophical cultural environment in which the Constitution developed was **permeated by the premise of natural law at the core of the Constitution.**"[252] (bold added for emphasis)

Right of privacy

In *Zimmermann v. Wilson*,[253] the federal Court of Appeal reviewed a District Court's order dismissing the taxpayer's request to protect them from a subpoena and deposition regarding their banking records. The Court summarized the facts as follows:

> "... [T]he pleadings disclose a case where, three and four years after a due examination by the government

---

251 Id. at 56.

252 Ibid.

253 (3rd Cir. 1936) 81 F.2d 847.

agents, the income returns of both husband and wife were approved, where no allegation is now made of fraud, concealment, or wrongdoing of any kind by the taxpayers, and no contention made that the revenue agents who approved the returns made any mistake, oversight, or did not do their duty and, it may be added, where, on the hearing by this court, counsel were asked by the court what was the purpose and reason for their asserted right of a second search three and four years thereafter, they could give none save that they acted on the orders of their superiors."[254]

The Court ruled that the rights of the taxpayers, and not of the brokers, were at issue:

"We rest on substance when we regard the rights of Zimmermann and his wife and their rights as the real parties in interest are the questions at issue, and their bankers and brokers as mere agents. [Citations omitted] It is the right of the taxpayers, and not the course pursued by their bankers, that is here involved. It is the information the banker's books contain, and not the books in which that information is recorded, that is the property right of these taxpayers, a property right this court protects by injunctive relief."[255]

Zimmermann then pointed to natural law as being the basis of the privacy right which was violated by the governmental intrusion:

---

254 Id. at 848.

255 Id. at 849.

> **"[W]e regard the search here asserted as a violation of
> the natural law of privacy in one's own affairs which
> exists in liberty loving peoples and nations** – for no right
> is more vital to 'liberty and the pursuit of happiness' than
> the protection of the citizen's private affairs, **their right
> to be let alone.** And that right extends to the records
> of his transactions from the unreasonable inspection
> and examination thereof by unwarranted governmental
> search. **If due protection of this natural right be denied
> him by the courts, his other rights and his citizenship
> lose their value."**[256] (bold added for emphasis)

The Court reversed the District Court, remanding the case with instructions to reinstate the taxpayers "bill" and to grant the requested injunction.[257] *Cited with approval by* the California Supreme Court's Opinion in *Taus v. Loftus* (2007) 40 Cal.4th 683, 732.[258]

In *Toffoloni v. LFB Publ'g Group*,[259] a right of privacy and of publicity was raised by the mother of Nancy Benoit, a professional wrestler who had been murdered. When the wrestler was 20-years old, she posed as a model for nude photographs, but had immediately asked for such photographs to be destroyed. After her murder, the photos were published with a brief story about the murder itself. The Court wrote:

---

256 Ibid.

257 Ibid.

258 In *Taus*, the California Supreme Court confronted a claim that defendants improperly invaded appellant's privacy by *investigating her background* and *discovering and disclosing information concerning her private life* without her consent.

259 (11th Cir. 2009) 572 F.3d 1201.

"The right of publicity grew out of a long-standing recognition of the right to privacy under Georgia law. See *Pavesich v. New England Life Ins. Co.* (1905) ... 50 S.E. 50, 69-81... Rooted in the right to privacy, the right of publicity is also characterized by an economic concern that individuals be allowed to control the use of their image in order to maximize the profit they can receive from its publication. ....

As the Supreme Court of Georgia has explained, 'to each individual member of society there are matters private, and there are matters public so far as the individual is concerned.' *Pavesich* [*v. New England Life Ins. Co.* (1905)], 50 S.E. [50,] at 69. 'All will admit that the individual who desires to live a life of seclusion can not be compelled, against his consent, to exhibit his person in any public place, unless such exhibition is demanded by the law of the land.' *Id.* at 70. **Thus, '[t]he right of privacy within certain limits is a right derived from natural law**, recognized by the principles of municipal law, and guaranteed to persons in [Georgia] by the constitutions of the United States and of the State of Georgia, **in those provisions which declare that no person shall be deprived of liberty except by due process of law.'** *Id.* at 71. ...

The tort of invasion of privacy protects the right 'to be free from unwarranted publicity, ... or the unwarranted appropriation or exploitation of one's personality, the publicizing of one's private affairs *with which the public had no legitimate concern*.' [citation omitted] From this right to be free of the public's illegitimate gaze, Georgia extrapolated a right of publicity—a right to control if, when, and under what circumstances one's image is made public and subject to scrutiny."[260] (bold added for emphasis)

Based upon the natural law right of privacy, as embodied in the U.S. and Georgia constitutions, the Court *Reversed* the lower court, finding as a matter of law that the story of the daughter's death was *incidental to the photos*, and not *vice versa*. Thus, the Court Held that the photos were not conceivably related to the incident of public concern of the daughter's death and remanded the case for further proceedings on the mother's claim for damages and injunction.[261] *See also*, to the same effect, *Colgate-Palmolive Co. v. Tullos*[262] ("the right of privacy within certain limits is derived from natural law").

Right to bear arms
Teixeira v. Cnty. of Alameda[263] held that the right to keep and bear arms for self-defense was not only a fundamental right, but *also* an enumerated one and is more appropriately analyzed under the Second Amendment than under the Equal Protection Clause.

Privilege against self-incrimination
In *United States v. Gecas*,[264] appellant, a resident alien, was *subpoenaed to testify concerning his war activities*, which, if proven, would be grounds for appellant's deportation. The court enforced the subpoena, holding that the Fifth Amendment to the United

---

260 *Toffoloni*, at 1205-1206.

261 Id. at 1213.

262 (5th Cir. 1955) 219 F.2d 617, 619.

263 (9th Cir. 2016) 822 F.3d 1047.

264 (11th Cir. 1997) 120 F.3d 1419.

States Constitution did not afford appellant the right *as against the world* not to testify, enforceable through United States courts, but only applied to fear of domestic criminal court proceedings. In arriving at this conclusion, **the Court discussed the *origin*** of the privilege against self-incrimination:

> "Beginning in the 1690s, however, common-law courts began to describe the pre-existing, implied privilege against self-incrimination **as a reflection of natural law.** See [M.R.T.] MacNair [, *The Early Development of the Privilege Against Self-Incrimination, 10 Oxford J. Legal Stud., Spring 1990]*, at 84 (quoting Geoffrey Gilbert, The Law of Evidence 99 (Garland ed., 1979 (1754). Courts also began to interpret the privilege as a limitation on the power of centralized government."[265] (bold added for emphasis)

The *Gecas* Court continued:

> "Defendants first began to invoke the implied, common-law privilege as a shield against the inquisitional techniques of the prerogative courts of the seventeenth century. The common-law courts used the privilege as a pretext for curtailing the jurisdiction of rival tribunals. Religious and political nonconformists asserted the privilege in an effort to undermine the prosecution of crimes of conscience. **Through their combined efforts, the common-law privilege came to represent a defining difference between common-law criminal trials and inquisitional proceedings of the seventeenth century.** When the common-law courts made explicit their own

---

265   Id. at 1450-1451.

implied privilege against self-incrimination, they viewed it through the lens of seventeenth-century events. **They concluded that it would violate natural law** for the government to prosecute crimes of conscience using inquisitional techniques, techniques which undermined the procedural protections of the common law."[266] (bold added for emphasis)

The *Gecas* Court explained:

"**The common-law courts later emphasized the natural law roots of the right.** 'To furnish testimonial evidence against himself, with or without oath, was likened to drawing one's blood, running oneself upon the pikes, or cutting one's throat with one's tongue.' Lord Chief Baron Geoffrey Gilbert, whose *Law of Evidence* was well-known in the American colonies, wrote that although a confession was the best proof of guilt, "'this Confession must be voluntary and without Compulsion; for our Law in this differs from the Civil Law, that it will not force any Man to accuse himself; **and in this we do certainly follow the Law of Nature, which commands every Man to encourage his own Preservation.**""[267] (bold added for emphasis)

Indeed, the Court noted the privilege against self-incrimination to have *natural law roots* long before English common law:

---

266 Id. at 1457.

267 Id. at 1473-1474.

"The self-preservation rationale for the **natural law roots of the right against self-incrimination** harkens back to ancient Talmudic law, which provided that '"a man cannot represent himself guilty, or as a transgressor."' *See Moses v. Allard*, 131 Bankr. 328, 779 F. Supp. 857, 870 (E.D.Mich. 1991)...."[268] (bold added for emphasis)

Restraints against retroactive laws

In *South East Chicago Com. v. Department of Housing & Urban Development*,[269] the Court affirmed a district court's grant of summary judgment in favor of the Department of Housing and Urban Development (HUD). The Court found that regulations (24 C.F.R. Sects. 200.700 *et seq.*) setting forth project selection criteria for a commitment to fund a low-income housing project in Chicago *could not apply retroactively* to the HUD director's decision since retroactive application would interfere with the antecedent rights of the developer. In so-holding, the Court observed:

> "...[B]oth the natural law and the Constitution were seen to place restraints on the government in enacting retroactive laws. The language quoted from [United States v. The] Schooner Peggy [(1801) 5 U.S. 103] [(that a French vessel was not "definitively condemned" and thus falling within the terms of a France-United States treaty for return of seized vessels seized as a prize of war by a naval vessel of the United States)] **may thus have been directed to the obstacle of the natural law.** Today, of course, the decision would go off solely on **the Constitution**, the

---

268   Id. at 1474, fn. 94.

269   (7th Cir. 1973) 488 F.2d 1119.

bounds of which have been expanded since *Fletcher* **to take in many principles long thought to be natural law.**"[270] (bold added for emphasis)

Ban against cruel and unusual punishment

Mukmuk v. Commissioner of Dep't of Correctional Services[271] dealt with a prisoner's civil rights claim of cruel and unusual punishment within New York prisons, where he had spent 15 years. His claims concerned extensive solitary confinement and confinement in "strip cells." The Court *Reversed* a lower court's grant of summary judgment for defendants, ruling that the plaintiff/prisoner had raised legitimate factual issues on his claims of improper prison practices when he was placed in solitary confinement and in strip cells. In arriving at this holding, the Court reasoned:

> "The **conception of what is meant by 'cruel and unusual punishment' in the language of the Eighth Amendment has been evolving** in the past two decades. ... No man can say today what the Eighth Amendment may mean tomorrow. **If the Eighth Amendment is governed by natural law, that law is itself chameleon in character.** It reflects an evolving view of society as interpreted by the Supreme Court. Nevertheless, when we deal with situations involving 'cruel and unusual punishment' one may argue that if the 'violation' charged is not so shocking to the conscience as to be readily perceived, it is not an Eighth Amendment violation in any event. See *United States ex rel Hyde v. McGinnis*, 429 F.2d 864 (2 Cir. 1970).

---

270 *South East Chicago Com*, 488 F.2d at 1124, fn. 4.

271 (2nd Cir. 1975) 529 F.2d 272.

And if it is so perceived, there is no need to declare it in advance of imposing liability."[272] (bold added for emphasis)

Parental rights and duties

In *Bell v. Leonard*,[273] the Court granted a mother's writ of *habeas corpus*, holding that the **mother's right as a natural guardian** was paramount to an ex-custodian's rights, insofar as the ex-custodian had presented no evidence of the mother's want of natural affection or lack of fitness for the charge.[274] In so holding, the Court observed:

"... [S]ee *People ex rel. Portnoy v. Strasser*, 1952, ... 104 N.E.2d 89, 896: 'No court can, for any but the gravest reasons, transfer a child from its natural parent to any other person ... **since the right of a parent, under natural law, to establish a home and bring up children is a fundamental one and beyond the reach of any court**, *Meyer v. State of Nebraska*, 262 U.S. 390, 399 ....'"[275] (bold added for emphasis)

Right to engage in interstate commerce

In *Young v. Coloma-Agaran*,[276] the issue was whether the State of Hawaii had lawfully imposed conditions[277] within its police power

---

272 Id. at 277-278.

273 (D.C. Cir. 1958) 251 F.2d 890.

274 Id. at 895.

275 Id. at 895, fn. 17.

276 (9th Cir. 2003) 340 F.3d 1053.

277 In fact, Hawaii had categorically banned issuance of conditional use permits to any commercial vessel whatsoever for operating, "at or on the Hanalei River or Hanalei Bay ocean waters...."

which adversely affected issuance of federal "coasting" licenses, or whether such conditions imposed by the State of Hawaii violated the Supremacy Clause by unlawfully negating federal powers regarding shipping laws pursuant to 46 U.S.C. Section 12106. A vessel must have a coasting license to engage in the "coastwise trade," and coastwise trade includes the transportation of passengers.[278] The Court observed,

> "The sweeping nature of the coasting license is premised on the idea that **the right to engage in interstate commerce derives from natural law**[,] and the Constitution confers absolute control of its regulation to Congress. ... It is well-settled that '[a] state may not exclude from its waters a ship operating under a federal license.'"[279] (bold added for emphasis)

The Court held that Hawaii's refusal to issue permits effectively rendered it impossible for operators to comply with both federal and state law in order to ply their trade.[280]

International Reach of United States to Enforce Natural Law/Human Rights

In recent case law, the pendulum was swinging toward the United States as constituting a viable forum for enforcement against extraterritorial human rights violations—*i.e.*, violations taking

---

278   Id. at 1056.

279   Ibid.

280   Id. at 1057.

place *outside* of the United States. And U.S. "jurisdiction" as such was based in part on the viability of natural law.

United States v. Yousef,[281] was an appeal of judgments of *criminal* conviction, for conspiracy to bomb 12 United States commercial airliners in Southeast Asia and the February 1993 bombing of the World Trade Center in New York, entered in the District Court for the Southern District of New York in two separate jury trials. A preliminary issue was **whether the United States properly extended federal *jurisdiction* to the overseas conduct**. The Court wrote:

> "In determining whether Congress intended a federal statute to apply to overseas conduct, 'an act of Congress ought never to be construed to violate the law of nations if any other possible construction remains. ... Nonetheless, in fashioning the reach of our criminal law, 'Congress is not bound by international law.' ... 'If it chooses to do so, it may legislate with respect to conduct outside the United States, in excess of the limits posed by international law.' ..."[282]

The Court observed that unrestricted, "universal" jurisdiction (in federal, criminal prosecutions) exists only as to piracy, war crimes and "crimes against humanity":

> "The class of crimes subject to universal jurisdiction traditionally included only piracy. ... In modern times, the class of crimes over which States can exercise universal jurisdiction has been extended to include war

---

281   (2ⁿᵈ Cir. 2003) 327 F. 3d 56.

282   Id. at 86.

crimes and acts identified after the Second World War as 'crimes against humanity.'"[283]

The Court noted,

> **"The universality principle permits a State** [meaning: a sovereign nation] **to prosecute an offender of any nationality for** an offense committed outside of that State and without contacts to that State, but only for the few, near-unique offenses uniformly recognized by the 'civilized nations' as an offense against the **'Law of Nations.'"**[284] (bold added for emphasis)

Explaining, the Court revealed *the basis* for this far-reaching United States jurisdiction in criminal prosecutions:

> "The phrases 'international law' and the 'law of nations' frequently are used interchangeably..., but these terms are not entirely synonymous. 'International law' is of a far more recent vintage than 'law of nations.' **'Law of nations' derives from the Latin *jus gentium*, meaning literally 'law of nations'** (the root of *gentium* being gens, meaning a race, clan or people) and was used to refer to the law applied by Roman magistrates in foreign lands. **The *jus gentium* is closely related to the concepts of natural law and natural reason**, *jus naturale* and *naturale ratio*. ...Thus[,] while Benthamite 'international law' and its progeny are concerned with lawmaking in any area that

---

283 Id. at 104.

284 Id. at 103.

could improve the condition of, and relations between, States, **the 'law of nations' historically consisted of a finite set of principles believed** by commentators (primarily Grotius, Vattel, Pufendorf, and Burlamaqui) **to be derived** from the divine order, or **from abstract reason and natural law.**"[285] (bold added for emphasis)

Thus, *Yousef* acknowledged the *existence and judicial viability* of the "law of nations," which is *derived* from the Latin "jus gentium," which in turn is "closely related to ... natural law and natural reason." Finding extraterritorial jurisdiction for this *criminal* prosecution, the *Yousef* Court *Affirmed* the convictions and sentencing in virtually all respects.[286]

In a later case, a trial court ruled against the plaintiffs, holding that federal District Courts had no subject-matter jurisdiction for *civil* **claims** stemming from **extraterritorial** human rights violations. Plaintiffs had sued defendant corporation under the Alien Tort Statute ("ATS"), 28 U.S.C. 1350, for, among other causes of action, genocide and war crimes claims. On appeal, in what purported to be a landmark appellate ruling for enforcement of human rights violations, the Court, in *Sarei v. Rio Tinto, PLC*,[287] *reversed* **the District Court's dismissal**, holding that federal District Court jurisdiction over civil claims of extraterritorial genocide and war crimes **did** exist.

The complaint alleged genocide against the indigenous population of the island of Bougainville in violation of the Convention on the Prevention and Punishment of the Crime of

---

285 Id. at 103, fn. 38.

286 Id. at 170-173.

287 (9th Cir. 2011) 671 F.3d 736.

Genocide,[288] and alleged that the *jus cogens* prohibition of genocide extends to corporations.[289] In *Sarei*, the complaint adequately pled facts, which if believed, would support a finding that the defendant corporation acted to kill, inflict serious bodily harm and create conditions of starvation with an intent to destroy, in whole or part, a national, ethnic, racial or religious group.[290] The complaint describes,

> "the residents of Bougainville by reference to their 'native way of life,' ancestral attachment to the land, distinct culture, and black skin color."[291]

The complaint further alleged war crimes, as defined by the Geneva Conventions, committed by the corporation. The *Sarei* Court held that corporations may be liable under the ATS for war crimes claims.[292] *Sarei* further held that the complaint had adequately alleged that war crimes had been committed by the corporation, since it alleges, "murder of civilians during the civil war between the people of Bougainville and the PNG..."[293] There,

> "...[the corporation,] Rio Tinto[,] 'understood that it had a great deal of the control over the situation' and 'knew'

---

288 Id. at 758.

289 Id. at 759-760.

290 Id. at 761.

291 Id. at 762.

292 Id. at 764-765.

293 Id. at 766.

NATURAL LAW AND INALIENABLE HUMAN RIGHTS

that this was the only way it could reopen its profitable mine. Plaintiffs allege that Rio Tinto solicited the military action for its own private ends and directed the military response even 'while reports of war crimes surfaced.'"[294]

Plaintiffs alleged that,

> "Rio issued the PNG government 'an ultimatum': displace the local residents interfering with its mining operations, no matter the means, or Rio would abandon all investments on PNG."[295]

Subsequent to the *Sarei* decision, however, the *pendulum for justice* took a **dramatic swing backwards**, toward restraint and political correctness. In the U.S. Supreme Court case of *Kiobel v. Royal Dutch Petroleum Co. (Shell)*,[296] the Court held that the ATS did **not** grant federal courts jurisdiction over claims relating to conduct occurring outside the United States *without evidence of a substantial nexus* to the United States. This decision **decisively changed** the playing field, for the *worse*, as to affording **civil remedies** within the U.S. for extraterritorial war crimes and human rights abuses.

There, plaintiffs alleged that Shell aided and abetted the Nigerian military dictatorship in shootings, torture, rapes, arrests and murder of unarmed protesters in the 1990s. Defendants argued that there is no precedent for corporations being sued under international law and thus, there is no international principle to support such a

---

294   Ibid.

295   Ibid.

296   (2013) 569 U.S. 108.

lawsuit in the U.S. pursuant to the ATS. *Plaintiff* framed the question as being whether the notion of "free trade" includes a freedom to commit, with impunity, grievous human rights violations including torture, rape, false arrest, imprisonment, slave labor and murder as standard operating procedures of doing business. However, the *Court* shaped the issue differently, as follows:

> "The question presented is whether and under what circumstances courts may recognize a cause of action under the Alien Tort Statute, for violations of the law of nations occurring within the territory of a sovereign other than the United States."[297]

In answering this question, *Kiobel* referred to its holding in *Sosa v. Alvarez-Machain (2004)* 542 U.S. 692:

> "... *Sosa* limited federal courts to recognizing causes of action only for alleged violations of international law norms that are "'specific, universal, and obligatory." *Id.*, at 732, 124 S.Ct. 2739"[298]

Kiobel recounted that *Sosa* stated that the issue,

> "is not whether a federal court has jurisdiction to entertain a cause of action provided by foreign or even international law. The question is instead **whether the court has authority to recognize a cause of action under**

---

297   Id. at 112-113.

298   Id. at 117.

U.S. law to enforce a norm of international law."[299]
(bold added for emphasis)

Kiobel pointed out that concerns over meddling into the foreign affairs of another sovereign nation,

"are not diminished by the fact that *Sosa* limited federal courts to recognizing causes of action only for alleged violations of international law norms that are "'specific, universal, and obligatory'" … [I]dentifying such a norm is **only the beginning** of defining a cause of action …. Each of these decisions carries with it **significant foreign policy implications**."[300] (bold added for emphasis)

On this reading of legislative intent as to the reach of the ATS, *Kiobel* held that the ATS does **not** afford a U.S. forum for Nigerian human rights victims who were harmed when Shell Oil purportedly assisted the Nigerian government in attacking them and their family members. The Court wrote:

"In the end, nothing in the text of the ATS evinces the requisite clear indication of extraterritoriality."[301]

The Supreme Court considered the fact that the ATS afforded jurisdiction **over acts of piracy** committed on the High Seas, but wrote:

---

299 Id. at 119.

300 Ibid.

301 Ibid.

"Petitioners contend that because Congress surely intended the ATS to provide jurisdiction for actions against pirates, it necessarily anticipated the statute would apply to conduct occurring abroad.

Applying U.S. law to pirates, however, does not typically impose the sovereign will of the United States onto conduct occurring within the territorial jurisdiction of another sovereign, and therefore carries less direct foreign policy consequences. Pirates were fair game wherever found, by any nation, because they generally did not operate within any jurisdiction. See 4 Blackstone, *supra*, at 71. We do not think that the existence of a cause of action against them is a sufficient basis for concluding that other causes of action under the ATS reach conduct that does occur within the territory of another sovereign; pirates may well be a category unto themselves."[302]

The Supreme Court, in *Kiobel*, dismissed the notion that Congress intended the United States to be the **policeman of the entire world** regarding to human rights violations:

"Finally, there is no indication that the ATS was passed to make the United States a uniquely hospitable forum for the enforcement of international norms. As Justice Story put it, "No nation has ever yet pretended to be the *custos morum* of the whole world...." *United States v. The La Jeune Eugenie*, 26 F. Cas. 832, 847 (No. 15,551) (C.C.Mass.1822). It is implausible to suppose that the First Congress wanted their fledgling Republic—

302   Id. at 121.

struggling to receive international recognition—to be the first. Indeed, the parties offer no evidence that any nation, meek or mighty, presumed to do such a thing."[303]

Accordingly, *Kiobel Affirmed* the Court of Appeals dismissal of plaintiffs' complaint, holding:

> "On these facts, all the relevant conduct took place outside the United States. And even where the claims **touch and concern** the territory of the United States, **they must do so with sufficient force** to displace the presumption against extraterritorial application. See *Morrison,* 561 U.S. 247, 130 S.Ct., at 2883-2888. Corporations are often present in many countries, and it would reach too far to say that mere corporate presence suffices. If Congress were to determine otherwise, a statute more specific than the ATS would be required."[304] (bold added for emphasis)

In this manner, *Kiobel* strongly inferred that unless the alleged misconduct adequately *touches and concerns* the United States, the federal courts did not have subject-matter jurisdiction, in enforcement of the (civil) ATS, over allegations of human rights violations, by corporations, *occurring within a foreign entity,* such as those facts raised in *Sarei.* [305]

---

303 Id. at 123.

304 Id. at 124-125.

305 A Concurring Opinion by Justice Breyer approached the issue in *Kiobel* without reliance on any presumption against extraterritoriality, and by use of more of a *facts and circumstances test.* Justice Breyer also pointed out that piracy against a vessel under the United States flag **does**, in fact, take place *within the*

Upon Petition for Certiorari, the Supreme Court subsequently ordered the Court of Appeals Decision in *Sarei* to be **Vacated** and for the Court of Appeals to reconsider the case in view of *Kiobel*. Thereafter, on June 28, 2013, the *Sarei* Court of Appeals upheld the District Court dismissal of plaintiff's case, citing *Kiobel's* holding against extraterritorial application of the ATS, and *Remanded* to the District Court, which court thereafter dismissed the case on lack of jurisdiction grounds.

As reported in EarthRights International,[306]

"territory" of the United States since that flagged vessel is *deemed* to be within the United States. (569 U.S. at 130-131) Justice Breyer nevertheless concurred in the result of the case, finding an *insufficient nexus* of the human rights violations with the United States:

"Applying these jurisdictional principles to this case, however, I agree with the Court that jurisdiction does not lie. The defendants are two foreign corporations. Their shares, like those of many foreign corporations, are traded on the New York Stock Exchange. Their only presence in the United States consists of an office in New York City (actually owned by a separate but affiliated company) that helps to explain their business to potential investors. See Supp. Brief for Petitioners 4, n. 3 (citing *Wiwa v. Royal Dutch Petroleum Co.*, 226 F.3d 88, 94 (C.A.2 2000)); App. 55.

The plaintiffs are not United States nationals but nationals of other nations. The conduct at issue took place abroad. And the plaintiffs allege, not that the defendants directly engaged in acts of torture, genocide, or the equivalent, but that they helped others (who are not American nationals) to do so.

Under these circumstances, even if the New York office were a sufficient basis for asserting general jurisdiction, but see *Goodyear Dunlop Tires Operations, S.A. v. Brown*, 564 U.S. ----, 131 S.Ct. 2846, 180 L.Ed.2d 796 (2011), it would be farfetched to believe, based solely upon the defendants› minimal and indirect American presence, that this legal action helps to vindicate a distinct American interest, such as in not providing a safe harbor for an 'enemy of all mankind.' Thus I agree with the Court that here it would 'reach too far to say' that such 'mere corporate presence suffices.' *Ante*, at 1669.'" (569 U.S. at 139-140)

306   EarthRights International, *KIOBEL V. SHELL: SUPREME COURT LIMITS COURTS' ABILITY TO HEAR CLAIMS OF HUMAN RIGHTS ABUSES COMMITTED ABROAD.*

"'The [*Kiobel*] Supreme Court's decision further exposes how human rights abuses are given a low priority in US courts. This decision will ignite the Ogoni campaign for justice against Shell Oil and the Nigerian government,' said plaintiff **Charles Wiwa.** 'We will never give up fighting for our day in court.'

'Today's opinion was a missed opportunity to send a crystal[-]clear message: the world's torturers and war criminals are not above the law—and neither are their accomplices,' said **Pamela Merchant**, Executive Director of the **Center for Justice and Accountability**. 'In spite of the Court's decision, the human rights community will continue our work to ensure that U.S. courts give victims what they were denied abroad: a chance to seek truth, healing, and a measure of redress.'"

Plaintiff's counsel in *Kiobel* announced that the fight was not over for the Ogoni plaintiffs:

"'Today's decision is contrary to the development of customary international law since Nuremberg and is a step backwards for the United States standing as venue for the impartial adjudication of egregious human rights violations. The United States was never meant to harbor the "enemies of mankind" and this decision only gives solace to the perpetrators. This unfortunate decision will not deter the Ogoni plaintiffs from pursuing justice against

Shell.' **Carey R. D'Avino**, Plaintiffs' Counsel, **Eaton & Van Winkle LLP.**"[307]

The *Kiobel* subject-matter jurisdiction question became: What constitutes adequate "touch and concern" facts to justify a federal District Court in asserting jurisdiction over civil allegations of extraterritorial acts of genocide and crimes against humanity? This question has been the subject of five Circuit Court of Appeal opinions. Their approaches differ greatly. The Fifth Circuit simply holds that the ATS fails to provide jurisdiction for international law violations which occur abroad.[308]

In the Second Circuit, for ATS jurisdiction to arise, a defendant's domestic conduct must be enough to, "giv[e] rise to a violation" of the law of nations.[309]

The Fourth, Ninth, and Eleventh Circuits, on the other hand interpret *Kiobel*'s "touch and concern" test more favorably toward federal enforcement of international breaches of natural law. In *Al Shimari v. CACI Premier Tech., Inc.*,[310] the Fourth Circuit ruled that federal subject-matter jurisdiction pursuant to ATS did exist:

> "The plaintiffs' claims reflect extensive 'relevant conduct' in United States territory, in contrast to the 'mere presence' of foreign corporations that was deemed

---

307 Center for Constitutional Rights, "Kiobel v. Shell: Supreme Court Limits Courts' Ability to Hear Claims of Human Rights Abuses Committed Abroad," April 17, 2013, https://ccrjustice.org/home/press-center/press-releases/kiobel-decision-supreme-court-limits-us-courts-ability-use-human.

308 *Adhikari v. Kellogg Brown & Root, Inc.* (5th Cir. 2017) 845 F.3d 184, 197.

309 *Balintulo v. Daimler AG* (2d Cir. 2013) 727 F.3d 174, 192.

310 (4th Cir. 2014) 758 F.3d 516.

insufficient in *Kiobel.* When a claim's substantial ties to United States territory include the performance of a contract executed by a United States corporation with the United States government, a more nuanced analysis is required to determine whether the presumption has been displaced. In such cases, it is not sufficient merely to say that because the actual injuries were inflicted abroad, the *claims* do not touch and concern United States territory.

Here, the plaintiffs' claims allege acts of torture committed by United States citizens who were employed by an American corporation, CACI, which has corporate headquarters located in Fairfax County, Virginia. The alleged torture occurred at a military facility operated by United States government personnel.

In addition, the employees who allegedly participated in the acts of torture were hired by CACI in the United States to fulfill the terms of a contract that CACI executed with the United States Department of the Interior. The contract between CACI and the Department of the Interior was issued by a government office in Arizona, and CACI was authorized to collect payments by mailing invoices to government accounting offices in Colorado. Under the terms of the contract, CACI interrogators were required to obtain security clearances from the United States Department of Defense.

Finally, the allegations are not confined to the assertion that CACI's employees participated directly in acts of torture committed at the Abu Ghraib prison. The plaintiffs also allege that CACI's managers located in the United States were aware of reports of misconduct abroad, attempted to 'cover up' the misconduct, and 'implicitly, if not expressly, encouraged' it." [311]

The *Al Shimari* Court held that plaintiff's complaint made adequate allegations for ATS subject matter jurisdiction, explaining:

> "Although the 'touch and concern' language in *Kiobel* may be explained in greater detail in future Supreme Court decisions, we conclude that this language provides current guidance to federal courts when ATS claims involve **substantial ties to United States territory**. We have such a case before us now, and we cannot decline to consider the Supreme Court's guidance simply because it does not state a precise formula for our analysis." [312] (bold added for emphasis)

Then, in *Warfaa v. Ali*, [313] the Fourth Circuit repeated its emphasis on a "fact-based analysis" as to ATS subject-matter jurisdiction. The Court's stated:

> "... [I]n *Kiobel*, the 'petitioners' case seeking relief for violations of the law of nations occurring outside the United States [wa]s barred.' *Id.* at 1669. The Supreme Court emphasized that the ATS can create jurisdiction for such claims only where they 'touch and concern' United States territory 'with sufficient force to displace

---

311   Id. at 529.

312   Ibid.

313   (4th Cir. 2016) 811 F.3d 653.

the presumption against extraterritorial application.'
Id."[314]

Warfaa attempted to distinguish *Al Shimari* from the facts in
Warfaa:

"*Al Shimari* thus is best read to note that the presumption
against ATS extraterritorial application is not irrefutable.
A plaintiff may rebut the presumption in certain, narrow
circumstances: when **extensive United States contacts**
are present and the alleged conduct bears such **a strong
and direct connection to the United States** that it falls
within *Kiobel's* limited "touch and concern" language."[315]
(bold added for emphasis)

In *Mujica v. AirScan Inc.*,[316] the Ninth Circuit wrote,

"that a defendant's U.S. citizenship or corporate status
is one factor that, in conjunction with other factors, can
establish a sufficient connection between an ATS claim
and the territory of the United States to satisfy *Kiobel*."[317]

---

314   Id. at 660.

315   Ibid.

316   (9th Cir. 2014) 771 F.3d 580, *cert. denied sub nom. Mujica v. Occidental
Petroleum Corp.*, 136 S. Ct. 690 (2015).

317   Id. at 594.

The Eleventh Circuit, in *Doe v. Drummond Co.*,[318] held that an ATS claim satisfies the test for subject-matter jurisdiction pursuant to ATS if the claim has,

> "a U.S. focus and [if] *adequate* relevant conduct occurs within the United States."[319] (emphasis added)

Not only is the *location* of the defendant's conduct relevant, the defendant's *U.S. citizenship* and *potential national interests* in allowing the case to proceed are *also relevant* to the jurisdictional issue.[320]

International Courts

There is an international tribunal for litigation of European civil **human rights cases**. It is known as the European Court of Human Rights, previously the European Commission on Human Rights (collectively, "ECtHR"). The ECtHR is based in Strasbourg, France. Its mission is to guarantee respect for human rights and to rule on alleged violations of the 1950 European Convention on Human Rights committed by a Member State of the Council of Europe. Case-law exists at ECtHR as to whether, and under what circumstances, compulsory vaccination is compatible with the European Convention on Human Rights (ECHR).[321]

---

318   (11th Cir. 2015) 782 F.3d 576, *cert. denied*, 136 S. Ct. 1168 (2016).

319   Id. at 592.

320   *Id.* at 592, 594, 596.

321   Spyridoula Katsoni, *Do compulsory vaccinations against COVID-19 violate human rights?: An assessment of the measure's compatibility with the*

Requests for injunctive relief against France's and Greece's compulsory Covid-19 vaccination statutes were filed with ECtHR between August and September 2021. Pursuant to those statutes, French firefighters and Greek healthcare workers were required to vaccinate in order to continue their employment. Both filings, however, were rejected by ECtHR on procedural grounds. The legality of vaccine mandates against SARS-CoV-2 under the European Convention of Human Rights has not been directly resolved.

The petitioners in those cases argued that subjecting public employees to Covid-19 vaccination is in violation of multiple ECHR's provisions, ranging from Article 2's "right to life" and Article 5's "right to liberty and security," to Article 4's "prohibition of slavery and forced labour." The primary argument against the lawfulness of the statutes was based, however, on Article 8's "**right to respect for private and family life**," which is interpreted as ensuring, "freedom from interference with physical and psychological integrity."[322]

Article 8 states that,

> "Everyone has the right to respect for his private and family life, his home and his correspondence."

This proviso, however, is subject to two conditions, one of which is that there needs to be *a legitimate aim* that justifies the interference with Article 8 rights. Also, the interference must be, "necessary in a democratic society." These exceptions to the Article 8 rule are inordinately vague, and evidence neither a standard of proof nor even a requisite level of necessity.

European Convention on Human Rights, Völkerrechtsblog, 02.12.2020, doi: 10.17176/20210107-183113-0.

322   Rainey, B, McCormick, P, Ovey, C. *Jacobs, White, and Ovey: The European Convention on Human Rights*, Eighth Edition, (Oxford University Press; 2020).

In American jurisprudence parlance, an issue becomes—Is proof by a mere "preponderance of the evidence" adequate to justify injunctive relief, or must the case be proven by "clear and convincing evidence," or even "beyond a reasonable doubt"? This aspect of presenting a petitioner's case would be crucial in convincing the ECtHR of the right to an injunction. As to the requisite standard of proof, it has been argued,

> "Taking into account Franck's theory of procedural fairness, ... [the ECtHR's] **assignment or application of the standards of proof** largely fails to meet the relevant criteria, and **are opaque and incoherent.**"[323] (bold added for emphasis)

In 1984, the ECtHR affirmed that,

> "a requirement to undergo medical treatment or a vaccination, on pain of a penalty, *may* amount to interference with the right to respect for private life."[324]

Article 8(2) sets forth the circumstances under which an interference with privacy can be deemed justified. In *Boffa and others v San Marino*,[325] the Commission first set forth the essential claims of the applicants for injunction:

---

323 *Deference in International Courts and Tribunals,* Chapter 13, "The European Court of Human Rights and Standards of Proof: An Evidentiary Approach towards the Margin of Appreciation," Mónika Ambrus, (Oxford Academic, October 2014).

324 *Acmanne and others v. Belgium,* at 251, 255.

325 No. 26536/95, January 15, 1998.

"The applicants complain of the existence of laws making it compulsory for residents of San Marino to undergo vaccinations. They argue that the risk of death associated with vaccinations is high and claim a violation of Article 2 of the Convention. Further, they complain that parents' inability freely to choose whether or not to have their children vaccinated constitutes an unjustified interference with their freedom of thought and conscience, contrary to Article 9 of the Convention. Finally, the applicants complain that their inability to choose whether or not to be vaccinated constitutes an unjustified infringement of their right to liberty as guaranteed in Article 5 of the Convention and their right to respect for their private and family life as protected by Article 8 of the Convention."[326]

The Commission then proceeded **to *deny*** the applicants' requested relief, in a *conclusionary* summary opinion:

"The first applicant complains of the dangers associated with the relevant vaccinations. He alleges a violation of Article 2 of the Convention. Under that provision everyone's right to life is to be protected by law. No one is to be deprived of his life intentionally save in the execution of a sentence of a court following his conviction of a crime for which this penalty is provided by law. The Commission recalls that this Article primarily provides protection against deprivation of life. Even assuming that it may be seen as providing protection against physical injury, **an intervention such as a vaccination does not, in itself, amount to an interference** prohibited by it.

---

326   Pages 29-30.

Moreover, the applicant has not submitted any evidence that, in the particular case of his child, a vaccination would create a real medical danger to life."[327] (bold added for emphasis)

ECtHR concluded that protecting the public's health was a legitimate public interest and that the plan to mandate inoculation against hepatitis B was "necessary" to accomplish that purpose.[328]

The ECtHR has established that "necessity in a democratic society" implies a pressing social need and that this interference would be *proportionate* to the public interests pursued.[329] In *Solomakhin v Ukraine*,[330] an applicant's health deteriorated and he eventually died after receiving a "compulsory" vaccination against diphtheria during an epidemic. His mother continued with the action claiming medical malpractice. The Court first admitted that the victim's privacy had been infringed upon:

"The Court has emphasised [sic: emphasized] that a person's bodily integrity concerns the most intimate aspects of one's private life, and that compulsory medical intervention, even if it is of a minor importance, constitutes an interference with this right (see Y.F. v. Turkey, no. 24209/94, § 33, ECHR 2003IX, with further references). Compulsory vaccination – as an involuntary

---

327 Page 33.

328 Page 34.

329 *Dudgeon v. the United Kingdom*, paras 51-53. This manner of expressing a comparison of individual *human rights* with any public interest *contravening* such human rights, is very confusing.

330 No. 24429/03 Para 33, March 15, 2012.

medical treatment – amounts to an interference with
the right to respect for one's private life, which includes
a person's physical and psychological integrity, as
guaranteed by Article 8 § 1 (see Salvetti v. Italy (dec.),
no. 42197/98, 9 July 2002, and Matter v. Slovakia, no.
31534/96, § 64, 5 July 1999)."[331]

Factors concerning the victim were noted by the Court:

"The applicant insisted that he had been vaccinated during
the acute stage of an illness and that the doctors had not
checked all relevant contraindications to vaccination in
his case. He claimed that he had been administered an
expired vaccine of poor quality and that it had been done
against his will. All of these failings had resulted in his
serious health problems, which the doctors at fault and
judges had conspired to conceal and who had therefore
falsified medical records and court documents. He
considered that there had been no reason for interfering
with his private life, as there had been [sic] not been an
outbreak of diphtheria in his home town at the relevant
time and the vaccine had been strongly contraindicated
for him."[332]

The Court then embarked into an *ad hoc* **balancing test**
between the (now-deceased) victim's private life, on the one hand,
and society's hypothetical risk of a mass diphtheria outbreak, on the
other hand:

---

331 Id. at para. 33.

332 Id. at para. 30.

"In the Court's opinion the interference with the applicant's physical integrity could be said to be **justified by the public health considerations and necessity to control the spreading of infectious diseases** in the region. Furthermore, according to the domestic court's findings, the medical staff had checked his suitability for vaccination prior to carrying out the vaccination, which suggest that **necessary precautions had been taken to ensure that the medical intervention would not be to the applicant's detriment to the extent that would upset the balance of interests between the applicant's personal integrity and the public interest of protection health of the population.**"[333] (bold added for emphasis)

On the issue of the proof of the need for compulsory vaccinations, the government contended that the **public assessment should be considered as final and beyond dispute**:

"They [meaning: the government] considered that the **findings of the domestic authorities**, who had had the primary task of interpreting the law and assessing the proof adduced, **should not be called into question.**"[334] (bold added for emphasis)

Nonetheless, apparently the "necessary precautions" to assure that the compulsory inoculation would not be to the victim's "detriment" were obviously *inadequate*, considering the fact that he later died from complications to his being in an "acute stage" of a

---

333   Id. at para. 36.

334   Id. at para. 32.

preexisting illness at the time of vaccination. But the **greater errors** in this ECtHR decision were that:

- The case took **over nine years** to conclude, by which time the 34-year old applicant had died;

- There was no particular rule, articulated by the court, as to which party had the *burden* **of proof** in any of the factual issues;

- There was no particular *standard* **of proof** as to any of the factual issues—such as a preponderance of the evidence, clear and convincing evidence or beyond a reasonable doubt standard;

- There was no specific test defining **what constitutes** the requisite "necessity" justifying the invasion of privacy and liberty (such as a "compelling" state interest versus merely a "rational basis" supporting the public interest);

- There may have been some sort of *priority or deference* given to public officials in "interpreting the law and assessing the proof adduced" in resolving any factual/expert opinion disputes; and,

- There was no articulation of a need for the defendants to prove **the absence of any** *alternative measures* to accomplish the public policy in question which would be **less intrusive** on the victim's liberty and privacy.

Regarding the requirement that restrictions of individual privacy must be "necessary in a democratic society," the elephant in the room is: *how* necessary? As shown *supra*, when a "State actor" abridges a "fundamental right" in the United States, it must prove a "compelling" state interest and further prove that the infringement is the *least intrusive means* of accomplishing such interest. Whether the compulsory vaccination satisfies a compelling state interest would involve **a detailed assessment of both the advantages and disadvantages** of the vaccine. However, merely tipping the balance toward the public interest in the privacy infringement would not necessarily prove that the government's action is necessary to achieve a compelling governmental interest.

For example, it appears to be undisputed that there had been **no outbreak** of diphtheria within the victim's town at the time he was forced by law to submit to the vaccination. Significantly, then, there was no evidence showing **a specific necessity** for mass vaccinations *in the victim's region*. There was no showing of the **particular efficacy** and **durability** of the diphtheria vaccine. There was no discussion of the **gravity and rate of major side effects** *risks* from the diphtheria vaccine. Exceptional danger of **collateral illness or immune system degradation** created by the vaccine itself would mitigate against the need. Any impact of **Antibody Dependent Enhancement** on the targeted virus would mitigate against the need to vaccinate. There was no showing that the victim had any **particular personal vulnerability** to diphtheria. There was no discussion as to whether the victim had **preexisting immunity** to diphtheria. There was no comment on whether there existed **widespread natural immunity** to diphtheria. There was no showing that should the victim became infected with diphtheria, he was likely to **spread it to people** who had already been vaccinated. There was no showing that if he were *unvaccinated*, he could **not be isolated** or otherwise use **N95 masks** and **frequent handwashing** in order to significantly reduce the risk of his spreading the disease. There was no showing as to **what drugs**, if any, could be used **to effectively *treat* persons** infected by diphtheria. There was no discussion as to **whether and why** *other countries declined to engage* in mass, compulsory inoculation for diphtheria. There was no showing of what **particular age groups** were particularly prone to becoming infected with diphtheria. In short, it appears as if the ECtHR simply took **the legislative decision** to require mass, indiscriminate diphtheria vaccination as **the** *final, indisputable word* that such a policy was sufficiently important so as to *per se* **override** every individual's personal medical privacy.

Concluding Remarks

During the rich history of American positive law and related jurisprudence, **natural law** has both **been recognized** as the source of fundamental human rights and **implemented** in countless statutory administrative and constitutional enactments. The continuing presence and impact of natural law has encompassed such far-reaching areas of life and society as:

- A right of self-preservation (self-defense; defense of others; defense of property)

- Duties of parental protection and nurturing of their children

- Corresponding rights of parents to raise and to establish a home for their own children

- "Life and Liberty"

- Property rights

- "Safety, happiness and privacy"

- Substantive and procedural due process of law

- A child's right to a free, equal and public education

- Right to education, as offered in one's native language

- Right to trial by jury

- Right to marry and to procreate

- Right of marital privacy

- Right of medical privacy

- Right of financial affairs privacy

- Right of privacy in private personal affairs such as intimate photographs

- Right of privacy in day-to-day affairs on a college campus

- Right of freedom from discrimination based on "suspect" classes such as ancestry

- Right to bear arms

- The "public trust" doctrine of rights

- Privilege against self-incrimination

- Restrictions against retroactive laws

- Ban against cruel and unusual punishment

- Right to engage in interstate commerce

The positive law proscriptions into which human rights have in some instances evolved are gaining more and more structure. The "elephant" in the natural law sculpture is gaining greater and greater visibility and clarity over human history. All of the human rights commissions, proclamations of positive law and innumerable lawsuits in enforcement of natural law combine to create an **enduring roadmap** for future enforcement efforts. Violators of natural law **are and will** *continue* **to be** held accountable, so long as people stand tall against a rising tide of tyranny and oppression.

Access to United States Courts for *civil* enforcement of extraterritorial violations of natural law and inalienable human rights was limited by *Kiobel, above.* However, a pathway does exist for determining what manner and scope of conduct adequately "touches and concerns" the United States in order to justify ATS subject-matter jurisdiction.

Moreover, innumerable statutes continue to extend the long-arm of American Justice to horrendous human rights abuses. Ultimately, however, **international enforcement of human rights and redress for human rights abuses** may require sovereign States **to cooperate** in creating uniform positive laws and treaties articulating the proscribed conduct, setting forth the appropriate forum(s) for redress and enumerating adequate procedures for litigating these claims of human rights abuses. This may well be the requisite future in any successful endeavor to comprehensively protect the natural law rights at stake.

Notwithstanding the foregoing, the **ECtHR has fallen behind** in the sophistication of its analysis of the lawfulness of infringements against human rights. It needs to undertake a **much more detailed analysis of the pros and cons** of forced inoculations, for example. It needs to adopt and apply a **test** similar to the U.S. **strict scrutiny test** as to violations of fundamental human rights. The ECtHR should immediately adopt a *standard* **of proof** of **beyond a reasonable doubt** as to any attempt to defend against human rights violations. Moreover, the ECtHR should place the *burden* **of proof** directly **upon the person or entity infringing** upon fundamental human rights.

In June 2017, Professor Obiora C. Okafor[335] (Nigeria) was appointed by the Human Rights Council of the United Nations as the "Independent Expert" on human rights and international solidarity. He assumed his functions on August 1, 2017. It has been reported to the Human Rights Council of the United Nations, that Professor Okafor surmises,

> "that while the world is increasingly interconnected, territorial States remain primarily responsible for realising [sic: realizing] human rights. This has resulted in **gaps in protection**, especially regarding the actions of transnational corporations in the global South.[336] (Bold added for emphasis)

The UN report continued, stating:

---

335   Mr. Okafor is the Edward B. Burling Chair in International Law and Institutions at the School of Advanced International Studies, Johns Hopkins University, Washington DC. He is also a former Chairperson of the UN Human Rights Council Advisory Committee.

336   United Nations, United Nations Human Rights, "Extraterritorial application of human rights requires multilateral approach – UN expert," June 24, 2022, https://www.ohchr.org/en/press-releases/2022/06/extraterritorial-application-human-rights-requires-multilateral-approach-un.

"Relying on lawsuits in foreign courts may promise more than it can deliver, the expert warned. 'Too many victims of human rights violations may end up being prevented – in practice – from accessing justice, as it may be impossible for affected communities to litigate their cases abroad,' he said."[337]

Concluding,

"Okafor's report said good practices in promoting human rights abroad in the context of increased globalization, such as the Global Deal initiative addressing labour market challenges, **are anchored in *multi-stakeholder negotiation processes***, which include workers and those directly affected from all parts of the world.

To promote international solidarity on transnational issues, **States should avoid** unilaterally enacting legislation, **and instead favour multilateral regulatory efforts**, including a **business and human rights treaty**. True solidarity requires participation and involvement of workers, affected communities and host States, the expert said."[338] (Bold and italics added for emphasis)

Complex problems require complex solutions. Contrary to the conclusion of Mr. Okafor, statutes enacted by the United States in affording U.S. jurisdiction over some, limited extraterritorial

---

337 Ibid.

338 Ibid.

human rights abuses, certainly constitute positive steps toward enforcement of natural law.

However, as described in *Kiobel, above*, it is both unlikely and impractical that *any one State* would *desire to be*, much less *be able to be*, a global custodian and enforcer of natural law. Accordingly, the Okafor proposal of a *multi-stakeholder approach* to securing human rights, regulatory measures and enforcement procedures *may well provide* the best and primary solution to human rights abuses in years to come. This assumes, of course, that corporate collaboration and assent is realistically attainable. Can the fox be trusted to guard—or to set rules for the lawful operation of—the henhouse? Maybe not but time will tell.

CHAPTER SEVEN

Evolving Standards of Human Rights Abuse

Israel-Palestine War of 2023

THE ISRAEL-PALESTINE WAR of 2023, on the coattails of Russia's invasion of Ukraine, has launched issues of War Crimes and Crimes Against Humanity into tight focus throughout the world. Outraged by the October 7, 2023 wanton Palestinian attacks against music-festival goers and other military and civilian targets in Israel, Israel commenced a virtual scorched-earth campaign against the Gaza Strip. [339] In that Israeli assault, despite advance Israeli warnings for Palestinians to evacuate to the south, thousands of civilians were killed as bombs rained down, leveling entire cities in the Strip. Competing allegations of human rights violations swept the Media. Waves of pro-Palestine and pro-Israel protestors throughout the world vied for the moral high-ground. Was one of the issues as simple as it seemed?

---

339 The Gaza Strip is a 25-mile-long by 6-mile-wide enclave, bounded by the Mediterranean Sea to the west, Israel to the north and east and Egypt to the south.

Does Israel have a right of self-defense to use *any means necessary* to rid itself, once and for all, of the brutal terrorist organization known as Hamas?

And for that matter, are virtually all Arabs in and around Israel committed to killing all Jews or otherwise ousting them from Israel? In a recent *ad hoc* street poll of Arabs residing in Israel, a question was posed, asking whether a two-State solution would be acceptable to them if it resulted in an enduring peace between Palestinian Arabs in the area and Jews.[340] The uniform response was: absolutely not, and the reason given was that Jews were outsiders who stole Arab lands. One man responded,

> "Of course not. This is our land. They occupied it, and at the end of the day, we are the owners of the land."

Another man stated,

> "Of course not. That's our land. And something for me, I don't like to share it, especially when it comes by force. … Well, they started by the wrong way. They started with the force. So, it's already late to come with a [peace] solution."

One of the women responded,

> "No. Because it's our land, it's not *their* land. We don't share it. … They are not [from here]."

---

340   TikTok, https://www.tiktok.com/t/ZT8fgrArs/ The verbatim question posed was: "Would you be willing to share the land equally with the Jews if you had peace and equality?"

After generations of indoctrination, Arabs in and around Palestine contend that all Jews are trespassing on Arab land. Moreover, these Arabs believe that Jews *enforce* their presence with military oppression over the indigenous victim-Arab population.

Following a personal visit to Israel, Elon Musk stated, in a November 27, 2023 interview,[341]

> "Essentially, these people were fed propaganda since they were children. And, it's remarkable what humans are capable of if they're fed falsehoods from when they are children. They will think that the murder of innocent people is a good thing. That is how much propaganda can affect people's minds. … Obviously, there are three things that need to happen in the Gaza situation. There's no choice but to kill those who insist on murdering civilians. There's no choice. They're not going to change their mind. And then the second thing is to change the education, so that a new generation … is not trained to be murderers. And then the third thing, which is also very important, is to try to build prosperity."

A Concise History of the Enduring Conflict Between Israel and Palestinian Arabs

For well over one-hundred years, Israel and Arabs known as Palestinian Arabs, or simply, Palestinians, have been locked in what appears to be **a zero-sum game** of life and death.[342] The conflict

---

341 TikTok, https://www.tiktok.com/t/ZT8fguc7b/.

342 Palestinians and Israelis alike view the land between the Jordan River and the Mediterranean Sea as their own, and Christians, Jews and Muslims all consider parts of that territory as sacred.

encompasses the land between the Jordan River to the east and the Mediterranean Sea to the west, and is shaped by conflicting religious mandates and statehood claims between the Israelis and the Palestinians, supported by various international agendas. The land which would become Israel was for centuries part of the Turkish-ruled Ottoman Empire.

It perhaps started with the late 19th-century Jewish migration— within the Ottoman Empire—to escape the pogroms[343] and other persecutions in eastern Europe – and the rise of Zionism. Another key turning-point would be what is known as the "Balfour Declaration"[344] in 1917, during World War I, by the British government in support of establishing a **"national home for the Jewish people"** in Palestine. Unfortunately, a thriving Arab population already resided in that location, together with a small minority of Jewish settlers.

The United Kingdom had declared war against the Ottoman Empire in November 1914 and the British War Cabinet immediately commenced consideration of the future of Palestine and partition of the Empire. A memorandum was circulated to the Cabinet by a Zionist Cabinet member, Herbert Samuel, in which he proposed British support of Zionist ambitions in order to encourage support by Jews in the wider war.

---

343 No, it is not a misspelling of "programs." According to Wikipedia, a pogrom is a violent riot incited with the aim of massacring or expelling an ethnic or religious group, particularly Jews. The term is derived from Russian to describe 19th- and 20th-century attacks on Jews in the Russian Empire. Similar attacks against Jews which also occurred at other times and places became known retrospectively as pogroms.

344 This unilateral declaration was contained in a November 2, 1917 letter from the United Kingdom's Foreign Secretary **Arthur Balfour** to Lord Rothschild, a leader of the British Jewish community, for eventual transmission to the Zionist Federation of Great Britain and Ireland.

By late 1917, leading to the Balfour Declaration, the war had reached a stalemate. In Southern Palestine, within the Middle Eastern theatre of World War I, that stalemate was broken by the Battle of Beersheba on 31 October 1917.[345] The verbiage of the Balfour Declaration constituted perhaps the first official expression of support for Zionism by a major political power. Reference to a "national home" had no established meaning, and was deliberately vague in order to avoid opposition as intending to establish a Jewish State. The geographic boundaries of this national home were left largely unspecified, but were purportedly not intended to cover all of Palestine. In a throwback to the principles of freedom set forth in the 6th Century B.C. Cyrus Cylinder, the Balfour Declaration outlined safeguarding civil and religious rights for the indigenous Palestinian Arabs, though it fell short of assuring *political rights.*[346]

In the immediate aftermath of the Allied victory in WWI, a "League of Nations" was formed which, in 1919, declared (among other "mandates") a "Mandate for Palestine." This particular mandate called for British administration, in trust for the native populations, of the territories of Palestine and Transjordan, both of which had been conceded by the Ottoman Empire. Regarding Palestine, the Mandate expressly required *implementation* of the Balfour Declaration's "national home for the Jewish people," alongside of indigenous Palestinian Arabs.

The Mandate for Palestine lasted for some three decades. During this period, there was a 1936–1939 Arab revolt in Palestine

---

345 In this battle, fought on October 31, 1917, the British Empire's Egyptian Expeditionary Force (EEF) comprised of British and Australian troops, attacked and captured the Ottoman Empire's Yildirim Army Group garrison at Beersheba, and in the process, commenced the Southern Palestine Offensive of the Sinai and Palestine campaign of World War I.

346 *See* discussion of the Cyrus Cylinder in Chapter One of this book, *supra.*

and a 1944–1948 Jewish uprising in Mandatory Palestine. By 1948, a greater larger portion of territory had come under Israel's control, not including the areas of the West Bank and Gaza Strip. Some 700,000 Palestinians escaped to Gaza in what Palestinians refer to as the "Nakba," or "catastrophe."

On November 29, 1947 the **United Nations** voted to enact a **Partition Plan** for Palestine which purported to unilaterally create *separate Jewish and Arab states*, with Jerusalem annexed to trusteeship by the United Nations.[347] The plan was never implemented after rejection by the Arab contingent, which stated that it is unfair to their majority community. On May 15, 1948, the date marking the final day of the Mandate, an **Israeli Declaration of Independence** was announced and executed by the Palestine Jewish community. **Once the 1947–1949 Palestine War** ended, Palestine was divided between Israel, Jordan (annexed the West Bank) and Egypt (established an All-Palestine Protectorate in the Gaza Strip).

Thus, in the stroke of a fountain pen, the Balfour Declaration and resulting Palestine Mandate, had upgraded Zionism worldwide to an internationally supported concept. It also led to both the emergence of Israel and an enduring dissention between Israel and indigenous Palestinian Arabs. The chronology of conflicts between Israel and Palestinian Arabs, however, had only begun.

Ensuing Hostilities

Hostilities continued, virtually unabated, in one tragic manner or another. The June, 1967, there was the so-called "Six-Day War," in which Israel seized control of the Gaza Strip, Sinai, the West

---

347 This well-intended UN declaration closely followed the historical annihilation of millions of Jews in the WWII Holocaust.

Bank, Golan Heights and most of Palestinian East Jerusalem. Arab armies suffered massive losses.

Then, in the 1972 "Munich Massacre," Palestinian extremists (8 members of the Black September group) took over an Olympic Village dorm where Israeli athletes were housed. Two athletes were murdered and nine others are taken as hostages, all of whom were soon murdered during a West German rescue attempt.

In October, 1973 a coalition of Arab nations sympathetic to Palestinian Arabs attacked Israel on a sacred religious holiday, Yom Kippur. Led by Egypt and Syria in what is now known as the Yom Kippur War, the aggressors gain some territory but are pushed back by Israel, aided by supplies provided by the United States. Both Israel and the Arab aggressors suffer heavy losses.

In September 1978, U.S. President Jimmy Carter mediates a peace agreement, to become known as the Camp David Accords, between Egyptian President Anwar Sadat[348] and Israeli Prime Minister Menachem Begin. The Accord lays the framework for peace between Israel and Egypt the next year, including Israel's gradual withdrawal from the Sinai Peninsula and a process of Palestinian self-government in the West Bank and Gaza. Although the pact led to the signing of a 1979 Israel-Egypt Peace Treaty, the Camp David Accord was criticized for **not involving Palestinian Arabs in the negotiations**, and consequently, the peace proposals for Palestine were never carried out. The UN General Assembly rejected the *Framework for Peace in the Middle East*, because it had been concluded without participation of UN and PLO and failed to include a Palestinian right of return, of self-determination and to national independence and sovereignty. In defense of the mediation, there did not then exist a Palestinian leader with adequately

---

348 In retaliation, by other Arab States, Egypt was subsequently suspended from the Arab League from 1979 until 1989.

widespread political support of "Palestine" who was interested in, and capable of, negotiating peace effectively on its behalf.[349]

In December, 1987, in what is known as the First Intifada, territory-wide Palestinian protests erupted against Israel's occupation and control of the West Bank, Gaza and even Israel itself. The Israeli military response was swift and destructive, though the protests and unrest continue for several years.

In 1993, the initial **Oslo Accord** is signed by Israel and the Palestine Liberation Organization (PLO).[350] The Accord established a limited Palestinian self-rule in the West Bank and Gaza Strip. The PLO was expressly recognized by the parties, and by the United States, as the official negotiating party for Palestinian Arabs, but key issues of Israeli settlements in the West Bank and the status of Jerusalem were not included in the Accord. The Oslo process involved multiple agreements, negotiations, suspensions and resumption of negotiations, designed to fulfill the "right of the Palestinian people to self-determination". However, the Oslo process ended after the failure of the Camp David Summit in 2000 and the outbreak of the Second Intifada.

On November 4, 1995, a peace rally was underway, attended by more than 100,000 in Tel Aviv. Yitzhak Rabin, 73, then Prime Minister of Israel, was in the process of leaving the rally when he was fatally shot by a right-wing Jewish extremist intent on stopping the

---

349 In the late 1950s, Yasser Arafat cofounded Fatah, a secular paramilitary organization **seeking the removal of Israel** and its replacement with a Palestinian state. Then, in 1969, Arafat was elected Chair of the Palestine National Council—the legislative organization responsible of developing policies and programs for the Palestine Liberation Organization. It was not until 1988 that Arafat acknowledged Israel's right to exist and sought a two-state solution to the Israeli–Palestinian conflict.

350 Menachem Begin, Jimmy Carter, Anwar Sadat participated. A renewal, or follow-up, accord was signed in 1995.

peace process with Palestinians. The shooter, Yigal Amir, opposed the Oslo accords on religious grounds, claiming that he acted on "orders of God" to stop holy land from being granted to Palestinians.

In 2000, the Second Intifada arose following a visit by right-wing Israeli political figure Ariel Sharon (later prime minister) to a compound in Jerusalem that is considered to be sacred in Judaism, Islam and Christianity. Violence and resulting deaths continued until 2005.

In 2005, Israel **withdrew its troops from Gaza**, while continuing to occupy the West Bank. Elections were held and in 2006, a militant Palestinian group, HAMAS (acronym for the Arabic words for Movement of Islamic Resistance, in Arabic), won the legislative elections. The election of Hamas members led, in turn, to serious political issues with the more moderate Fatah party controlling the West Bank (home to 3 million Palestinians and 500,000 Jews).[351] In a series of mid-2007 bloody battles between Hamas and Fatah contingents, Hamas wrested complete political and military control away from Fatah.

In response to this political shift in Gaza, in 2007, Israel proceeded to implement a complete blockade of the Gaza Strip. The blockade would stand to limit mobility of goods and people in and out of the territory for 16-years to date. The overcrowded Gaza Strip was home to some 2 million Palestinian Arabs and the already-stressed economy was dependent on the free flow of goods and services.

A 2022 Amnesty International report stated that it had observed,

> "Israel's intent to create and maintain a system of oppression and domination over Palestinians, … [through] territorial fragmentation; segregation and

---

351 The Jewish settlements by one view are deemed unlawful under international law.

control; dispossession of land and property; and denial of economic and social rights."

Amnesty International determined: "This is apartheid."

In the month of November and December of 2008, Israel sustains over 800 rocket attacks originating in Hamas-controlled Gaza. On December 27, 2008, Israeli warplanes retaliate with an unprecedented wave of airstrikes on dozens of security compounds in Gaza. Hundreds of combatants and hundreds of civilians are killed.

In 2012, Israel kills the Hamas military chief, Ahmed Jabari, igniting over a week of rocket fire from Gaza and retaliatory Israeli airstrikes. As a result, over 150 Palestinians and six Israelis die in these exchanges.

April 23, 2014 Hamas and the PLO sign a reconciliation agreement for a "unity" government, but no unity government materializes and internal tensions rise as rival political entities continue to control the disconnected West Bank and Gaza Strip.

Stoking the fire, in the summer of 2014, Hamas militants kidnap and murder three Israeli teenagers from a Jewish settlement in the West Bank. This atrocity prompts an Israeli military response. Hamas thereupon answers with more rocket attacks from Gaza. This seven-week conflict results in more than 2,200 Palestinians dead in Gaza and 73 Israelis dead.

On July 8, 2014 Israel invades the Gaza Strip, in Operation Protective Edge. Lasting for over 50 days, the incursion results in the deaths of two thousand Gazans, sixty-six Israeli soldiers, and five Israeli civilians. Palestinian rocket fire targets major Israeli cities.

In December, 2017, changing a decades-old foreign policy, U.S. President **Donald Trump formally recognizes Jerusalem**[352] **as the**

---

352   Since the end of the Six Days War, East Jerusalem, within the West Bank, has been considered to have been a part of Israel.

capital of Israel and declares that the U.S. intends to shift the U.S. Embassy there from Tel Aviv. Palestinians were incensed from this arguably-thoughtless disregard of Palestinians' political rights.

In 2018 Palestinian protestors hurl rocks and gasoline bombs across the border of Gaza. Israel responds with a clandestine raid in Gaza, killing seven suspected Palestinian militants and sustaining the loss of one senior Israeli army officer. Hamas responds by firing hundreds of rockets into Israel.

On January 28, 2020 President Trump announced his administration's Israeli-Palestinian peace plan. The plan was devised through collaboration of the United States and Israel, but incredibly, without any input from representatives of Palestine. The plan proposed, again, to establish the proverbial two-state solution—Israel and Palestine—with financial aid to Palestinians, and prerequisite requirements for Palestine statehood. It proposed a road/tunnel linking the Gaza Strip with the West Bank. The plan also commented on an eventual annexation of the West Bank by Israel. In lockstep, Israel's Prime Minister, Benjamin Netanyahu, promptly declared Israel's plan to annex portions of the West Bank. To no one's surprise, Palestinian authorities immediately reject the peace plan.

> "Despite Trump's promise "to be fair" to Palestinians in his speech, the actual document itself represents a far less conciliatory if garbled vision, often reading like a series of Israeli government talking points. The overall message [of Trump's peace plan], however, is that what the Trump administration has in mind is something far less meaningful than the two-state solution conceived by previous administrations or Oslo, with emphasis being

placed on Israel's security rather than Palestinian self-determination."[353]

Palestinian participation in planning "land swaps" with Israel would be conditioned upon the eradication of Hamas as the governing body of Palestine:

> "Palestinians in Gaza, currently ruled by Hamas, would be offered land swaps in Israel close to the Egyptian border but remain largely excluded from planning until a ceasefire and the removal of Hamas."[354]

In May, 2021, evictions of Palestinians in East Jerusalem and clashes at al-Aqsa Mosque[355] once again spark renewed conflict between Israel and Hamas. Israeli police raid the al-Aqsa Mosque, prompting Hamas to fire thousands of rockets toward the city Israel retaliated with hundreds of airstrikes. In excess of 200 are killed within Gaza, with no fewer than 10 killed in Israel.

A spate of violence on Israelis by Palestinians leaves 14 Israelis dead in a handful of attacks between March 22 and April 8, 2022. In response, Israel clamped down on militants and activists, and launched the "Break the Wave" military operation in the West Bank. Israeli forces kill 146 Palestinians in the West Bank in 2022, a death toll higher than in any other year since the United Nations began

---

353 The Guardian, *Trump's Middle East peace plan: key points at a glance*, Peter Beaumont, January 28, 2020.

354 Ibid.

355 This Mosque is one of the holiest landmarks in Islam.

keeping records in 2005. Israel's Foreign Ministry says Palestinians killed 29 Israelis that year.[356]

In December, 2022, Benjamin Netanyahu is sworn in for his sixth term as Israel's Prime Minister. He proceeds to craft the most far-right coalition of politicians in Israel's history.

> "It's also the most pro-settler government, with some members encouraging an expansion in settlement activity in occupied Palestinian territories."[357]

In January, 2023, Israeli military enters the Palestinian city of Jenin, where nine Palestinians are killed in a shootout. The following day, during prayers at an East Jerusalem synagogue, a Palestinian gunman slaughters seven people, including children.

Summer of 2023—the mutual destruction of life and property **substantially escalates**, unabated.

> "Israel launches surprise airstrikes across the Gaza Strip in May, killing three top militants and 10 others, including women and children, health officials say. That sets up a five-day bout of violence that kills at least 33 people in Gaza and two in Israel.

> On June 19, Israeli forces raid Jenin, deploying helicopter gunships to the West Bank for the first time since the second intifada.

---

356 The Washington Post, *The Israeli-Palestinian conflict: A chronology*, Sammy Westfall, Brian Murphy, Adam Taylor, Bryan Pietsch and Andrea Salcedo, October 9, 2023.

357 Ibid.

The next day, two Hamas gunmen open fire at a hummus restaurant at an Israeli settlement, killing four Israelis.

Hundreds of Israeli settlers then rampage through Palestinian villages, torching homes and cars, and shooting at residents, according to local officials. Israel also carries out its first drone strike in the West Bank since 2006, killing three suspected militants.

In July, Israel stages an air and ground attack with 1,000 soldiers backed by drone strikes against a refugee camp inside Jenin, killing 12 people. The operation marks the start of an "extensive counterterrorism effort" that the Israel Defense Force says will continue indefinitely.[358]

October 7, 2023 Hamas Attack

Far from being an isolated event, the ongoing conflict between Israel and Palestine **exploded** on October 7, 2023. At 6:30 a.m., rockets were launched from the Gaza Strip into southern Israel, as far north as Tel Aviv. Hamas claims it launched 5,000 rockets in total.

Some 3,000 Hamas militants breached the Gaza–Israel barrier on motorbikes, on foot, and by hang glider into Israeli towns – as well as to the open-air Tribe of Nova music festival in southern Israel near Re'im – killing some 1,210 men, women, and children in all, including 30 Americans, and injuring over 5,400. Hamas also took a reported 240 hostages.

"The assault came on a Saturday morning, on the Jewish holiday of Simchat Torah — the end of a two-week string

---

358 Ibid.

of holidays — ravaging a sleeping nation that had been assured repeatedly by its top security officials that Hamas posed no immediate threat.

...."Their success wasn't tech; it was preparation,' said Miri Eisin, a former senior intelligence officer in the IDF. They 'used military tactics to carry out a terror attack.'" [359]

Hamas spokesperson Khaled Qadomi claimed that the Hamas military operation was,

"in response to all the atrocities the Palestinians have faced over the decades. We want the international community to stop atrocities in Gaza, against Palestinian people, our holy sites like Al-Aqsa. All these things are the reason behind starting this battle." [360]

The following day, Netanyahu **declared war** on Hamas, launching aerial assaults on the densely populated Gaza Strip and preparing for a potential ground invasion of the territory, home to over 2 million Palestinians.

Ahead of the closed-door, October 8 meeting of the 15-member Security Council, Israel's UN Ambassador, Gilad Erdan, stated,

"These are war crimes, blatant documented war crimes,".
... The era of reasoning with these savages is over. ... Now is the time to obliterate [the] Hamas terror infrastructure,

---

359 The Washington Post, *How Hamas broke through Israel's border defenses during Oct. 7 attack*, Shira Rubin and Loveday Morris, October 27, 2023.

360 Aljezerra, *Why the Palestinian group Hamas launched an attack on Israel? All to know*, October 7, 2023.

to completely erase it, so that such horrors are never committed again."[361]

After the Security Council meeting, Deputy U.S. Ambassador to the U.N. Robert Wood remarked,

"What's important now is [that] the international community show its solidarity with Israel. We have Israel's back fully. … The condemnation of Hamas needs to continue until they end this violent terrorist activity against the Israeli people."[362]

In the initial six days of the war, Israel dropped a reported[363] 6,000 bombs on Gaza. Electricity was cut by Israel to Gaza and fuel and food was blocked from entering Gaza as well. On October 13, Israel issued an order for (some 1 million) civilians **to evacuate northern Gaza**. The bombing of Gaza continued and more civilians perished. [364] Israel planned an invasion of Gaza in order to target underground tunnels in which Hamas had sought refuge.

On October 20, 2023, trucks containing medicine, medical equipment, and food entered Gaza through the Rafah. Rafah is an

---

361 Reuters, *Israel UN envoy decries 'war crimes,' UN Security Council meets*, Michelle Nichols, October 8, 2023.

362 Ibid. *But query:* whether the IDF *deliberately* permitted the October 7 atrocities.

363 The Guardian, *Al-Ahli Arab hospital: piecing together what happened as Israel insists militant rocket to blame*, Manisha Ganguly, Emma Graham-Harrison, Jason Burke Elena Morresi, Ashley Kirk and Lucy Swan, October 18, 2023.

364 AP, *Israel bombs Gaza region where civilians were told to seek refuge, as mediators try to unlock aid*, Ajib Jobain, Samya Kullab and Ravi Nessman, October 17, 2023.

Egyptian border crossing, and the only crossing into and out of Gaza which is not controlled by Israel.

On October 27, before launching a ground incursion into northern Gaza, Israel shut down most of Gaza's internet and cellphone service. Telecommunication companies in Gaza also ceased operations from lack of fuel.[365]

Deborah Brown, senior technology researcher at Human Rights Watch, commented:

> "Prolonged and complete communications blackouts, like those [now] experienced in Gaza, can provide cover for atrocities and breed impunity while further undermining humanitarian efforts and putting lives at risk."[366]

Rasha Abdul-Rahim, director of Amnesty Tech. remarked:

> "People will be deprived of access to lifesaving information, such as finding areas of safety or contacting emergency services. ... The critical work of humanitarian agencies will also be severely disrupted as workers lose contact with each other."

UNRWA chief Philippe Lazzarini stated,

> "It is appalling that fuel continues to be used as a weapon of war."[367]

---

365 Aljezeera, *Telecommunications cut off in Gaza after fuel runs out amid Israeli siege*, November 17, 2023.

366 Ibid.

367 Ibid.

BBC News reports that medical and food supplies for innocent Palestinian Arabs were not being allowed into the Gaza Strip where they were sorely needed. The International Criminal Court's top prosecutor, Karim Khan, stated that impeding aid deliveries for Gaza might constitute a war crime:

> "Civilians must receive food and water. … I saw trucks full of goods, full of humanitarian assistance, stuck in Egypt where no one needs them. Stuck in Egypt, away from hungry mouths and bleeding wounds. These supplies must get to civilians in Gaza without delay."[368]

Karim Khan explained that Israel had,

> "clear obligations in its war with Hamas. Not just moral obligations but **legal obligations** to comply with the laws of armed conflict. …"[369] (bold added for emphasis)

Khan added that "this principle [also] applies to Hamas, in firing indiscriminate rockets into Israel".[370]

Tuesday, October 31, 2023, Israeli airstrikes hit Jabalia, a densely populated, and the largest, refugee camp in Gaza. The bombing

---

368 BBC, *Doctors in Gaza say Israel has told them to evacuate key hospital*, Rushdi Abualouf in Gaza; Jeremy Bowen, Anna Foster and Lucy Williamson in southern Israel; Yolande Knell, Paul Adams, Wyre Davies and Alice Cuddy in Jerusalem; and Hugo Bachega in southern Lebanon, October 29, 2023.

369 Ibid.

370

killed at least 50 Palestinians and a Hamas Commander.[371] The camp was bombed again on November 1, 4, and 18.

On November 3, 2023, an ambulance convoy was directly targeted by Israeli-fired missiles from the Israeli occupation forces while it was transporting casualties. The convoy consisted of 5 ambulances, 4 of which belong to the Gaza Ministry of Health ("MoH") and one belonging to Palestine Red Crescent Society ("PRCS"—similar to the Red Cross).[372]

Israel has consistently held that the Al-Shifa hospital sits above a Hamas headquarters, a supposition which the United States confirmed was supported by its own intelligence. On Wednesday, November 15, Israeli military *invaded* the hospital, subsequently reporting that it located a Hamas operation-headquarters and technological assets within tunnels beneath the facility. Israel released a video displaying seized weapons, grenades, ammunition and flak jackets from underneath the hospital. Hamas (preposterously) denied the smoking gun claims as constituting, "lies and cheap propaganda."[373] Israeli Defense Force ("IDF") later confirmed that it had arrested Dr. Mohammad Abu Salmiya, Director of Al-Shifa hospital, and had transferred him to the Shin Bet domestic security service for questioning. IDF explained that Al-Shifa, "under his [Abu Salmiya's] direct management, served as a Hamas command

---

371   Reuters, *Israel strikes dense Gaza camp, says it kills Hamas commander,* Nidal Al-Mughrabi and Emily Rose, October 31, 2023.

372   United Nations, Office of the Coordination of Humanitarian Affairs ("OCHA") Services, *PRCS Statement on The Israeli Occupation Force's shelling of the Ambulance Convoy transporting the injured for the aggression on Gaza towards Rafah crossing border on November 3rd 2023*, November 5, 2023.

373   Reuters, *Hamas command centre, weapons found at Gaza hospital, Israeli military says,* Nidal Al-Mughrabi, November 15, 2023.

and control centre," and that Hamas fighters had sought refuge in the hospital.[374]

According to Gaza's Health Ministry, over 13,000 Palestinians have been killed to date since October 7, 2023. Another 6,000 or so are reported as "missing" and are feared buried under the rubble left by IDF bombings of Gaza.[375]

As of November 27, 2023, some humanitarian inroads were met by Israel:

> "Limited phone and internet services began working again Friday across Gaza after fuel was delivered to restart generators that power the networks. Israel announced that it will allow two tanker trucks of fuel into Gaza each day for the United Nations and communication systems. That amount is half of what the U.N. said it needs for lifesaving functions including powering water systems, hospitals, bakeries and the trucks delivering aid."[376]

In addition, it was confirmed by OCHA that from October 7, 2023 through November 19, 2023, in the West Bank (controlled not by Hamas but by the more moderate "Palestinian Authority"),

---

374 The Guardian, *Israel arrests Gaza hospital director and bombs 300 targets amid truce delay*, Dan Sabbagh, November 23, 2023.

375 The Guardian, *Israel-Hamas war live: Israel vows to continue 'intense' fighting after ceasefire; Hamas reportedly to release 23 Thai hostages* ("ISRAEL-HAMAS WAR LIVE"), Helen Livingstone, Léonie Chao-Fong, Maya Yang, and Martin Belam, November 23, 2023.

376 AP, *Live updates | Limited telecom services return to Gaza, but the UN lacks fuel for aid delivery*, November 17, 2023.

including East Jerusalem, Israeli forces had killed 200 persons, including 52 children.[377]

Although the Hamas attack was quickly likened to America's 9/11, the comparison is weak considering that historically, Israel has yet to address the underlying causes of the popularity and resilience of Hamas within Palestine.

> "The greatest differences between 10/7 and 9/11 grew out of very different strategic contexts. 9/11 stemmed from Bin Laden's hostility towards both the Western way of life, and the United States' presence in the Middle East. By contrast, while the roots of the 10/7 attack lie partly in Hamas's long-standing commitment to Israel's destruction, they also grew out of Israel's decades-long failed strategy of "mowing the grass" in Gaza— which attempted to both contain and deter Hamas in Gaza, **while simultaneously not addressing any of the underlying economic and political conditions that had helped bring Hamas into power and keep it there.** While Hamas's core supporters may not have changed, a more far-sighted Israeli policy could have at least undercut Hamas's popular support."[378] (bold added for emphasis)

A Pause in Hostilities

In negotiations between Israel and Hamas representatives, a 4 to 5-day ceasefire commencing on Friday, November 23, 2023 at

---

377 OCHA, *Hostilities in the Gaza Strip and Israel | Flash Update #44,* November 19, 2023.

378 The RAND Blog, *Why the Oct. 7 Attack Wasn't Israel's 9/11,* Ralph S. Cohen, November 13, 2023.

7:00 a.m. local time, and limited hostage exchange, was to occur that afternoon. Hamas was set to release 50 hostages (of the 240 hostages), most of whom are women and children. Ten hostages were to be released by Hamas for each day of the truce.[379] Israel and its allies, including the United States, hoped that the exchange would take place as agreed and that it would lead to further exchanges. Under the terms of the agreement, Israel was to release at least 150 Palestinian prisoners as well as allowing up to 300 trucks of humanitarian aid into Gaza.[380]

In a separate agreement mediated by Iran, Hamas agreed to unconditionally release an additional 23 Thai hostages.[381]

The IDF, and presumably Hamas as well, likely used the ceasefire to organize and resupply arms and logistics for a continued battle following the short pause in hostilities.[382] Technically, however, no military advantage was to result from the short ceasefire. Qatar's chief negotiator in ceasefire talks, Minister of State at the Foreign Ministry Mohammed Al-Khulaifi, described that under the ceasefire agreement, there would be, "no attack whatsoever. No military movements, no expansion, nothing."[383]

Concerning the permanency of any ceasefire and rumors that the ceasefire could lead to an abandonment of the war, Israel made it clear that there would be no permanent ceasefire in Gaza until

---

379 Los Angeles Times, *Israel, Hamas agree to temporary cease-fire to free 50 hostages*, Jeffrey Fleischlman, Laura King, November 21, 2023.

380 *ISRAEL-HAMAS WAR LIVE.*

381 Ibid.

382 Ibid.

383 Reuters, *Israel–Hamas war: The hostage deal and ceasefire explained* (*"HOSTAGE DEAL AND CEASEFIRE EXPLAINED"*), November 23, 2023.

Hamas is finally and fully defeated.[384] Prime Minister Netanyahu assured Israelis:

> "Let me make clear: we are at war, and we will continue the war until we achieve all our objectives – eradicating Hamas, bringing back all our hostages and MIAs, and guaranteeing that there will be no figure in Gaza that threatens Israel."[385]

Human Rights Issues

IDF and Hamas paused to exchange hostages for prisoners of war. Israel vowed to continue the war until Hamas was wiped out, or surrendered. Negotiations previously for a 'two-State" solution had failed miserably, partly due to the fact that no one leader of the Palestine-Arabs had universal authority of and credibility with the Palestinians.[386]

> "The two-state solution calls for establishing an independent state for Palestinians alongside that of Israel. And U.S. support for it is nothing new: For decades, it has been the primary proposed framework for resolving the Israeli-Palestinian conflict.

---

384 *ISRAEL-HAMAS WAR LIVE*; and, *HOSTAGE DEAL AND CEASEFIRE EXPLAINED.*

385 The Guardian, *Netanyahu avoids political rebellion over Hamas hostage deal but ally calls it 'immoral',* Peter Beaumont, November 22, 2023.

386 The Ezra Klein Show, Podcast, *The Best Primer I've Heard on Israeli-Palestinian Peace Efforts,* November 21, 2023.

But failed peace talks, logistical questions, expanded Israeli settlements, Palestinian attacks and recurring clashes have kept it from becoming a reality. The two-state solution has seen dwindling support from both Palestinians and Israelis over the years. And its prospects now seem dimmer than ever, in light of Hamas' attack on Israel and Israel's response."[387]

Meanwhile, the population of Israeli settlers in the occupied West Bank, including East Jerusalem, had grown from 520,000 to more than 700,000 between 2012 and 2022 further complicating the concept of a 2-State solution.[388]

What will the endgame be for a final solution in Israel? They are intractably bound to Arab States on their borders, and to Palestine-Arabs within Israel itself and its occupied or blockaded territories. Hamas believes that its 1988 founding charter compels the Palestine Arabs to literally obliterate Israel.[389] Israelis believe that they will never be safe until Hamas, somehow, is eradicated as a force of terror on its borders and within Israeli. Meanwhile, Egypt, Jordon and other Arab countries are understandably skeptical about

---

387 NPR, *Biden wants a two-state solution for Israeli-Palestinian peace. Is it still possible?*, Rachel Treisman, October 27, 2023.

388 United Nations Human Rights Office of the High Commissioner, *Human Rights Council Hears that the Current Israeli Plan to Double the Settler Population in the Occupied Syrian Golan by 2027 is Unprecedented, and that 700,000 Israeli Settlers Are Living Illegally in the Occupied West Bank*, March 28, 2023.

389 BBC NEWS, *How much of a shift is the new Hamas policy document?*, Olande Knell, May 2, 2017. A new Hamas Charter softens the anti-Semitic rhetoric of the original Charter, but still restates the mantra of, the Palestinians' claim to all the land "from the River Jordan in the East to the Mediterranean Sea in the West". The new document, however, does formally accept the creation of a Palestinian state in Gaza, the West Bank and East Jerusalem - what are known as pre-1967 lines.

welcoming Palestinian refugees into their countries.[390] And what war crimes and crimes against humanity will take place during the continuing conflict by Israel and by Hamas?

War Crimes and Crimes Against Humanity

Regarding "**War Crimes**", according to the International Committee of the Red Cross ("ICRC"), a distinction must always be made between **who or what may be attacked**, and **who or what must be spared and protected**. Civilians must *never* be targeted. To do so is a war crime. Care must be taken to avoid harming civilians, or destroying things essential for their survival. Moreover, civilians have a right to receive help when they need it.

Detainees are no longer a threat and must neither be "tortured" nor subjected to retribution. In order to preserve their dignity and lives, detainees must be provided food and water, shelter, and a means of communicating with family.

The sick and the wounded must be allowed *to receive medical attention*. Medical workers must be permitted to do their jobs, and the Red Cross or Red Crescent must not be attacked. The sick or wounded have a right to be attended to, regardless of whether they are friend or foe.

Weapons of war are constantly evolving and regardless of their sophistication, it is mandatory that they be utilized within the rules of war.[391]

---

390 *See*, AP, *Why Egypt and other Arab countries are unwilling to take in Palestinian refugees from Gaza*, Jack Feffrey and Samy Magdy, October 18, 2023.

391 War Crimes have been further defined and discussed *supra* in this book, Chapter Five, All's Fair in War?, *The Holocaust and Nuremberg*, and *The Tokyo Trial*.

Regarding **"Crimes Against Humanity"**, the principles of International Humanitarian Law are complex and reflect a lengthy history of international warfare and a plethora of diverse war crimes. There are **four** "core" *humanitarian* principles: humanity; impartiality (non-discrimination in the manner in which relief is provided); neutrality and independence.[392]

In 1991, through United Nations General Assembly (HN) Resolution #46182, the first three, core, humanitarian principles of humanity, impartiality and neutrality were adopted. In 2003, in Resolution #58114, the principle of independence was added as a core humanitarian principle. Subsequently, nation-states implemented these four, core, humanitarian principles as they were reflected in their policies and practices. An example of this was the 2008 European Consensus on Humanitarian Aid.

Humanitarian principles reflect the sanctity of human life and the essential equality of humans. In order to render nondiscriminatory care and treatment of injured persons, there must be access, and open and independent lines of communication with persons needing medical care and treatment. Humanitarian aid is comprised of more than material assistance of health, food and shelter, but also assuring that human rights are protected.

Impartiality assures that help is presented based on the severity and urgency of the need. To the greatest extent possible, the medical worker must exclude personal bias from his or her decision-making.

Neutrality is required in order for the medical worker to continue to enjoy the confidence of all sides. Without trust, access will be compromised. Neutrality, in turn, is two-fold. First, there must be military neutrality by the medical worker or organization.

---

392 In contrast, there are *seven* "core" Red Cross/Red Crescent principles: voluntary service; unity; universality; humanity; impartiality; neutrality and independence.

This means, of course, not taking sides in the underlying military conflict itself. Secondly, there must be both ideological and religious neutrality. This requires that the medical worker or organization refrain from expressing or otherwise engaging in political, religious, ideological or racial dogma and controversies.

A succinct ICRC definition of **Crimes Against Humanity** is as follows:

> "The legal definition of crimes against humanity, as they are understood today, can be found in the ICC Statute. A crime against humanity is one of the acts listed below when committed 'as part of a widespread or systematic attack directed against any civilian population, with knowledge of the attack': murder; extermination; enslavement; deportation; persecution on political, racial, national, ethnic, cultural, religious, gender or other grounds; apartheid; arbitrary imprisonment; torture; rape, sexual slavery, enforced prostitution, forced pregnancy, enforced sterilization or any other form of sexual violence; enforced disappearance of persons; or other inhumane acts intentionally causing great suffering or serious injury to the body or to mental or physical health."[393]

Crimes in the Course of the 2023 Israel-Hamas War

In order for perpetrators of crimes against humanity and of war crimes to be held accountable, the suspect conduct must be first investigated, then prosecuted within the internationally-recognized structures.

---

393   ICRC, How Does Law Protect In War?, *Crimes Against Humanity.*

"All parties involved in the conflict are governed by a body of law drawn from a system of conventions, treaties and war crimes tribunal rulings known as 'international humanitarian law' (IHL) or the 'law of armed conflict'"[394]

In the Hague, the **International Criminal Court** ("ICC") is the judicial body recognized in that system as having the jurisdiction to entertain **prosecutions of war crimes and crimes against humanity**.[395] However, The United States is *not a party* to the Rome Statute of the International Criminal Court (Rome Statute), which founded the ICC in 2002. The United States had many legitimate reasons to not choose to be signatory to the Rome Statute:

"The primary objection given by the United States in opposition to the treaty is the ICC's possible assertion of jurisdiction over U.S. soldiers charged with "war crimes" resulting from legitimate uses of force, or its assertion of jurisdiction over other American officials charged for conduct related to foreign policy initiatives. The threat of prosecution by the ICC, it is argued, could impede the United States in carrying out military operations and foreign policy programs, impinging on the sovereignty of the United States."[396]

---

394 The Guardian, *Have war crimes been committed in Israel and Gaza and what international laws apply?* ("*Have War Crimes Been Committed*"), Chris McGreal, October 31, 2023.

395 Ibid.

396 EveryCRSReport.com, *U.S. Policy Regarding the International Criminal Court (ICC)*, July 9, 2002 – August 29, 2006.

Other issues with the Rome Statute included, for example, the Unaccountable Prosecutor, the Usurpation of the Role of the U.N. Security Council, and the lack of Due Process guarantees in the criminal prosecution procedures.[397]

Nevertheless, the question remains, in this currently ongoing violent conflict whether Israel or Hamas, or both have committed or are currently committing crimes against humanity and/or war crimes.

Hamas
It was reported:

"The UN said that Hamas's indiscriminate killing of hundreds of noncombatants, including children, and the abduction of about 200 others as hostages and human shields in Gaza, is a crime under international humanitarian law.

'Reports that armed groups from Gaza have gunned down hundreds of unarmed civilians are abhorrent and cannot be tolerated. Taking civilian hostages and using civilians as human shields are war crimes,' it said.

Legal experts said that Hamas and other groups such as Islamic Jihad may also be guilty of war crimes for firing thousands of rockets from Gaza into Israel."[398]

---

397 Ibid.

398 *Have War Crimes Been Committed?*

The widespread slaughter on October 7, 2023 by Hamas of civilians, including men, women, children and even infants, was horrific for lack of a better word expressing horror. On his podcast, Ben Shapiro showed captured videos of much of the depravity, after which he felt obliged to give an explanation for exposing this highly egregious level of evil to his viewers[399]:

> "I know the past few days have been really hard to watch. I know this show has been really difficult to watch and to listen to. So, I want to take a moment to explain why I'm showing you all this video and playing all the audio and showing you all the pictures of the atrocities that the terrorist group Hamas has taken and released. Why I'm showing you the abduction of raped women, the kidnapping of families, and the murder and burning of children—there's a reason I'm doing this—because there is an intellectual self-centeredness that predominates among a lot of us in the West. We think that everybody thinks like us. So, we see somebody do something truly evil, and we think to ourself: well, that is terrible, but the only reason I would do something like that is if something truly awful like that happened to me. After all, people are generally reasonable, generally peaceable, generally decent. Everyone I know is. So, what awful circumstance could force someone into such terrible, evil behavior? We think, well if only someone had just made a few concessions, dismantled a few settlements, offered a little more land. After all, we all want the same thing. Right?

---

399 TikTok, https://www.tiktok.com/t/ZT8fgYDb6/.

Well, no. No, we don't. *That* is the point. We can all tell ourselves these comforting little lies, before you see the pictures of what true evil does. But you can't tell those lies to yourself *after* you see the pictures, *after* you see the videos, *after* you listened to the audio, because here's the thing: Nothing anyone has ever done *to* you, or *could* ever do to you, would cause you to do these things. No territorial dispute would cause you to butcher babies. No squabble over territory would cause you to rape and abduct women. No so-called 'occupation' would cause you to kidnap entire families, or burn them alive in their home. The only type of person who would do something like that is a person who *isn't* like you. A person who *thinks differently* than you do. A person who does *not* value life or children or decency the same way that you do. A person who might proclaim, for example, that they love death like you love life. Actually [not] care about their children the way you do. Which is why they hide rocket-launchers behind their own kid. [People w]ho will willingly murder Jewish babies, just because they are Jewish babies. [People w]ho have been indoctrinated, cult-like since youth, in a system of cancerous-hatred so strong, they are willing to commit the worst atrocities since the Nazis, and then post them online and *celebrate* them. Hamas is *not* like you. Those who celebrate Hamas are *not* like you."[400]

---

400 Western *rejection of Islam* is not limited to the atrocities committed by Hamas. European nations in droves are rejecting the influence of Islam and opposing immigration of Islamists into their territories. The new Prime Minister of the Netherlands recently announced: "Today, I have a message for the Turks. Your government is fooling you into believing that one day you will become a member of the European Union. Well, forget it. You are no [sic: not] European

Regarding the exchange of hostages for military prisoners—although Hamas initially embarked upon returning some of the hostages to their host countries, that may have mitigated the harm, but did not constitute a complete legal defense to the international crime of taking *even a single civilian hostage*. Essentially, Hamas captured civilian hostages for the *express purpose* of using them as bargaining chips. This is **strictly prohibited** by international law. Moreover, any wartime incidental-harm which comes to the hostages *while in Hamas' custody* will be the responsibility of Hamas and its leaders. This is similar to the manner in which the "felony-murder" rule operates in American Jurisprudence. If anyone, including perpetrators, is killed during the course of a violent felony (such as, burglary, robbery, kidnapping, arson, and rape) being committed—whether the death is at the hand of perpetrators, Good Samaritans, or law enforcement—then each surviving perpetrator is held legally responsible for murder, for that loss of life.[401]

On November 28, 2023 it was announced by IDF, that instead of releasing a 10-month-old infant, his 4-year-old brother, mother and father from custody as October 7 hostages, Hamas has "transferred" them to another terrorist faction in Southern Gaza.[402] Hamas requested additional cease fire days. It is well-known that the IDF is moving from

---

and you will never be. An Islamic state like Turkey does not belong to Europe. All the values Europe stands for—freedom, democracy [and] human rights are incompatible with Islam. Turkey voted for Erdogan, a dangerous Islamist who raises the flag of Islam. We do not want more, but *less* Islam. So Turkey, stay away from us. You are not welcome here." TikTok, https:www.tiktok.com/t/ZT8fguc7b/.

401   *See, e.g., Tison v. Arizona,* 481 U.S. 137 (1987), where the co-conspirator's actions showed a reckless indifference to human life and played a "major" part in the felony.

402   FOX News, *Hamas transfers 10-month-old Israeli hostage, family to separate Palestinian terror group in Gaza: IDF,* Chris Pandolfo, November 28, 2023.

north to south in Gaza, and it is apparent that this kidnapped family is being unlawfully transported and used as a shield against Israeli attacks to the south. Again, **using civilians as a shield** is not only a **blatant War Crime**, but using an infant and a 4-year-old boy as hostage shields also **exemplifies** the vile and wanton disregard for life and absence of any semblance of human decency practiced by the terrorist organization, Hamas. If its objective is to influence public opinion in the Israeli-Palestinian conflict—it is certainly accomplishing that goal, but decidedly AGAINST Hamas. Suffice it to say that if any hostages, much less these children, are harmed in any way and not swiftly returned to Israel or their home countries, the weight of the world will be directed squarely down on the Gaza Strip and its oppressors, Hamas.

Israel

The UN has reported that Israel may have committed the war crime known as "collective punishment," through its relentless attack of northern Gaza. The ICRC stated,

> "The instructions issued by the Israeli authorities for the population of Gaza City to immediately leave their homes, coupled with the complete siege, explicitly denying them food, water and electricity are not compatible with international humanitarian law."[403]

The ICRC stressed,

> "When military powers order people to leave their homes, all possible measures must be taken to ensure the population has access to basic necessities like food

---

403   ICRC, *Israel and the occupied territories: Evacuation order of Gaza triggers catastrophic humanitarian consequences*, October 31, 2023.

and water and that members of the same family are not separated."[404]

Significantly, ICRC was **not** taking the position that civilian populations **may never** be ordered to leave their homes. The ICRC simply states that when civilians are ordered to leave their homes in order to avoid harm, such persons must be afforded the "basic necessities like food and water" and that members of the same family must not be separated.

In the case of the northern areas of the Gaza Strip, it is apparent from the Al-Shifa hospital situation, *supra*, that Hamas has actively utilized an elaborate system of underground tunnels, combined with using civilians as shields, to avoid harm from IDF attacks. Where the enemy hides under buildings and circulates in and about civilian areas, a direct ground attack without destruction of overlying buildings may be unacceptably dangerous to a combatant-State's troops. In that case, in modern warfare, orders to civilians to evacuate to the south cannot properly constitute the war crime of a collective punishment. As to food, water and shelter, the accounts are conflicting as to whether IDF has willfully violated this humanitarian mandate.[405] Jordan's King has called for an end to the war, and he claims that the Israeli siege on the Gaza Strip that prevented for weeks the entry of medicine, food, and fuel and cut electricity supplies, amounted to war crimes. The monarch stated,

---

404 Ibid.

405 *See*, Ibid., and AP, *The UN stops delivery of food and supplies to Gaza as a communications blackout hinders coordination*, Wafaa Shurafa, Jack Jeffery and Lee Keath, November 17, 2023, "Israel has barred entry of fuel since the start of the war, saying it would be diverted by Hamas for military means. It has also blocked food, water and other supplies except for a trickle of aid from Egypt that aid workers say falls far short of what's needed."

"These are war crimes. We cannot stay silent."[406]

Prior to the October 7, 2023 assault by Hamas, Israel **blockaded the Gaza Strip**, carefully screening supplies of goods, services, exports, food and water.

> "The Israeli government has argued that its blockade of the Gaza Strip is necessary to prevent the smuggling of weapons and other military supplies to Hamas, the Palestinian militant group that controls the territory. ... Whether or not Israel's cutting off food, water, and fuel supplies to 2 million Palestinians violates international law is a complex question that is still under debate. However, there is a strong consensus among international law experts that the blockade is illegal."[407]

The Blockade

The Gaza Strip, a narrow slice of land on the Mediterranean Sea, is inhabited by an estimated 2,300,000 Palestinian Arabs. The strip is located between the sea to the west, Israel to the north and east, and Egypt's Sinai Peninsula to the south. The strip is distant from the other Palestinian territory, the West Bank, and Palestinians cannot freely travel between the two.

Most Palestinians who live in Gaza are refugees or the descendants of refugees who moved to Gaza during the 1947-1949

---

406 Reuters, The Jerusalem Post, *Jordan's king says Israeli actions in Gaza and West Bank negate human values*, November 28, 2023.

407 Reddit, r/geopolitics, *Does Israel's cutting off food, water and fuel supplies to 2 million Palestinian civilians violate any international laws?*, Georgeo57, September 2023.

Palestine War, *supra*. Roughly half the people in Gaza live in refugee camps – tented communities.

Israel thereafter captured Gaza during the Six Day War, *supra*, taking it from Egyptian forces. The IDF remained there until 2005, when the then-Prime Minister of Israel, Ariel Sharon, "disengaged", withdrawing more than 8,000 Jewish settlers from the area. In order to shore up Israeli support for his unilateral withdrawal from Gaza, Sharon declared an intent to greatly expand Israeli settlement-presence in the West Bank.[408]

As noted *supra*, Hamas won a 2006 Palestinian election and in 2007 defeated the secular Palestinian Authority for complete political and military control of the Gaza Strip. However, Israel continued its overall control of Gaza and the UN considered Gaza to still be occupied.

People, food, fuel, internet, power and water cannot leave or enter Gaza without express permission from Israel. Egypt enforces the only entry area not otherwise controlled by Israel. The blockade has been characterized as being, "an open-air prison." Israel routinely justifies the blockade by pointing to missile strikes from Gaza and the need to keep terrorism in check on its borders. However, life inside the Gaza strip is grim, to say the least, and without doubt, Israel is itself responsible for much of the abject misery of Palestinians living there.

In an *eye-opening*, 2019 research article,[409] Yaser Alashqar[410] chronicles conditions of life inside the Strip. Mr. Alashqar explained,

---

408 The Guardian, *Sharon pledges to expand in West Bank*, Chris McGreal, August 22, 2005.

409 The Conversation, *Gaza: what life is like under the continuing Israeli blockade* ("*What Life is Like*"), Yaser Alashqar, November 9, 2019.

410 Mr. Alashqar is a Lecturer in Conflict Studies and Middle East Politics at Trinity College Dublin.

"I returned to Gaza, the place where I grew up and lived for 22 years, in July 2019 for a research project on the humanitarian and political dimensions of the crisis there, carrying out interviews with people from across society. My trip provided a real window on the realities of occupation, blockade and suffering in Gaza."

Military sojourns into Gaza keep the Gazan residents in fear.

"They have been subjected to brutal military assaults since 2008, in the context of the Israeli policy of 'mowing the lawn', military attacks and bombardment which indiscriminately kill civilians and cause massive levels of damage to civilian infrastructure in Gaza. This Israeli campaign continues under the pretext of undermining the military power of Hamas, the Palestinian political armed movement which runs Gaza."

The complete and comprehensive blockade of Gaza is accomplished by pervasive Israeli surveillance and force:

"The blockade is enforced by military means on the ground as well as by air. The movement of Israeli military airplanes, the sound of invisible drones and night explosions are a major source of stress, fear and anxiety."

Movement of people and goods in and out of Gaza is severely restricted:

"The possibility of travelling out of Gaza via the Rafah crossing with Egypt remains limited and fraught with security risks and restrictions. The movement of people between Gaza, the West Bank and Israel continues to be restricted to 'exceptional cases' and subject to Israeli permits, which are denied in many cases on unspecified security grounds. There are also multiple and complex Israeli restrictions on the shipment of commercial items and the movement of goods in and out of Gaza. Any attempt to break the blockade is met with severe punishment."

And as of 2019, the Gaza situation was worsening, not improving:

"The past two years have witnessed a severe worsening of the economic and humanitarian conditions in Gaza. The UN Relief and Works Agency (UNRWA) for Palestine Refugees reported that the number of Palestinian refugees relying on it for food aid in Gaza increased from less than 80,000 in 2000 to about 1m in 2018. As a result, 80% of Gaza's population have become dependent on international aid, and 95% of the population also lack direct access to clean water. Severe and damaging power shortages continue."

The adverse socio-economic impact of this cycle of despair and hopelessness cannot be overestimated:

"Data from the World Bank indicates that the unemployment rate among the youth in Gaza has reached over 70%. Adding to this crisis mode, basic services such as healthcare, water and sanitation have significantly deteriorated since 2014.

The blockade is a state of physical imprisonment and human despair. It not only shatters collective hopes for a better future among the people of Gaza but it also prevents access to professional and educational opportunities abroad. The social fabric is being torn apart. During my research interviews, I heard about increasing cases of domestic violence, suicide and addiction."

Nevertheless, Mr. Alashqar believes that despite the disheartening conditions of life in Gaza,

"...the desire for freedom and a better future remains very strong inside this besieged territory."

The foregoing accounting of the Gaza humanitarian circumstance, however, clearly does not address the existential threat posed by Hamas, and by Palestinian supporters of Hamas, to Israel and to Israeli Jews. From *their* perspective, they were driven out of their land, granted territorial rights to a homeland by the League of Nations and later, by the United Nations, as discussed, *supra*, their homeland status was re-confirmed. They defended and established their contemporary borders in conflicts with their neighbors in the Six Days War. Israel has offered peace to Palestinian Arabs through the optimistic *two-State solution* on multiple occasions, always to be met with ardent Arab refusals and ensuing Palestinian attacks.

While part of the solution suggested by Mr. Musk, *supra*, is education of the newest generation of Palestinian Arabs, the fact is that since 2006, Gaza has been run by the iron fist of Hamas, an organization that sanctions baby-killing, rape, murder and kidnapping. It is completely unrealistic to expect any kind of progressive, historically accurate and redeeming **education** in a Hamas-controlled Gaza Strip concerning race relations, religious tolerance, the historical basis for a legitimate claim on territories comprising the State of Israel, and the mutual interests to be advanced by peace.

An assumption that this brand of enlightened education would even be *remotely* possible while Hamas is in power in Gaza would be a proverbial "pipe-dream" of deadly consequences for Israel. As Mr. Shapiro convincingly pointed out, *supra*, Hamas and supporters of Hamas **do not** think like Westerners and they fully intend that the **only** local solution to the problem at hand is to destroy Israel and to kill all Jews in or about Israel.

Keeping the Palestinian Arabs weak, on the other hand, is hardly a long-term solution to the conflict since violence will continue unabated, and once Hamas is eliminated, another Hamas will intervene. What Israel may need to accomplish in order to normalize life in Israel is to **force Palestinian Arabs to relocate out of Gaza** and into another Arab nation. Then, Israel would convert Gaza to an agricultural mecca, with no cities and few if any Arab residents. It may be that in past generations, forced relocations of mass-civilian populations would have constituted a crime against humanity. But in the case of the current Israeli-Palestinian horror story in race-relations, mass forced relocation may indeed represent the most humanitarian solution practically available.

Compelled Inoculations

In Chapter Five, we saw the widespread and catastrophic global *socio-economic effects* resulting from a nation, such as the United States, covertly engaging in prohibited biological warfare research. The *human rights* **aftermath** of the Covid-19 so-called "pandemic" has been equally devastating for the fundamental right of medical privacy inherent in natural law.

In August, 2021 and effective October 15, 2021, the Board of Directors for the Los Angeles Unified School District (LAUSD, or, the "District")[411] created a highly controversial policy (the Vaccine Mandate) whereby **all employees** of the District had to be vaccinated against the Covid-19 virus with any of the mRNA, Experimental Use Application ("EUA") approved vaccines [Pfizer, Moderna and Janssen (Johnson & Johnson)], *subject to* any approved claims of exemption (religious and medical), and all employees must *register* their vaccine status with the District's "Daily Pass" system. The County of Los Angeles rescinded a similar vaccine mandate effective September, 2023.

> "[On]…September 13, [2023,] the California Department of Public Health (CDPH) announced that the Order of the State Health Officer, Vaccine Verification for Workers in Schools, issued August 11, 2021, will be rescinded effective September 17[, 2023]."[412]

Some two weeks later, on September 26, 2023, the District Board of Directors followed suit and voted to forthwith cancel its Vaccine Mandate. The Vaccine Mandate had been in effect against employees of the District for two-full-years.

During this period of time, hundreds of "Certificated" teachers and "Classified" educators resisted the Vaccine Mandate by timely filing their respective requests for exemptions based on grounds of

---

411 LAUSD is the second-larges school district in the country. During the 2022-2023 school year, it employed 24,769 teachers and 49,231 other employees. Wikipedia, Los Angeles Unified School District, https://en.wikipedia.org/wiki/Los_Angeles_Unified_School_District.

412 County of Los Angeles, Public Health, September 14, 2023 letter of Robert A. Gilchick, M.D., M.P.H., Child and Adolescent Health Section Chief.

"sincerely held religious beliefs" ("SHRB") in direct conflict with the Vaccine Mandate. The **author represented** many of these Certificated and Classified employees of the District. With few exceptions, the SHRB claims themselves went *uncontested* by LAUSD and instead were conceded by the District. However, the District then contended that as an "essential function" of employment, and regardless of any SHRB claims, only employees **with the Covid-19 vaccination** could work at any physical facility of the District.[413]

A procedure known as an interactive process of reasonable accommodation commenced for each SHRB claimant, whereby the claimant would eventually[414] appear remotely, with counsel if represented, before a so-called Committee on Reasonable Accommodations Based on Sincerely Held Religious Beliefs (the "SHRB Committee"). The SHRB Committee would thereafter issue its unilateral "Decision." Classified employees would be granted no work assignment whatsoever. Teachers would either be granted assignment in a remote position, or denied work.

As to those employees of the District not assigned to a remote work position, they would be *processed for disciplinary proceedings.* Over strenuous objections based primarily on medical privacy and religious freedom grounds, SHRB claimants in these disciplinary

---

413 Some Certificated teachers were assigned to remote teaching positions in the District's online academy known as "City of Angels", but no Classifieds received such an assignment. In the second year of the Vaccine Mandate, the remote assignments for even Certificated teachers were drastically cut back when the City of Angels program of "distance learning" was impacted by State law and changed to an "Independent Study" approach where teacher interaction with students was substantially reduced, and remote student enrollment fell precipitously.

414 There was at least one earlier procedural step, where the SHRB claimant would meet with their Supervisor, but this step was merely *pro forma* as the Supervisor had *absolutely no authority* to provide any reasonable accommodation whatsoever for an SHRB claimant's request for work.

proceedings were found guilty of "insubordination" for failure to vaccinate[415] and later terminated by the District's Board of Directors, retroactive to the date of the disciplinary proceedings.

Those denied reasonable accommodation would then seek employment elsewhere. If these efforts to find new employment failed as to SHRB claimants, many of the unemployed former employees of LAUSD thereafter sought unemployment insurance ("UI") benefits. The District, however, would routinely send letters to the California Employment Development Department ("EDD") asserting that the applicant was *ineligible* for UI benefits since they had supposedly been terminated from employment for "good cause" and "willful misconduct," to wit: refusing to submit to the Vaccine Mandate. This unlawful gambit by the District was successful *until* LAUSD employee Coretta Miller appealed an EDD "Determination" denying benefits.

The Coretta Miller EDD Case

In *Coretta Miller v. LAUSD*,[416] Administrative Law Judge ("ALJ") Honorable Susan Johnson ruled that the applicant, Miller,

---

415   This disciplinary process for approved SHRB claimants was akin to a *kangaroo court*, where District's administrators callously ignored constitutional law objections and *steamrolled* the SHRB claimants with express, written findings that **despite the District-approved SHRB claims of exemption**, the employees had *failed to comply* with the District's Vaccine Mandate, were thereby "insubordinate," and were to be terminated from employment based thereon for "good cause." The terminated employees thereafter filed complaints against the District with either the Civil Rights Department of the State of California, or the Equal Employment Opportunity Commission, or both. Those complaints were *uniformly rejected* by the respective agency, which merely provided each of the claimants with their "right to sue" letter, needed in what is known as "exhaustion of administrative remedies."

416   California Unemployment Insurance Appeals Board, Case No. 7276111, October 3, 2022.

for Unemployment Insurance benefits, was **NOT disqualified from entitlement** simply because she failed to comply with the LAUSD Covid-19-related Vaccine Mandate, since Miller had filed an unopposed or approved claim of exemption from the mandate based upon her sincerely held religious belief which was in direct conflict with the mandate.

The District had initiated disciplinary proceedings against Miller, alleging that because of her failure to comply with the Vaccine Mandate, she was purportedly guilty of "Insubordination." Once the Disciplinary Committee *found its own allegation to be true*, the LAUSD Board of Directors proceeded to suspend Miller and forthwith terminate her from employment, retroactively to the disciplinary hearing date.

In the EDD application proceedings for UI to follow, LAUSD opposed Miller's claim for UI on the grounds Miller had been terminated *for misconduct*. However, an initial EDD ruling in favor of LAUSD was REVERSED on appeal. ALJ Susan Johnson wrote:

> "'Misconduct connected with the work' is a substantial breach by the claimant of an important duty or obligation owed the employer, willful or wanton in character, and tending to injure the employer. [Citation]...The employer has the burden of proving misconduct. [Citation]."

Citing, *Hobbie v. Unemployment Appeals Commission of Florida* (1987) 480 U.S. 136 [Seventh-Day Adventist believer unlawfully terminated for refusing to work Friday sunset to Saturday sunset], Judge Johnson concluded:

> "Here, the final incident that led to the claimant's employment termination does not rise to the level of misconduct connected to the claimant's work. Requiring

the claimant to get the Covid-19 vaccine would violate the claimant's right to free exercise of religion. Additionally, the claimant substantially complied with the employer's Covid-19 protocols and procedures and the employer had even approved the claimant's religious exemption. ... The claimant is not disqualified under [Insurance Code ... section 1256."

The actions of State Boards of Education, School Districts, and even Charter Schools constitute "state actors" for purposes of enforcing the U.S. Constitution, Fourteenth Amendment guarantees of equal protection of the laws and due process of law.[417] Human rights abuses from these governmental entities *come in all forms*— such as school district schemes to unlawfully deprive terminated employees of unemployment insurance benefits, or as to unlawful bases for the termination of employment itself.

In the United States, an employment vaccine mandate accompanied by discipline of employees for noncompliance, violates

---

417 *See, Brown v. Board of Education* (1954) 347 U.S. 483 [Segregation of white and Negro children in the public schools of a State solely on the basis of race, pursuant to state laws permitting or requiring such segregation by the State Board of Education, denies to Negro children the equal protection of the laws guaranteed by the Fourteenth Amendment -- even though the physical facilities and other "tangible" factors of white and Negro schools may be equal]; *Butt v. State of California* (1992) 4 Cal.4th 668, 680-681, 679, 688 [equal protection guaranties of the California Constitution (art. I, § 7, subds. (a), (b); art. IV, § 16, subd. (a)) require State intervention to ensure that fiscal problems do not deprive a local district's students of basic educational equality]; and, *Peltier v. Charter Day Schools* (4th Cir. 2022) 37 F.4th 104 [Charter school policy of requiring girls to wear skirts to school violates Fourteenth Amendment guarantee of equal protection of the laws by discriminating against girls on the basis of gender and violates their right to the full benefits of their education; *cert. den., Charter Day Schools v. Peltier* (June 26, 2023) 20-1001, 20-1023; *but see, Wells v. One2One Learning Foundation* (2006) 39 Cal.4th 1164 [Charter school is not a state actor where there is *de minimus* State control].

the employee's State and Federal constitutional rights of Due Process of Law, Equal Protection of the law, (potentially) Freedom of Religion, and fundamental rights of Liberty and Privacy, including *inter alia*, the **right of medical privacy**.

Right of Privacy

As discussed *supra*, in Chapter 6, privacy was determined to constitute a ***fundamental personal right*** by the United States Supreme Court in *Griswold v. Connecticut* (1965) 381 U.S. 479. Moreover, as we have seen, Article 1, Section 1 of the California Constitution specifically recognized privacy as being one of the **essential inalienable rights**. Moreover, in *White v. Davis*,[418] referring to Article 1, Section 1, the California Supreme Court held:

> "…[T]he amendment does not purport to prohibit all incursion into individual privacy but rather **that any such intervention must be justified by a compelling interest**… [and that] **the constitutional provision**, in itself, '**creates** a legal and enforceable **right of privacy** for every Californian.'"[419] (bold and underlining added for emphasis)

Forcing employees to undergo the Covid-19 "vaccines" violates an employee's **fundamental right** of medical privacy.[420] Without turning this book into a forum for expert testimony and studies,

---

418   (1975) 13 Cal.3d 757.

419   Id. at 234.

420   The constitutional right to Due Process of Law would also mandate application of the strict scrutiny test.

any need for compulsory use of Covid-19 vaccines is *far less than compelling*, and *reasonable alternatives* absolutely do exist.

The Case Against the EUA Covid-19 Vaccines

The vaccines in question undeniably **do *not* prevent a person from contracting COVID-19** and **do *not* prevent a vaccinated person from passing on the infection to others.** Spain's study on the Omicron variant found that vaccinated people spread COVID-19 at **the same rate** as unvaccinated people. The most consequential finding in the extensive research project[421] is that vaccines did not appear to reduce the spread of the virus.

Moreover,

> "... a yearlong study of 621 people in the U.K. with mild Covid-19, scientists found that their **peak viral load** was similar regardless of the vaccination status, according to a paper published Thursday in The Lancet Infectious Diseases medical journal. ... The results go some way toward explaining why the delta variant is so infectious even in nations with successful vaccine rollouts, and **why the unvaccinated can't assume they are protected because others have had shots.**" (bold added for emphasis)[422]

---

421   The study was based on 622 Omicron cases (and their 1,420 contacts) detected in Cantabria, a region on Spain's north coast, in December 2021.

422   Bloomberg US Edition, *Vaccinated People Also Spread the Delta Variant, Yearlong Study Shows*, Suzi Ring, October 28, 2021. This is consistent with the UC Davis, Genome Center, UC San Francisco and Chan Zuckerberg Biohub study in around October 2021 which found that there is no significant difference in viral load between vaccinated and unvaccinated people who tested positive for the delta variant of SARS-CoV-2, and no significant difference between infected

This is in **stark contrast** to the *unqualified misinformation* spread on mass media by the CDC when Dr. Rochelle Walensky, director of the CDC, stated on MSNBC on Tuesday, March 30, 2021:

> "Our data from the CDC today suggests that vaccinated people do not carry the virus, they don't get sick. And that it's not just in the clinical trials, but it's also in real-world data."[423]

Internal Pfizer documents from a Court-ordered document dump show[424] that Pfizer acknowledged *at an early date* that **Natural Immunity antibodies** are *at least as strong* as antibodies created by its Covid-19 vaccine and that *Pfizer knew it*. In the limited trial, none of the vaccinated, nor those with previous infection, resulted in severe disease as defined by either the FDA or the CDC (zero cases in the natural immunity group, whether they were vaccinated or not). The Pfizer data also showed that **natural immunity was**

---

people with or without symptoms. The same result/finding occurred in the Massachusetts study which concluded that people with so-called breakthrough infections carried approximately the same amount of the coronavirus as those who did not get the shots.

423   On April 2, 2021, it was reported that the CDC had walked back from this outrageous claim, stating that, "the evidence isn't clear" and that Walensky was "speaking broadly." NEW YORK POST, *CDC walks back claim that vaccinated people can't carry COVID-19*, April 2, 2021, nypost.com.

424   www.youtube.com/watch?v=5eJ5TIT6zvk Kim Iversen reporting on *THE HILL rising*. According to The Lancet, 16-year-olds have a 99.993% chance of surviving Covid-19, a 30-year-old is at 99.943%, a 50-year-old is at 99.572% and only when the age level is above 60-years-old does the survivability drop below 99% with neither vaccine nor natural immunity.

statistically identical to the vaccine against COVID-19 infection.[425] Recent studies show further that **Natural Immunity antibodies last 2 to 3 times longer** than antibodies created by any of the COVID-19 vaccines.[426]

Natural immunity is spontaneous and robust when exposed to Covid-19. According to a study examining anecdotal evidence from "tens of thousands of doctors in Europe,"

> "rapid and efficient memory-type immune responses occur reliably in virtually all unvaccinated individuals who are exposed to SARS-CoV-2. The effectiveness of further boosting the immune response through vaccination is therefore highly doubtful. Vaccination may instead aggravate disease through antibody-dependent enhancement (ADE)."[427]

It is been established that some unvaccinated people have **natural immunity** *even without* exposure to Covid-19. Because of **repeated exposure *to the common cold***, and resulting T-cell immunity, it is likely that people of all ages will have some immunity since there will be some "cross-reactivity" within the T-cells.

---

425 Pfizer then *misled* consumers by instead reporting, "**Overall Conclusions** Final efficacy results show that BNT162b2 at 30 ug provided protection against COVID-19 in participants *with or without evidence of prior infection* with SARS-CoV-2, including across demographic subgroups, with severe cases observed predominantly in the placebo group."

426 https://www.news-medical.net/news/20220512/Messenger-RNA-COVID-19-vaccines-induce-high-levels-of-short-lived-antibodies-compared-to-natural-infection.aspx.

427 PECKFORD42, *Letter to Physicians: Four New Scientific Discoveries Regarding the Safety and Efficacy of COVID-19 Vaccines*, July 17, 2021.

"Much of the study on the immune response to SARS-CoV-2, the novel coronavirus that causes COVID-19, has focused on the production of antibodies. But, in fact, immune cells known as memory T cells also play an important role in the ability of our immune systems to protect us against many viral infections, including—it now appears—COVID-19. An intriguing new study of these memory T cells suggests they might protect some people newly infected with SARS-CoV-2 by remembering past encounters with other human coronaviruses. This might potentially explain why some people seem to fend off the virus and may be less susceptible to becoming severely ill with COVID-19."[428]

Regardless of inherent, T-cell cross-reactivity, however, **natural immunity** in *recovering from Covid-19* **is robust and enduring.**

"The Brownstone Institute lists 81 of the highest-quality, complete, most robust scientific studies and evidence reports/position statements on natural immunity as compared to the COVID-19 vaccine-induced immunity. We should not force COVID vaccines on anyone when the evidence shows that naturally acquired immunity is equal to or more robust and superior to existing vaccines. Instead, we should respect the right of the bodily integrity of individuals to decide for themselves. Public health officials and the medical establishment with the help of the politicized media are misleading the public

---

428 NIH Director's Blog, *Immune T Cells May Offer Lasting Protection Against COVID-19*, July 28, 2021.

with assertions that the COVID-19 shots provide greater protection than natural immunity. ... "[429]

Examining the ramifications of the Israeli experience of the Pfizer vaccine and viral spread, it was reported,

"'With a total of 835,792 Israelis known to have recovered from the virus, the 72 instances of reinfection amount to 0.0086% [i.e., *less* than 1/100th of 1%] of people who were already infected with COVID. By contrast, **Israelis who were vaccinated were 6.72 times more likely to get infected after the shot than after natural infection**, with over 3,000 of the 5,193,499, or 0.0578%, of Israelis who were vaccinated getting infected in the latest wave.' With over 60% of their respective populations now fully vaccinated, Israel and the U.K. are perfect case studies demonstrating that **vaccines are not playing the predominate role in slowing down the viral spread**. If you compare all of the European countries by recent cases per million to vaccination rates, you will find zero correlation, and in fact, eastern European countries with low vaccination rates seem to have fewer cases. [Instead,] ... infection-induced immunity is much deeper and broader. 'A natural infection induces hundreds upon hundreds of antibodies against all proteins of the virus, including the envelope, the membrane, the nucleocapsid, and the spike,' said Dr. Cole, who has spent the past 16 months examining and culturing SARS-CoV-2

---

429   The Burning Platform, *81 Research Studies Confirm Natural Immunity to COVID "Equal" or "Superior" to Vaccine Immunity* ("*81 Research Studies*"), October 21, 2021.

specimens. ... However, in vaccine-induced immunity, according to Cole, 'we mount an antibody response to only the spike and its constituent proteins.' He explains how this produces much fewer neutralizing antibodies, and 'as the virus preferentially mutates at the spike, these proteins are shaped differently and antibodies can no long "lock and key" bind to these new shapes.' **It is simply criminal for the global governments to suggest ...that those with deeper and broader natural immunity should risk the side effects of a vaccine that is now expected to wane in effectiveness.** Much of the focus now is on scaring people about the 'Delta variant,' but it could very well be that the vaccine effectiveness was bound to wane (unlike what they predicted with natural infection) over time, regardless of the mutations. ... Contrast that with immunity from infection, which has been shown to be impervious in every study. ... 'Yes, our antibody levels drop over time, however, scientifically, the memory B cells that make **antibodies** have been proven to be present **in our lymph nodes and bone marrow**,' explained Dr. Cole. 'They are primed and ready to produce a broad array of antibodies upon viral pre-exposure."[430] (bold added for emphasis)

Also, there is *strong evidence* that the COVID-19 vaccines themselves create *vastly more risk of serious bodily injury or death* than does COVID-19 in any of its variants. *For example,* a **Pfizer consent-form**, dated December 15, 2021, for a child clinical trial

---

430 NEWS+RESCUE, *Delta Variant: Natural Immunity 700% Greater Protection Than Shot, Data from Israeli Govt. Shows,* July 15, 2021.

of the Pfizer vaccine contains admissions of the serious side effects from the vaccine:

> "**Myocarditis** Myocarditis (inflammation of the heart muscle) and pericarditis (inflammation of the lining outside the heart) have occurred in some people who have received BNT162b2. Cases have mainly been reported in males under 30 years of age and following the second vaccination, however, there have been some cases reported in older males and females as well as following the first vaccination. ... While some severe cases have been reported most cases have been associated with full resolution of symptoms in the short term, however, long-term follow-up is limited. It is not known whether the risk of myocarditis or pericarditis is increased following additional doses of the vaccine, e.g. following a booster dose."

The document indicates that the incidence rate of these heart conditions is **10 in 100,000 people**, a *5x higher rate* than the previously reported Pfizer information of 1 in 50,000 people. The consent form further states that the effect of the vaccine on sperm, a nursing child, or pregnancy are *not known*. **The consent form makes another *startling admission*** as to the potential of an **ADE reaction** (*see, infra*) to the Pfizer mRNA vaccine. In this regard, the form advises that although not seen to date, it is not ruled out that the studied vaccine could make a *later COVID-19 illness more severe*! The consent form further admitted that in clinical trials *white cell count* temporarily *dropped* following vaccination (i.e., a *weakened immune system* for a week following the vaccination):

"1.4.2.1.1. Phase 1 Safety ... Clinical laboratory evaluations showed a transient decrease in lymphocytes that was observed in all age and dose groups after Dose 1, which resolved within approximately 1 week ... [but] were not considered clinically relevant."

Also, **brain damage reports** for *encephalopathy*, across the board, have *increased in excess of 20X* since introduction of the Covid-19 "vaccines" into the United States in approximately December 2020:

> "But how do reports of brain damage following COVID-19 vaccines compare to the rate of brain damage reported with all other vaccines administered for the previous 30 years before the roll-out of the COVID-19 experimental shots?

> To develop a baseline, I chose to search VAERS (VACCINE ADVERSE EVENTS REPORTING SYSTEM) for all cases reporting "encephalopathy" following vaccination. 'Encephalopathy' is a term for 'any diffuse disease of the brain that alters brain function or structure.' This term alone does not represent all the cases of neurological damage to the brain that are reported in VAERS, but it does give us a point of reference to compare cases reported after COVID-19 shots as compared to all other FDA-approved vaccines for the previous 30+ years. And what I found was that there is **a 2,000%+ increase in brain injuries being reported after COVID-19 shots**. Here are the results based on a search for 'encephalopathy' symptoms after COVID-19 vaccines. Notice the high rate of death among these cases of 'encephalopathy.'

This is the result from 17 months of COVID-19 vaccine distribution since December of 2020, when the vaccines were given emergency use authorization, which is *over 64 cases per month.*

By way of contrast, for the previous 30 years (360 months) before the COVID-19 vaccines started, there were 1,068 cases of 'encephalopathy' reported after all other FDA-approved vaccines, an average of *less than 3 per month.* That is an increase of over 2000%."[431]

The Covid-19 vaccines caused a **horrendous spike in deaths**.

"Israel doesn't have a high rate of full vaccination (66%), but the country eagerly embraced all proposed boosters: four. Despite all that Israel experienced the **highest COVID-19 death rate on record** this year."[432] (bold added for emphasis)

According to *Data Show,*

"...Finland, Denmark, Iceland and Norway [84%, 83%, 81% and 79% vaccinated] each documented their highest

---

431 GOODLY LAWFUL SOCIETY, *CASES OF BRAIN DAMAGE IN CHILDREN SKYROCKET FOLLOWING COVID-19 VACCINES*, Joshua Flint, May 27, 2022.

432 [your] NEWS, *Data Show Just How Ineffective are the COVID-19 Vaccines Around the World* ("*Data Show*"), June 16, 2022. *Data Show* examines data from numerous countries, worldwide, including Israel, Norway, Iceland, Finland, Denmark, Canada, Australia and Japan.

death rates, some beating their records multiple times in the last few weeks."[433]

Canada is 86% vaccinated, and yet,

"...the latest wave started a month earlier and has thus far left a similar number of victims than last year. In other words, the vaccines did absolutely nothing."[434]

Japan is 82% vaccinated, and,

"...recently experienced its worst death rate this year, doubling its all-time record. Masks and isolation didn't help either."[435]

Australia, home of governmental tyrants over the Covid-19 fiasco, is 87% vaccinated, but there,

"COVID-19 is running through Australia like a brushfire. The country recently experienced a death record **four times greater** than at any other point during the pandemic, and the fire is still raging. Maybe a 100% vaccination rate will help, or mandatory booster shots every time someone wants to step outside?"[436] (bold added for emphasis)

---

433 Ibid.

434 Ibid.

435 Ibid.

436 Ibid.

South Korea is 87% vaccinated, but peaked in June 2022 at 7 confirmed Covid-19 deaths per million people, a monstrous death rate.

> "Once a shining beacon on how to deal with COVID-19, today South Korea stands at the foot of a monster death spike. It accomplished this with 86.95% of the population fully vaccinated."[437]

Hong Kong, with 89% fully vaccinated, peaked in 2022 with over 35 Covid-19 deaths per million people.[438] And so on.

It is clear, moreover, that the **Covid-19 vaccines** are **statistically more dangerous** than the *disease itself*. These vaccines were promoted in the United States by claims of exceptionally high levels of supposed effectiveness in preventing deaths. The so-called *94.5% efficacy rated* touted by the vaccine makers, however, was **grossly misleading**. A peer-reviewed study published in Lancet, and other science publications, reveal that this vaccine efficacy rate was referring to ***"relative"* risk reduction** ("RRR"), rather than ***"absolute"* risk reduction** ("ARR"). The ARR of the vaccines for Moderna is 1.2%, for Johnson & Johnson is 1.2% and for Pfizer is .84% (i.e., less than 1%). This means that *after* a person *receives* the vaccine, he or she is, on average, still 99% *just as likely* to get Covid!

Obvious questions which arise are that if a person has natural immunity to Covid-19, as approximately 50% of the population most likely does, why would that person be required to get the vaccine, and if the vaccine doesn't stop the spread by the vaccinated, what would be the justification for a vaccine passport? Let's look at some official numbers.

---

437 Ibid.

438 Ibid.

The *inverse* of the ARR (for example 1/.84%) is called the *number needed to vaccinate* ("NNV")—which is to say: How many people do you *need to vaccinate* in order to prevent just *one* **case** of Covid-19?

The Pfizer NNV, calculated from its Phase 3 trials, is 119 (1/.0084), meaning that **119 people need to be vaccinated** *in order to prevent a single Covid-19 "case."* That's a Covid-19 *case*, not a Covid-19 death. The *median survival rate* of Covid-19 is 99.6% of all cases (*i.e.*, on average, .4% of cases result in deaths). Thus, 996 out of 1,000 *cases* survive and 4 out of 1,000 cases result in death. **So, how many people would have to be vaccinated with the Pfizer vaccine to** *save one life*? 1,000 cases = 4 deaths. 1,000 divided by 4 = 250, so 250 *cases* = 1 death. 119 vaccines required to save 1 case. Thus, to prevent 1 death requires 119 x 250 = 29,750 vaccinations. In other words, **29,750 vaccinations = 1 saved life**.

Yet, by the first half of 2021, about 134 million people in the U.S. have been fully vaccinated. During that time period, according to the CDC, 10,355 people *died* closely associated *with the vaccines.*[439] Taking the CDC numbers, 134 million vaccinated divided by 10,355 official deaths associated with the vaccines, result in 12,940.6. This means **the Covid-19 vaccines are closely associated with death**, at a minimum, in **1 out of every 12,940-vaccinated people.** So, if you **fully vaccinate** 29,750 people (required, as shown above, for the vaccine to save *one life*), **2.299 people** (29,750 divided by 12,940.6 = 2.299) **would** *die* from causes closely associated with the vaccine as opposed to **1 death** *saved* by the vaccine![440]

---

439 Due to under-reporting in the VAERS system, that number of deaths has been estimated by officials at the CDC and by whistle-blowers at 51,800.

440 And the irony is that *at least one* of the Covid-19 vaccine manufacturers is still running sophisticated television advertisements during NFL Football games encouraging people to take the jab, or updated variants thereof.

That means that for the Pfizer vaccine, as an average through the age groups, people are almost *2.3 times more likely to <u>die</u> from the vaccine* than to be saved by the vaccine from a Covid-19-related death. Moreover, with the *more likely* estimate of the *51,800-death toll* from the vaccines, the result is *even more startling* (134,000,000 divided by 51,800 = 2,586.87—meaning that the *vaccines are closely associated with the death of* approximately 1 out of every *2,586-vaccinated* people). So, if you fully vaccinate 29,750 people (1 life saved from the vaccine), then 11.5 people (29,750 divided by 2,586 = 11.504), on average will <u>die</u> from the vaccine. In *that* calculation, people are *11.5 times more likely to die <u>from causes closely associated with the vaccine</u>* than to be saved by the vaccine from a Covid-19-related death. And the likelihood of developing from the vaccine a lifelong debilitating disease, or future premature death from a severely weakened immune system, is *even greater*.

The **third EUA, FDA-approved vaccine (Johnson & Johnson) was never a safe and effective viable option** for Americans. Reports of *terrible side effects*, including death, were ongoing, and on May 5, 2022, the FDA took action.

> "The shot is now only available to people who are unable or unwilling to receive the other mRNA vaccine options. Johnson & Johnson's COVID-19 vaccine is now restricted to only a select group of people, the U.S. Food and Drug Administration announced Thursday. The vaccine's emergency use authorization is limited to people ages 18 and older for whom other vaccines are not accessible or appropriate, or for people who would not get a COVID-19 vaccine otherwise.

In a statement[441] announcing the change, the FDA said the new limitations are due to an **increased risk of the blood clotting** condition thrombosis with thrombocytopenia syndrome (TTS), a rare but potentially fatal side effect that can occur one to two weeks following the J&J vaccine."[442] (bold added for emphasis)

As variants to the virus developed, such as the "Delta" variants, studies showed that the vaccines *were even **less** effective* in ameliorating the effects of the disease than when the vaccines were originally introduced. And the vaccines had other problems as well:

"Unlike natural immunity, Israeli data[443] confirms that the Pfizer vaccine **wore off in just a few months** in all age groups. ... Data from the UK[444] finds vaccines are 'highly effective,' but effectiveness **wanes after as little as 3-4 months**. ... A study of health care workers in Vietnam[445] found vaccinated people infected with Delta Covid-19 carry 'unusually high viral loads' in their nostrils that are

---

441   FDA NEWS RELEASE, *Coronavirus (Covid-19) Update: FDA Limits Use of Janssen's COVID-19 Vaccine to Certain Individuals*, May 5, 2022.

442   HEALTH, *Why the FDA Restricted Use of Johnson & Johnson's COVID-19 Vaccine*, Korin Miller, May 6, 2022, https://medicine.buffalo.edu/research.host.html/content/shared/smbs/media/2022/05/covid-vaccine-jj-russo14994.detail.html

443   THE NEW ENGLAND JOURNAL of MEDICINE, *Waning Immunity after the BNT162b2 Vaccine in Israel*, October 27, 2021.

444   UK Health Security Agency, *COVID-19 vaccine surveillance report Week 40*, p. 7, October 7, 2021

445   THE LANCET, Transmission of SARS-CoV-2 Delta Variant Among Vaccinated Healthcare Workers, Vietnam, October 11, 2021.

251 times higher.' The study said that during a period **when the vaccinated patients are infected but don't yet know it, they could be responsible for heightened spread** to other vaccinated or the unvaccinated. [AstraZeneca] … According to Epoch Times,[446] in June 2021 nearly 4,000 fully vaccinated people in Massachusetts tested positive for Covid-19. … An analysis of data[447] in Israel which has one of the world's highest Covid-19 vaccination levels, showed **almost 60% of those hospitalized for Covid were fully vaccinated**. 'This is a very clear warning sign for the rest of the world.' Said Ran Balicer, CIO at Clalit Health Services, Israel's largest health maintenance organization. 'If it can happen here, it can probably happen anywhere.' The Pfizer vaccine is given in Israel." … A Study[448] by university and NIH scientists in the U.S. finds **Pfizer vaccine antibodies disappear after about 7 months** in many patients."[449] (bold added for emphasis).

What is known as **Antibody Dependent Enhancement ("ADE")** can make vaccinated people more susceptible to serious infection from the Covid-19 virus. With ADE, after people get vaccinated for an initial virus, infection by a subsequent variant

---

446 THE EPOCH TIMES, *Nearly 4,000 Fully Vaccinated People in Massachusetts Test Positive for COVID-19*, June 22, 2021

447 BECKER'S HOSPITAL REVIEW, *Nearly 60% of hospitalized COVID-19 patients in Israel fully vaccinated, data shows*, August 19, 2021.

448 bioRxiv, *Durability of immune responses to the BNT162b2 mRNA vaccine*, September 30, 2021.

449 SHARYL ATTKISSON, *Exclusive Summary: Covid-19 Vaccine Concerns*, October 29, 2021 (*"Exclusive Summary"*).

or strain of the virus can result in "increased viral replication and more severe disease, leading to major safety risks." ADE can also occur when neutralizing antibodies (which bind the virus and stop it from causing infection) are present at such low levels that they don't protect against infection. Instead, they can form immune complexes with viral particles, which in turn leads to worse illness.[450]

The danger of **physiological collateral damage from** ADE is *substantial*:

> "Clinically, this antibody-dependent enhancement … can cause a hyperinflammatory response (a 'cytokine storm') that will **amplify the damage** to the lungs, liver and other organs of our body. … The possibility of ADE was not adequately addressed in the clinical trials on any of the COVID-19 vaccines. It is therefore prudent to avoid the danger of inducing ADE through vaccination and instead rely on proven forms of treatment [fn.] for dealing with clinically severe COVID-19 disease."[451]

Moreover, the **statutory basis** for EUAs, in FDA approval of the Covid-19 vaccines, **no longer exists**. The Secretary of Health & Human Services ("HHS") **is obligated by law** to periodically review the *bases upon which* any Emergency Use Authorization-approvals have been granted by the U.S. Food & Drug Agency ("FDA").[452] One prerequisite for FDA issuance of an EUA approval, is that,

---

450 Ibid.

451 Ibid.

452 Public Readiness and Emergency Preparedness Act (*"PREP Act"*).

"there are no adequate, approved, and available alternatives."[453]

Regarding Covid-19 vaccines, each of the previously available vaccines in the United States[454] were authorized by the FDA upon an individual Emergency Use Authorization ("EUA"). Arguably, there may not have been any "adequate, approved and available alternatives" to the vaccines when,

- the Secretary of HHS issued a declaration of a public health emergency on March 27, 2020 (Federal Register, Emergency Use Authorization Notice of April 1, 2020), and,

- when the Secretary of HHS subsequently issued the Emergency Use Authorizations for the Pfizer, Moderna and Johnson & Johnson (Janssen) vaccines on December 11, 2020 for Pfizer, December 18, 2020 for Moderna, and February 27, 2021 for Johnson & Johnson (Janssen).

However, *since that time*, there have been **numerous scientific studies confirming the effectiveness** of the following **treatment protocols** as being *exceptionally effective* in **treating** Covid-19, caused by the SARS COV-2 virus:

1. **Ivermectin** "Conclusions: Moderate-certainty evidence finds that large reductions in COVID-19 deaths are possible using ivermectin. Using ivermectin

---

453   U.S Food & Drug Administration, *Emergency Use Authorization*.

454   "Comirnaty" may never have been available within the United States—*see*, e.g., 247SPORTS, *FDA Does a Bait and Switch with COVID Shots*, September 2, 2021.

early in the clinical course may reduce numbers progressing to severe disease. The apparent safety and low cost suggest that ivermectin is likely to have a significant impact on the SARS-CoV-2 pandemic globally."[455] "A focus of the manuscript was on the 27 controlled trials available in January 2021, 15 of which were randomized controlled trials...they found large, statistically significant reduction in mortality, time to recovery and viral clearance in COVID-19 patients treated with ivermectin."[456] "A 97% decline in Delhi cases with Ivermectin is decisive—period. It represents the last word in an epic struggle to save lives and preserve human rights."[457]

2. **Hydroxychloroquine** "A total of 43 reports were found that examined HCQ treatment for COVID-19 patients. Twenty-five reported positive clinical efficacy from providing HCQ to for COVID-19 patients; 15 showed no improvement with HCQ and three showed worse clinical results in patients who received HCQ."[458] "Big Tech continues to censor factual

455 AMERICAN JOURNAL OF THERAPEUTICS, *Ivermectin for Prevention and Treatment of COVID-19 Infection: A Systematic Review, Meta-analysis, and Trial Sequential Analysis to Inform Clinical Guidelines*, June 21, 2021.

456 Outbreak News Today, American Journal of Therapeutics, *Ivermectin is highly effective as a safe prophylaxis and treatment for COVID-19: Comprehensive review*, May 9, 2021.

457 The Desert Review, *Ivermectin obliterates 97 percent of Delhi cases*, by Justus R. Hope, MD, June 7, 2021.

458 U.S. NATIONAL LIBRARY OF MEDICINE, *Hydroxychloroquine is effective, and consistently so when provided early, for COVID-19: a systematic*

information related to use of hydroxychloroquine to treat or prevent Covid-19. That's despite two new studies that show the inexpensive drug works. A new study in MedRxiv found that hydroxychloroquine and zinc increased Covid-19 survival by almost three times. And a recent study published in the Journal of The Association of Physicians of India also found hydroxychloroquine is an effective treatment for Covid-19 … I think we have to look at the money. There's no big profits made in hydroxychloroquine It's very cheap, easy to manufacture, been around for 70 years. It's generic. Remdesivir is a new drug that could be very expensive and very lucrative if it's ever approved. So I think we really do have to consider there's some financial interest involved here. … [W]e checked financial ties among experts on the government panel devising coronavirus treatment guidelines—which had the effect of dialing back hydroxychloroquine use and giving an edge to Remdesivir. We found out that of 11 members reporting links to a drug company, nine of them named relationships to remdesivir's maker Gilead. Seven more, including two of the committee's leaders, have ties to Gilead beyond the 11 months they had to disclose. Two were on Gilead's advisory board. Others were paid consultants or received research support and honoraria. Nobody reported ties to hydroxychloroquine which

review, C. Prodromos and T. Rumschlag, October 5, 2020.

is now made by numerous generic manufacturers and is so cheap ...."[459]

3. **Monoclonal Antibodies**, "The study found that compared to the placebo group, COVID-19 patients who received sotrovimab had a significantly reduced risk of hospitalization or death and that the treatment, which was administered by intravenous infusion on an outpatient basis, was safe. Of the 583 study participants included in this analysis, three participants who received sotrovimab and 21 participants in the placebo group experienced disease progression that led to hospitalization or death, representing a risk reduction of 85% in people with COVID-19 who received the monoclonal antibody treatment."[460] "Monoclonal antibodies are immune molecules that are produced in a laboratory and designed to mimic the body's natural response to infection. In the case of COVID-19, the antibodies are made to recognize and bind to a part of the SARS-Co-V2 virus that enables it to infect human cells. Clinical trials conducted at Stanford Medicine and elsewhere indicate that this binding blocks the progression of the disease and reduces the chance of severe complications in high-risk people if administered early. The treatment is for

---

459 SHARYL ATTKISSON, *Hydroxychloroquine: Just the facts and a Follow the Money investigation*, June 13, 2021.

460 PRESS RELEASE, *Monoclonal antibody treatment highly effective at reducing COVID-19 hospitalizations*, October 28, 2021.

patients who have mild to moderate symptoms of the disease but an elevated risk of complications."[461]

4. **Other treatments** "...[C]ells infected with SARS-CoV-2 can only produce novel coronaviruses when a metabolic pathway called pentose phosphate pathway is activated. The researchers from the University of Kent in the UK and Goethe-University in Germany found that the drug **benefooxythiamine**, an inhibitor of this metabolic pathway, suppressed reproduction of SARS-CoV-2, and infected cells did not produce coronaviruses. ... 'Targeting virus-induced changes in the host cell metabolism is an attractive way to interfere specifically with the virus replication process,' Professor Jindrich Cinatl from Goethe-University added."[462] *See also*, THE WEEK MAGAZINE, *Novel drug treatment for COVID-19 identified*, October 30, 2021 (benefooxythiamine). United Nations, UN News, *WHO announces three new drugs for latest COVID-19 'Solidarity' trials*, August 11, 2021 (artesunate, imatinib and infliximab).

Although the federal Public Health Emergency was officially declared as "ended" as of May 11, 2023, Covid-vaccines are

---

461 Stanford MEDICINE, *Monoclonal antibody treatment available for early COVID-19 at Stanford Health Care*, June 21, 2021.

462 The Shillong Times, *Novel drug treatment for COVID-19 identified*, October 30, 2021.

still available.[463] However, because alternative treatments are in fact available, the EUAs for the Covid-19 vaccines in the United States are *no longer legally justifiable* and the vaccines are simply "experimental."

The **vaccinated are as likely to transmit the disease** as the unvaccinated.

> "The vaccinated are showing viral loads (very high) similar to the unvaccinated, and the vaccinated are as infectious." [464]

Individuals had high viral loads from nasal swabs irrespective of vaccine status:

> "The SARS-CoV-2 Delta variant and its sublineages … can cause high viral loads, are highly transmissible, and contain mutations that confer partial immune escape. Using PCR threshold cycle (Ct) data from a single large contract laboratory, we showed that individuals in Wisconsin, USA had similar viral loads in nasal swabs, irrespective of vaccine status, during a time of high and increasing prevalence of the Delta variant."[465]

Covid-19 vaccines simply do not prevent the vaccinated from spreading the Delta variant. The Lancet Infectious Diseases medical

---

463 Center for Disease Control and Prevention, *End of the Federal COVID-19 Public Health Emergency (PHE) Declaration*, updated September 12, 2023.

464 *81 Research Studies*, Ibid.

465 medRxiv THE PREPRINT SERVER FOR HEALTH SCIENCES, *Shedding of Infectious SARS-CoV-2 Despite Vaccination when the Delta Variant is Prevalent – Wisconsin*, July 2021.

journal reported a study which documented the health of 621 people with mild Covid-19 cases and found that the **vaccination did not significantly change the viral load**, which was similar regardless of vaccination status.

> "'Our findings show that vaccination alone is not enough to prevent people from being infected with the delta variant and spreading it in household settings,' said Ajit Lalvani, a professor of infectious diseases at Imperial College London who co-led the study."[466]

In fact, **vaccinations actually *prolong* the "pandemic" by *causing mutations which spread faster among the vaccinated*.**

> "The Delta mutation of the coronavirus can be easily spread from vaccinated to people who have contact especially at home. ... [A] new British study from Imperial College London ... shows that the highly contagious Delta mutation can spread even among vaccinated people. ... They found that the infection in the vaccinated **passes faster** but the maximum viral load remains similar to that of the unvaccinated."[467] (bold added)

A major study considered the effect of the Covid-19 vaccines when applied to the Delta variant. It found as follows,

---

466 TIMCAST NEWS, POLITICS, CULTURE, *VACCINATED PEOPLE ARE JUST AS LIKELY TO SPREAD DELTA VARIANT, YEAR-LONG STUDY FINDS* (*"Imperial College London Study"*) October 29, 2021.

467 THE KEFALONIA GREECE PULSE, *Coronavirus: Delta mutation also transmitted by vaccinated—Importance of booster doses*, October 31, 2021.

"A general principle in biology, vaccinology and microbiology is that if you put living organisms like bacteria or viruses under pressure, via antibiotics, antibodies or chemotherapeutics, for example, **but don't kill them off completely**, you can inadvertently encourage their mutation into more virulent strains. Those that escape your immune system end up surviving and selecting mutations to ensure their further survival."[468] (bold added)

The commentary quotes Geert Vanden Bossche, Ph.D., a vaccinology expert and former global director of vaccine programs such as the Bill & Melinda Gates Foundation:

"'It will have a very tough time ... and a lot of these microorganisms will die,' Bossche says. 'But if **you cannot really kill them all**, if you cannot prevent, completely, the infection and if there are still some microorganisms that can replicate despite this huge pressure, **they will start to select mutations that enable them to survive**.'"[469] (bold added for emphasis)

Dr. Peter McCullough, internist, cardiologist, epidemiologist and full professor of medicine at Texas A&M College of Medicine in Dallas, stated:

---

468 *The World We Live In*, a commentary, *BREAKING: Study Finds The Current Covid-19 Vaccines Will Cause "Vaccine Induced Enhanced Disease" When Infected With Delta* ("*BREAKING*"), September 16, 2021.

469 Ibid.

"If we keep this up with the injections, there is going to be one variant after another … **We're playing with fire here with this mass vaccination.** … I think this Delta outbreak that we have right now is the product of mass vaccination. **If we didn't have the jab, we would have been better off.** We had already treated this down to a very acceptable level."[470] (bold added for emphasis)

And none other than the CDC Director Rochelle Walensky, MD, made a "dire prediction," claiming that a new, more elusive variant in the Covid-19 virus,

"could be 'just a few mutations away.' … 'That's a very prescient comment,' Lewis Nelson, MD, professor and clinical chair of emergency medicine and chief of the Division of Medical Toxicology at Rutgers New Jersey medical School in Newark, tells Medscape Medical News. 'We've gone through a few mutations already that have been named, and each one of them gets a little more transmissible, he says. 'That's normal, natural selection and what you would expect to happen as viruses mutate from one strain to another.'"[471]

In short, there is *no compelling state interest* **for the draconian measure** by LAUSD (nor by any other governmental entity or private employer) in compelling the **exceptionally risky** Covid-19 vaccinations, where available, non-invasive, options for Covid-19, such as social distancing protocols, effective post-infection drug

470 Ibid.

471 WebMD, *"A Few Mutations Away": The Threat of a Vaccine-Proof Variant* (*"A Few Mutations Away"*), July 30, 2021.

treatments, and natural immunity would **overwhelmingly have satisfied** any related health and safety concerns.

Nuremberg Code

In 1947, a trial in Nuremberg, Germany took place involving several Nazi physicians accused of conducting inhumane and often deadly experiments on prisoners of concentration camps. At the conclusion, 16 people were found guilty. In the aftermath of that trial, what has become known as the "Nuremberg Code" was drafted and adopted with the aim of protecting human subjects in future medical research. The Nuremberg Code consists of 10 principles, including the vital principle that *free and voluntary consent* of the human subject is **absolutely essential** in any *experiment* on humans. In the case of vaccine mandates within the United States, the Covid-19 vaccines were approved by the FDA **only** as Emergency Use Authorization procedures as experimental drugs. Consent to taking an experimental and largely untested vaccine, under threat of employment termination (or other egregiously punitive consequences) as the alternative, is obviously not a free, knowing and voluntary consent.

Chapter Eight

Pathways to Enduring Freedom and Liberty

O N OCTOBER 14, 2021, over 3,000 people joined a "RightsForum21 – Where do we go from here?" in Vienna and online.

> "They were all united by one ambition – to build a vision of hope."[472]

The Director and Chair of this international symposium on human rights, Michael O'Flaherty, pointed to the need for widespread communication and understanding of human rights abuses and to technological ways of acquiring data and making "a business case for our claims."[473] Unfortunately, understanding and "spreading the word" is only the beginning in the promotion and preservation of human rights. It is similar to taking guns away from law-abiding citizens when criminals (or out of control governments,

---

472 European Union Agency for Fundamental Rights, *RightsForum21 – Where do we go from here?*, October 14, 2021.

473 Ibid.

such as in Australia today) happily ignore and bypass any such gun-restriction laws.

Recall, that human rights derive from the notion of **self-defense**, at both an individual and national level. ***How do we defend ourselves?*** It certainly commences by ***situational awareness***—recognizing the threat or potential threat. For example, a group of electors go after President Donald Trump in a five-day Court "trial" to prove that he *incited* "the January 6, 2021 Insurrection," to disqualify Trump from Presidential office and to justify Colorado in removing him from the primary Presidential ballot.

> "The lawsuit is viewed as a test case for a wider effort to disqualify Trump from state ballots under section 3 of the 14th Amendment, which was enacted after the U.S. Civil War to keep supporters of the confederacy from serving in the government."[474]

The trial court Judge made *findings against Trump* that the march on Congress on January 6, 2021 constituted "an insurrection" and that Trump's words on, and leading up to, January 6 "incited" that insurrection. Whether an "insurrection" *even took place* is a highly controversial subject. Trump's lawyers have pointed out, in any event, that his conduct in no way encouraged unlawful conduct and instead was *constitutionally protected free speech*.

> "Trump's lawyers argued that his speech to supporters on the day of the riot was protected by his right to free speech, adding that the constitutional amendment does

---

474 Reuters, *Trump barred from Colorado primary ballot for role in US Capitol attack* ("*Trump Barred*"), Andrew Goudsward and Jack Queen, December 20, 2023.

not apply to U.S. presidents and that Congress would need to vote to disqualify a candidate."

The trial court also found that Section 3 *did not apply to a President* and dismissed the case. The Colorado Supreme Court *reversed, in part* the trial court, holding that not only did Trump incite the "insurrection" but that a President was not exempt from Section 3.[475] All seven of the Colorado high court's justices were **appointed by Democrats**, but split 4-3 on the ruling. One dissenting Jurist, Carlos Samour, on the Colorado Supreme Court argued,

> "... in a lengthy opinion that a lawsuit is not a fair mechanism for determining Trump's eligibility for the ballot because it deprives him of his right to due process, noting that a jury has not convicted him of insurrection.
>
> 'Even if we are convinced that a candidate committed horrible acts in the past - dare I say, engaged in insurrection - there must be procedural due process before we can declare that individual disqualified from holding public office,' Samour said."[476]

The "trial," on an issue of extreme national importance, was a **truncated shamble of proceedings**:

> "It's worth noting that three of the judges on the Colorado high court agreed with some of Trump's arguments. They

---

475 *Anderson v. Griswold*, Colo Supreme Court, No. 23SA300, https://www.courts.state.co.us/userfiles/file/Court_Probation/Supreme_Court/Opinions/2023/23SA300.pdf.

476 *Trump Barred*, Ibid.

particularly chafed at the **rushed and improvised nature** of the groundbreaking case, which was heard by a district court judge in Denver judge in less than two months. That included a week of testimony from a handful of police and protesters who were at the Jan. 6 attack, two constitutional law professors and experts on a president's emergency powers and on right-wing political speech."[477] (bold added for emphasis)

The Colorado Supreme Court ruling applies only to Colorado, and other States are rushing to distance themselves from the case.

"Technically, the ruling applies only to Colorado, and secretaries of state elsewhere are issuing statements saying Trump remains on the ballot in their state's primary or caucus."[478]

And the U.S. Supreme Court will doubtless make a prompt and definitive *de novo* ruling on the pertinent Section 3 of the 14th Amendment issues.

"The justices will need to decide whether that provision applies to Trump as a former president, what constitutes an insurrection, and whether Trump participated in one."[479]

---

477 AP, *The Constitution's insurrection clause threatens Trump's campaign. Here is how that is playing out* ("*Insurrection Clause Threatens*"), Nicholas Riccardi, December 20, 2023.

478 *Insurrection Clause Threatens*, Ibid.

479 Los Angeles Times, Opinion: *Colorado's ruling against Trump raises questions only the Supreme Court can answer* ("*Only the Supreme Court Can*"

The U.S. Supreme Court has never ruled on the meaning and application of Section 3 of the 14th Amendment. Arguments against the applicability to Trump are numerous and compelling.

> "The arguments against disqualifying Trump are many. Trump's lawyers have argued that, technically, the president isn't an officer 'under the United States' — that it's a legal term of art that refers to government appointees and therefore the provision doesn't apply to him. Even if it did, they've argued the Jan. 6 attack wasn't an insurrection — it was more of a riot. And even if it was an insurrection, Trump didn't "engage" in it — all he did was exercise his rights to free speech under the First Amendment. And state courts, the argument goes, aren't in a position to determine whether Jan. 6 was an insurrection — it would take months at least to hold a trial and get all the facts, and most witnesses are out of their jurisdiction. Finally, even if the courts concluded Jan. 6 was an insurrection and Trump was barred, that's not their decision to make — it's a political question for Congress."[480]

Pundits quickly took sides on the issues, pending a U.S. Supreme Court Decision.[481]

Answer"), Erwin Chemerinsky, December 20, 2023.

480 *Insurrection Clause Threatens*, Ibid.

481 *See*, The Washington Post, Opinion, *The Supreme Court Should Toss the Colorado Case*, Ruth Marcus, December 20, 2023; and *Only the Supreme Court Can Answer.*

Is the Colorado Supreme Court ruling simply the result of a legitimate pursuit of a vision of Justice? Or, is it vindication of a bigger picture elucidated by the Trump campaign that the Justice System in the United States is being *systematically manipulated* by his opponents to target Trump for *purely political purposes*?

Indeed, prior to the Colorado Supreme Court, ruling **eight similar lawsuits** on Section 3, 14th Amendment grounds, in other States across the United States had been **dismissed** by the courts.[482]

> "Lawsuits citing the 14th Amendment were dismissed by nine courts: in Michigan, by the district court in Colorado -- leading to the appeals battle there -- and by the Minnesota Supreme Court, a district court in Washington and by federal courts in Arizona, Rhode Island, New Hampshire and Florida."[483]

Context is key in situational awareness. Context enables a vision for the means of defending against an existential threat to human rights.

That's an important start. Self-defense may continue also by *words*—a rational accounting of the situation communicated to our adversary. Maybe this will work. It may also progress to *physical resistance* in order to overcome the threat. Hence, for example, the evolution of martial arts. The Second Amendment Right to Bear Arms underlies the individual right to own and possess *weaponry* and in particular, firearms in self-defense and defense against tyrannical government. A nation's "escalation dominance" capability emerges

---

482 ABC News, *Trump ineligible to run for president in Colorado because of Jan. 6, court rules in historic move*, December 19, 2023, Isabella Murray

483 Ibid.

as a national security interest strategy, evolving now to "managing escalation in the midst of limited war."

But what happens when all of this fails? In Ukraine, Russia is undertaking a scorched-earth campaign to suppress that sovereign nation under the thumb of Russian control and hegemony.[484] Apparently the American CIA warned that Russia may employ "tactical nuclear weapons" in that conflict. The President of Ukraine, Volodymyr Zelensky, affirmed this potential development:

> "It can be the truth, because when they began to speak about one or an-other battles or involved enemies or nuclear weapons or chemical, some chemical, you know, issues, chemical weapons, they should do it—they *could* do it—I mean, they can, for them life of the people is nothing."[485]

Recent Russian missile attacks on the Ukrainian cities of Lviv and planned attacks on separatists in Donbas were noted. The commentator concluded,

> "So, Russia's scorched-earth policy continues, with no end in sight."[486]

On the **world** stage, what can be done to stop blatant, widespread and horrific human rights violations? When North Korean Leader, Kim Jong Un, was making threats against Guam and firing off

---

484 YOUTUBE, CNN, The Mehdi Hasan Show, April 18, 2022, *Russian's Scorched-Earth Policy Continues*, www.youtube.com.

485 Ibid.

486 Ibid.

missiles close to U.S. allies, then President Trump took a firm stance in his first address to the United Nations, September 19, 2017:

> "Rocket-man is on a suicide mission. ... The United States has great strength and patience, but if it is forced to defend itself or its allies, we will have no choice but to totally destroy North Korea."

Stanford scholar, Scott Sagan, argues that nuclear weapons are not simply an ultimate force used to *wage war or to deter* another state from attacking—**the weapons can also be used *as a shield*** which a nation can employ during its own aggression.[487] In the case of Russia's 2022 attack on Ukraine, Russian President Vladimir Putin has held NATO at bay with the *threat of nuclear war* in the event of direct intervention by any NATO country in the conflict.

> "Back in February [, 2022], Putin publicly ordered his Minister of Defense to put Russian nuclear forces into 'special combat readiness.' He also warned in a televised statement that if another nation interferes in the operation, 'Russia will respond immediately, and the consequences will be such as you have never seen in your entire history.' Was Putin threatening a nuclear war?"[488]

Most certainly, Putin's actions were intended as a credible threat of nuclear force. If the *effect* is to freeze opposition in its tracks, it

---

487 Stanford, News, *The U.S. must do what it can to prevent Russian military from crossing the nuclear threshold, Stanford scholar says*, April 20, 2022, https://news.stanford.edu.

488 Ibid.

makes no difference if the threat was genuine or a ruse. The *objective* of proactively disabling full resistance is achieved.

But can the world afford to bow to what amounts to *nuclear extortion*? Where does that extortion end? In Ukraine? In other Baltic nations which are a part of NATO? What if *China* adopts a similar policy and attacks Taiwan, or invades the Solomon Islands? If an intruder stands in front of your house with a shotgun and threatens to shoot you through the door if you do not open it, do you open the door and give up your weapon, or do you take cover and use your own shotgun to shoot back if necessary. Once a victim accedes to extortion, the aggressor can only assume that the tactic *will be successful again and again.*

Without attempting to outline a military and diplomatic strategy for NATO and the United States, it is apparent and obvious that a Russian threat of using nuclear weaponry **cannot** be a determining factor as to how the NATO organization and its member countries respond to Russian aggression in Ukraine. If the United States declining to enforce a "no-fly zone" over Ukraine is defensible, it should NOT be because of Russia's nuclear threat. That **Russian threat of nuclear strikes** in Ukraine, or against NATO members, **must be viewed as** *a neutral factor.*

> "... [T]he U.S. should remind Russian military leaders that any nuclear use against a Ukrainian city **will be treated as a war crime** and that they, not just Putin, will be treated as **war criminals**. The Russian military may not mind targeting civilians, as it has shown in its operations in Chechnya, in Syria, and now in Ukraine. But they do care about protecting themselves. Do they really want to live in a world in which they have broken the tradition of nuclear non-use that has existed since 1945? They may think twice about agreeing to drop nuclear bombs

if they know that **they may one day find themselves permanently imprisoned for their actions**. And if Putin gives such a reckless, dangerous order, it may just be the last straw that makes other leaders in Moscow decide that he finally has to go."[489] (bold added for emphasis)

Otherwise, the Western world is doomed to exist in fear of nuclear war and eventually will be subsumed by the forces of evil which make such threats of mutual annihilation.

Now, we're getting to the **heart** of protecting human rights on an international scale—enforcement of war crimes law in prosecutions of military leaders. Of course, this assumes that Russia and its leaders are *within the grasp* of an internationally recognized criminal justice body for implementing such prosecutions and punishment. Financial sanctions have been implemented against Russian oligarchs by the Biden Administration, and seem to have had some, at least minimal, effect against these (suspect) captains of industry in Russia.[490]

But does *financial punishment* of Russian oligarchs *actually influence* the choices Putin and his military generals make? Probably not. The wealth and sources of wealth for Putin and his

---

489   Ibid.

490   The Atlantic, *The Russian Elite Can't Stand the Sanctions*, Brooke Harrington, March 5, 2022, www.theatlantic.com, "And some of Russia's best-known oligarchs—business figures who have built up huge fortunes, in most cases through their connections to the state—are now calling for an end to the war [in Ukraine]." Recently, some of these oligarchs and their entire families, have suffered *untimely and unexplained deaths*—"the latest in a string of deaths among Russia's super rich since the beginning of Moscow's invasion of Ukraine." India Today, www.indiatoday.in, *Whodunnit: 2 Russian oligarchs, their families found dead within 24 hours*, April 25, 2022; Fortune, *Here are all the Russian oligarchs who've died under strange circumstances this year*, April 26, 2022, Andrew Marquardt.

administration are virtually limitless since the nation's resources are literally **there for the taking**.

As in almost any chronic bully situation, **fighting force with force** becomes the only viable solution. A line in the sand is drawn and fair notice is given, but once the line is crossed, *the consequences must be immediate and harsh.*[491]

Since the outset, the United States has refused to agree to be bound by the International Criminal Court ("ICC"). The ICC was formed by the "Rome Statute" in 1998 in an effort to prosecute the most egregious international war crimes, crimes against humanity and genocide. Apparently,

"The US … took umbrage at the – unlikely – prospect that the ICC could prosecute Americans."[492]

The founding nations, however, saw the ICC,

"as a step towards a world where no one has impunity for mass atrocities."[493]

---

491 As a personal anecdote, this situation arose one evening when walking to my office late at night. I was confronted with a snarling, aggressive, medium-sized dog. As it inched closer, I stepped back into what is known in karate as a "right neutral bow" and visualized a line across the sidewalk beyond which I would not allow the dog to cross. The moment that dog stepped beyond that line, without hesitation I kicked it in the chest with a right rear-leg thrust kick that sent the dog four feet in the air and eight feet back, end-over-end twice. When it landed, it quickly headed in the other direction. Problem solved.

492 European Council on Foreign Relations, *Why America is facing off against the International Criminal Court*, Anthony Dworkin, September 8, 2020, https://ecfr.eu.

493 Ibid.

The United States views prosecution of its citizens by the ICC as a violation of United States sovereignty. In *United States v. Balsys*,[494] the U.S. Supreme Court suggested that the United States may neither participate in, nor facilitate, a criminal trial in whole or in part under its own authority, unless the Constitution's guarantees are recognized and preserved. In many important respects, the ICC operates in a manner antithetical to the U.S. Constitution.[495]

If there is no viable international tribunal to prosecute war crimes, crimes against humanity and genocide, and assuming these violations of natural law continue to plague humans in this world at this time, **then *what is the solution?***

Force. Without *imminently available force*, there is no ultimate accountability. This is why we have bailiffs in courtrooms. If people misbehave, there is *immediate accountability*. Not a promise of accountability. Not a theory of accountability. Not a discussion of accountability, nor even scholarly articles about accountability with innumerable footnotes. *Direct, predictable and immediate accountability.* And because of this obviously present and available accountability in the courtrooms across America, incidents of misbehavior, in my experience as a trial lawyer, are relatively uncommon.

We can learn something from bailiffs. They are armed with some combination of gun, pepper spray, taser, baton and handcuffs. They have radios with which to request backup. They are attentive to the proceedings and to the people within the courtroom. They never

---

494   (1998) 524 U.S. 666.

495   The Heritage Foundations, *The International Criminal Court vs. the American People*, David Rivkin Jr. and Lee Casey, February 5, 1999, www.heritage.org For example—no right to trial by jury; violative of exclusive jurisdiction of American Courts; Jurists may be from enemies of the United States; and, invasive of right of United States to defend its interest by military action.

turn their backs on visitors to the courtroom. They are experienced and skilled in handling disruptions. They know their jobs and are courteous, yet firm. To me, the courtroom bailiff's every day protocol sound like a great metaphorical roadmap for each country within NATO when dealing with external threats against sovereign nations.

As President Theodore Roosevelt described his foreign policy, "speak softly but carry a big stick." Act decisively but fairly. Never coward to extortion. Recognize that natural law and human rights are *real*; they are *inherent* in the notion of self-defense. *We **defend** these rights and this defense becomes an **inherent aspect** of freedom.* We ***stand up*** for our freedoms, our rights and the rights of others. Again, as my song, *There Come a Time*, cries out,

> "Banding together, as proud as we're strong, that's
> how our enemies fell. We stand up and fight on,
> forever as one, ringing that Liberty *Bell*!"

www.ingramcontent.com/pod-product-compliance
Lightning Source LLC
Chambersburg PA
CBHW032050020426
42335CB00011B/274